Language Wars

Language Wars

The Role of Media and Culture
in Global Terror and Political Violence

Jeff Lewis

Pluto Press

LONDON • ANN ARBOR, MI

First published 2005 by Pluto Press
345 Archway Road, London N6 5AA
and 839 Greene Street, Ann Arbor, MI 48106

www.plutobooks.com

British Library Cataloguing in Publication Data
A catalogue record for this book is available from the British Library

ISBN   0 7453 2485 1 hardback
ISBN   0 7453 2484 3 paperback

Library of Congress Cataloging in Publication Data applied for

10   9   8   7   6   5   4   3   2   1

Designed and produced for Pluto Press by
Chase Publishing Services Ltd, Fortescue, Sidmouth, EX10 9QG, England
Typeset from disk by Stanford DTP Services, Northampton, England
Printed and bound in the European Union by
Antony Rowe Ltd, Chippenham and Eastbourne, England

For Belinda

Contents

Acknowledgements

I would like to express my profound gratitude to Belinda, Jay and Sian without whose support and friendship this book could not have been written. My thanks also to Liz Shuter, John Hill and Jordie Hill for providing such a conducive space in which to write *Language Wars*. Thanks to the School of Applied Communication at RMIT University and to the University's Research and Innovation sector for their direct financial support. Thanks to my colleagues at the Globalism Institute for their invaluable intellectual input and good humour. My gratitude is also extended to my many students and colleagues who have made my life as an academic so rich and rewarding. I would like to acknowledge David Castle and the team at Pluto Press for their considerable faith, enthusiasm and encouragement.

Introduction

TERRORISM AND LANGUAGE WARS

During the three-day siege in a small school in southern Russia, international audiences became absorbed by a narrative of increasingly familiar dread. The Beslan siege of September 2004 resolved itself in bloodshed. Our worst fears realized, images of injured, dead and dying children were beamed into living rooms across the world. Governments, reporters and publics were forced once again to give expression to a sense of grief and horror that tested the extremities of our comprehension. The motif of terror seemed to find a new level of depravity.

Around 360 people, mostly children, were killed in the siege, and as many more were injured. Survivors described the brutality of the hostage-takers who, wearing suicide bomb-belts and wielding sophisticated military weapons, had summarily executed anyone who spoke or moved without direction. But this was not a spontaneous operation. The Chechen rebels had laid weapons, ammunition and explosives in and around the school's gymnasium prior to the attack. The town of Beslan had been strategically selected by the rebels in order to maximize the symbolic force of their actions. Lying at the intersection of southern Russia's ethnic divisions – Ingush, Abkhaz, Ossetians and Georgians – Beslan clearly represented for the militants the brutal hegemony of Soviet and Russian imperialism. Within the region of Ossetia, Beslan had been part of Russia since the eighteenth century; neighbouring Ingushetia was annexed to the Soviet Union in 1917. During the First World War, Soviet Premier Joseph Stalin accused the Ingush and the Chechens of collaborating with Nazi Germany and forcibly deported the great majority of these people to the central Asian republic of Kazakhstan. Tens of thousands of Chechens died in these purges and the survivors were only allowed to return to their homelands after Stalin's death in 1953.

Clearly, the cultural memory of the Ingush and Chechen militants, who are suspected of carrying out the terrorist assault in Beslan, identifies the Ossetians with the oppression of Russian and Soviet imperial history. This memory, while constructed through various forms of tribal, linguistic and religious difference, has been more substantively generated through the political momentum of modernization – including the volition of ideology, nation and globalization. Thus, the formation of this difference as wars over 'culture' is profoundly political. The meaning of the siege in Beslan can never be disengaged from the historical, cultural and political circumstances that brought these players into conflict at this particular place and at this particular time. It is not, therefore, sufficient to reduce this complex matrix of causes to simple polemics – good against evil, the west against the east, Christianity against Islam. Rather, these agonisms are generated through the confluence of historical and contemporary cultural conditions that inevitably construct, deconstruct and challenge various modes of meaning and meaning-making. Our principal term for describing this effect is 'language wars'. These wars are constituted out of the human propensity for forming community, culture and meanings; these formative processes stimulate their own contentions both within particular social groups and between social groups. Tension, contention, dispute are all 'expressivities' of culture, the most acute of which manifest themselves as actual bodily violence. While language wars may be sporadic and instantaneous, marking the conflict between specific semantic moments, they may also be drawn through history and more durable social and cultural formations. A sporadic contention, however, can never be isolated from the broader dynamics of meaning-making. As we will discuss in detail in Chapter 2, this interconnection of discourses and texts has been characterized by various theorists as 'intertextuality', a process by which all utterances are connected ultimately to each other (see Barthes, 1977, Derrida, 1974, Kristeva, 1984, Orr, 2003).

In terms of 'language wars' we will focus on the congregation of discursive tensions that are evolving around the current phase of global terror and political violence. These tensions, however, are connected to texts and discourses that reach well back in history and which have become conscripted into current discussions and debates. In particular, we are interested in those discourses that are contributing to the construction of a revivified cultural polemic which we are calling 'the new east–west' divide. For the purposes of this book, 'language' refers to any meaning-making system – image, lexical and sound-based. While we will distinguish specifically between the language systems of writing and image-based broadcast mediation, we will nevertheless maintain a general view that 'language' (discourse, text, semiosis) is the principal mechanism for generating meaning and sustaining culture. We also distinguish between 'society' as the aggregation of individuals and communities, and 'culture' as the integration of meaning-making processes and these social formations (Lewis, 2002a: 12–18). While this definition of culture will be elaborated shortly, it is important to emphasize that culture is not the same as society, though language, society and culture are interdependent 'systems'.

It is also important to emphasize that language is an open and pervasively changing mode of meaning-making: any language system is inevitably in dispute with itself. As the fabric and superstructure of culture, language can never be disengaged from the material world or the world of phenomena. The notion of language wars in no way abrogates the validity of the physical conditions of human experience, most particularly as it is expressed through actual bodily violence. The approach of this book, rather, is to treat language and the phenomenal–material–corporeal as co-extensive. To this extent, we accept Foucault's view that 'discourse' (the compound of language, power and politics) provides access to the material–corporeal. While we might experience pain, distress or pleasure at the level of the individual body, we cannot 'know', 'explain', or inscribe that experience with meaning without the facility of language.

Language wars are not merely the articulations of corporeal violence; they are also the stimulant, conduit and conditions determining physical response. The actions of a suicide bomber in Gaza will produce direct physical effects, but these effects are entirely incomprehensible without reference to the discourses that have driven the action and the meanings that accompany the death and destruction: the biological effects on the bomber and the victim may seem identical, but their meanings are vastly different. Even so, agonies that have been suffered by the victims of political violence and terrorism are in no way compromised by our attention to the symbolic and cultural context of physical conflict. It is simply that language wars derive from circumstances that lie beyond the moment of suffering. They reach into history and through the complex matrix of cultural politics, mediated expression and power. They provide for us the lens of understanding and explanation required to unravel the constructed meanings that, in most circumstances, have generated the horror of events like the Beslan massacre.

In fact, the situating of the Beslan atrocities within the polemic of Islamic terrorism or George W. Bush's 'war on terror' indicates precisely how these language wars are formed and mobilized. As we have suggested, there is a complex tribal and regional history to the conflicts over Chechnya and Ingushetia. But it is the absorption and amplification of these 'language wars' into a national and global context that transforms local difference into violence. The children of a relatively unexceptional town are recruited by this symbolic amplitude into a vicious conflict over the meaning of territory, ethnicity and history. The Russian annexation of Chechnya is appended to an even more grave global dispute over Islam, the Middle East and international oil supplies. These oil supplies, even more particularly, are implicated in the historical disputes of US global hegemony which itself has been forged by hideous and brutal militarism and a global conquest by capitalist ideology. The 'end of history' which Francis Fukuyama so boldly declared on the fall of Soviet communism, announced in fact a new era of symbolic contention by which Russia would re-build its power and American access to oil would justify its moral, as well as military and economic, global primacy.

A number of organizations are suggesting, in fact, that the Chechen–Ingush militants who besieged the Beslan school were connected to the international Islamic organization al-Qa'ida. The US Council on Foreign Relations Report (2004) suggests that specific elements of the Chechen separatist movement have been trained and tactically influenced by al-Qa'ida. In particular, those Chechen rebels who had fought alongside the Taliban in Afghanistan's war against Russia, have been radicalized by the ideology of Islamic extremism and especially the notion of a global jihad or Islamic revolution. This influence is further confirmed by the presence of Arabic voices on the militants' own video recording of the Beslan siege. Thus, the relationship between the Chechen rebels and al-Qa'ida situates the atrocity within the broader discourses of terrorism that surround 9/11 and the US war on terror.

While various scholars and public commentators have sought to characterize these discourses, we can certainly suggest that they constitute a distinct constellation of cultural, linguistic and political effects. These effects, of course, are related to America's enhanced 'homeland' vulnerability to international political violence. More broadly, however, 9/11 marked the escalation of the language wars, which lay behind the attacks and which have their roots in historical and contemporary discourses of violence and terror. The media, in this sense, is a critical player in the current incarnation of these language wars – not merely as a conduit for their expression, but as a substantive contributor to their shape, direction and force of impact.

THE MEDIATION OF TERROR

While this point will be discussed in considerable detail in Chapter 1, we need to be clear that the current phase of global terror and political violence is absolutely embedded in the mediation of these language wars through the formation and contention of meaning. Indeed, as terrible as the murder of schoolchildren in Beslan may be, these deaths need to be configured against the estimated 100,000 noncombatants, mostly children and women, who have been killed during the US-led invasion and occupation of Iraq (Roberts et al., 2004) – a story which remains largely obscured within the discourses of liberation, democracy and freedom. Global media audiences were exposed to the narrative and dramatic events of the Beslan 'terrorist' massacre, but they have been largely denied access to the violence and horror of death in Iraq. As media audiences, in fact, our responses to political violence, terrorism and warfare are formed through interaction with the meaning-making capacities of the media, including the ways in which political discourses are constituted and disseminated throughout a culture.

A number of commentators are beginning to acknowledge the significance of the media in shaping and informing public views of political violence (Chomsky, 2001, 2003a, 2003b, Laqueur, 2003, Nacos, 2002, Philo & Berry, 2004, Silberstein, 2002, Tuman, 2003, Wilkinson, 1997); however, they have limited their focus to the message-bearing capacity of a mass media system and its power to influence public opinion. Noam Chomsky, for example, has been particularly critical of the mass media system (industry and institutions), which, he believes, tends to comply with the powerful interests of social elites. Nacos, Tuman and Silberstein have a more liberal and critical interest in the media, although they have also sought to analyse the capacity of media messages to influence public perception. Valuable as this work has been, the emphasis on the media's productive capacity and institutional status has tended to rarefy the various industries, technologies, techniques and professional personnel and isolate them from their political and cultural context of consumption and meaning-making. In this instance, meaning-making is not merely an exercise of media producers, but is absolutely implicated in the dynamics of context, production and consumption. This complex of associations can only be understood if we broaden our definition of the media in terms of a set of relationships and processes. The 'media' then becomes a collective noun defining the dynamic of the construction, contestation and deconstruction of meanings. Audiences, in this sense, are as critical to the media as producers, distributors and regulators. Figure I.1 summarizes these processes and relationships.

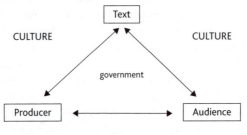

Figure I.1   Media triangle

The relationship between the text and context is largely constituted by 'representation'. For our purposes, representation refers to the various transformative processes which bind a subject to his or her phenomenal and semiotic–symbolic worlds. As noted above, the approach of this book assumes the interdependence of phenomena and language. Working through the traditions of phenomenology and poststructuralism, this approach denies a 'two realities' thesis which would distinguish between a 'true' and an 'imagined' reality. The human subject constitutes the nexus of phenomenal and imagined realities, convening the interdependence through the expressivities of language. Subjects draw on the available cultural resources in order both to produce and to 'read' a text. The act of reading (viewing, listening, consuming) is not a passive reaction to textual meanings, but is active and creative (Ang, 1996, de Certeau, 1984, 1988, Lewis, 2002a, Moores, 1993). This 'reading', in fact, constitutes a new text production through imagining, conversation, play or other expressive activities (Deleuze & Guattari, 1987). As we have noted, the phenomenal world may well exist outside the world of imagining and language, but it has no constitutive power of its own since we can only access it through language. Our focus in this current book, therefore, is on the ways in which language facilitates representation, most particularly through a culture which generates, and is generated by, a new global semiosis of mediated and televisualized political violence. Of course, political violence and warfare have been, and continue to be, represented in pre-televisual media; however, the focus of this book, as will be developed in the following pages, is on broadcast modes of communication, especially television. While the broadcast and narrowcast facilities of the Internet will be included for study in this book, television remains the most widespread and significant medium in the global communication of terror and political violence.

The argument of the book proceeds from the essential assumption that global terror and political violence are essentially formed in relation to these new modes of mediated meaning-making and language wars. We are not, however, content to say, as former British prime minister Margaret Thatcher has most famously remarked, that the media and publicity are the 'oxygen' of terrorism. It is certainly true, as we have suggested above, that the militants who besieged Beslan were engaged in a symbolic project which was designed to publicize their grievances against Russian and Soviet hegemony. It may also be true that the siege was implicated in a broader symbolic project of jihad and global Islamic revolution. There is no doubt that the spectacular brutality of the event was a conduit to media representation and the attention of global audiences. Certainly, Russian President Vladimir Putin has sought to deprive 'terrorists' of the 'oxygen' of publicity, most particularly through the introduction of new censorship laws. Reacting to the Moscow theatre siege of October 2002, Putin's new laws prohibited news agencies from reporting such events in any detail. While Putin may be partly motivated by security and strategic interests, there is also a strong claim that he was merely trying to camouflage the power of the state and the appalling mismanagement of the theatre siege. As in Beslan, significant questions are being asked about the strategy and skills of the Russian military authorities, who released gas pellets into the theatre in order to quell the attackers but ultimately killed around 120 hostages. As with the new Patriot laws in the United States, the authoritarian approach to censorship in Russia is problematized in a democratic state which is founded on the free flow of information and ideas in order to maintain its electoral and public competence.

While numerous commentators have discussed the issue of censorship in a modern democracy, a broader issue arises as governments seek to regulate the general momentum of a modernizing, global culture which has become so pervasively mediated. The aspiration of censorship seems a wind-drop against the implacable force of a rampantly pervasive televisual culture, as we have outlined it above. Thus, while President Putin was able to have the editor of the *Izvestia* newspaper dismissed for publishing photographs of the Beslan events, Russia's NTV and various Internet sites have also defied the ban by presenting the militants' own video of the siege. This impulse to represent may constitute a kind of 'oxygen', but it is an oxygen that is available to all; in fact, it is necessary for the sustenance of the entire culture.

CULTURE AND THE POLITICAL SIGNIFIER

The fundamental contention here is that culture is the aggregation of meanings within a social group. For contemporary globalizing culture(s), the broadcast networked media is central to the formation, distribution and consumption of these meanings. Martin Heidegger expressed his deep concerns about the technological transformation of modern societies, describing the emergence of the 'world as picture' in terms of an outbreak of 'the gigantic – the over-presentation of the world as image and spectacle' (1977: 135). While Heidegger was expressing these concerns in relation to the rise of photography and cinema, the comments relate equally to the primacy of television and other screen-based technologies in contemporary culture. The proliferation of the spectacle through televisualization is a theme that has been absorbed into the work of media theorists like Marshal McLuhan, Paul Virilio and Jean Baudrillard. What distinguishes their studies is a fascination with the transformative power of the televisual or 'oracular' technologies, and the ways in which societies and cultures have adapted them into their critical modes of self-definition and meaning-making. Virilio and Baudrillard have commented, in particular, on the relationship between mediation and political violence in terms of the constituent formation of history and culture – that is, the meaning-making of specific human groups. For Virilio, for example, the representation or expression of warfare is linked inextricably to the prevailing technologies and strategies of violence and the cultures which use them. The camera, according to Virilio, is the essential technology for warfare and information since it affected the very nature of 'power realization' in war, the process by which military activities are placed at a distance from the politics, authority and bodily engagement of combatants:

> By making attack unreal, industrial warfare ceased to be that huge funeral apparatus, denounced by moralists, and eventually became the greatest mystification of all: the apparatus of deception, the lure of deterrence. Already in the Great War . . . the industrialization of the repeating image illustrated this cinematic dimension of regional-scale destruction, in which landscapes were continually upturned and had to be reconstituted with the help of successive frames and shots, in a cinematographic pursuit of reality, the decomposition and recomposition of an uncertain territory in which film replaced military maps. Cinematic derealization now affected the very nature of power, which established itself in a technological Beyond with the space–time not of ordinary mortals but of a single war machine. (Virilio, 1989: 79)

The imaging of the violence, that is, becomes fundamental to its exercise; the very character of modern culture, Virilio claims, is transformed by this war machine – the abstract power of the camera.

Culture, in this sense, is a central concept for our understanding of contemporary terrorism, warfare and political violence. While we will explore the concept of culture in detail in Chapter 2, we need to establish at the outset that it is directly and essentially connected to the issues of global terror and political violence. As our model of the media confirms, culture is the overriding context within which social actions take place; it connects the subject to his or her social world, modes of social knowledge, communications processes, politics and history. To this end, we offer the following definition:

> Culture is the assemblage of imaginings and meanings that may be consonant, disjunctive, overlapping, contentious, continuous or discontinuous. These assemblages may operate through a wide variety of human social groupings and social practices. In contemporary culture these experiences of imagining or meaning-making are intensified through the proliferation of mass media images and information. (Lewis, 2002a: 15)

This definition releases culture from the notion of the 'web of meaning' thesis which in Weberian terms suggests a relatively closed context of meaning-making for a relatively integrated social group. Culture, according to the definition cited, is a more open and dynamic *process*, providing the resources for social harmony, disharmony and change. This definition allows cultural meanings and imaginings to struggle against one another, mutate, collapse and emerge through new modes of 'expressivity'. In other words, culture becomes a contingency of language wars by which various individuals and social formations struggle for discursive attention and primacy within a politically constituted 'mediasphere'. The mediasphere is that cultural site where the public and private dimensions of social life converge through the communications experiences of individual subjects: that is, the site where individuals and the media interact.

It is important to note that culture moves in multiple directions: toward and against stability. As I have argued elsewhere (Lewis, 2002a, Lewis & Best, 2002, 2005), the formation of meaning and culture necessarily implies its own de-formation or *deconstruction*, as Jacques Derrida calls it. Institutions seek over time to stabilize and fix signifiers to specific signifieds, creating the conditions for durable meaning. This attempt to stabilize meanings by fixing them to specific signs (concepts, symbols, images, discourses, texts and so on) is a political strategy as it necessarily involves the exercise of power: institutions marshal subjects and meanings in order to assert their own social, political and cultural primacy. During the course of this book, we will see how specific institutions, most notably political and social elites, have sought to fix the signifiers of concepts like 'terrorism', 'democracy', 'Islam' and 'freedom' to specific, politically determined signifieds (meanings). We will also see, however, that these signifiers are vulnerable to challenge – both quite conscious modes of resistance as well as intrinsic modes of semiotic unravelling or deconstruction.

While we might easily define and locate this first category of challenge, particularly through Muslim communities, global protest and alternative journalism, the latter forms of intrinsic deconstruction are less easy to define and locate. Nevertheless, it is important for our argument to acknowledge the ways in which the media and culture interact to produce specific kinds of semiotic flow which destabilize the political force of hegemonic institutions *and* their efforts to impose fixed and unassailable meanings over subjects and communities. Part of the intrinsic instability is explained by Jacques Derrida's reworking of Julia Kristeva's notion of intertextuality, a process by which any specific text (discourse, word, utterances, image) must refer to all other texts, since everything in language is ultimately connected to the meanings of the totality (Derrida, 1974, Lewis, 2002a, Orr,

2003). Thus, the meaning of the concept 'terror' will require reference to other words, news bulletins, books, histories and so on, leaving gaps for the unravelling of the original concept. Further to this perspective, however, it is arguable that the attempt by institutions to fix signifiers to signifieds within a durable and imposed semiotic system will ultimately collapse because it defies the intrinsic nature of language itself and the nexus that is created between subjects and their phenomenal, everyday experiences. As I have argued at length elsewhere (Lewis & Best, 2002, 2005), institutions, operating at a distance from everyday people and their discursive–phenomenal experiences, actually contribute to the instability of meanings and signifiers by seeking to override and ossify these experiences. To this extent, I am borrowing somewhat from Jacques Lacan (1977) and Michel de Certeau (1984, 1988), both of whom explore the 'imaginary' as a critical space for subject formation and modes of creative self-expression. Returning to the definition of culture cited above, we can see that this 'imaginary' is not easily captured by institutions and hegemonic discourses; the imaginary remains a space for the dynamic interchange of meanings, the creation of new meanings and the miraculous slippage that enables signifiers to dissociate from their signifieds.

In many respects, in fact, it is this discursive or pre-discursive space which enables subjects to irradiate meanings and elide the logical force of powerful institutions. As will be elucidated in the discussions of audience and public responses to mediated terrorism and other modes of political violence, subjects in the mediasphere can be remarkably unreliable. The very force of institutional power, in fact, creates the conditions for slippage and dissociation, allowing the signifier to scatter and metamorphose into the raw materials necessary for new semiotic experiences and meanings. Expressed through the aggregation of culture, this dynamic creates the instabilities necessary for social change – including changes in public opinion toward events like 9/11 and the invasion of Iraq. How we manage this change, of course, is a matter that is deeply embedded in the discursively forming relationships of power – that is, in language wars.

CULTURAL POLITICS AND GLOBALIZATION

Language wars are central to cultural counter-flows toward greater and lesser levels of social stability. Modern societies, in fact, are characterized by a tension which would create increasing aggregation of human groups, and a retreat toward fragmentary and a more individualized social formation: that is, between global and local flows. These movements express themselves within the double-coding of global terror by which the institutional force of American-dominated economic capitalism and cultural hegemony is confronting resistance from various incarnations of cultural localism. At its most dangerous and spectacular, this localism is forging its own institutional ideologies, exhorting violence against the perceived enemy. The double-coding should not surprise us, however, since globalization is itself a fundamentally paradoxical process. Arjun Appadurai (1990, 1996), in his seminal description of globalization, provides a useful basis for understanding this paradoxical and multilayered process. According to Appadurai: 'The new global economy has to be understood as a complex overlapping, disjunctive order, which cannot any longer be understood in terms of existing center–periphery models (even those that might account for multiple centers and peripheries)' (1990: 296). For Appadurai, globalization is constituted around a series of 'scapes', covering a range of overlapping global activities – finance, trade, media–telecommunications, the movement of people (tourism, business, migration, conflict) and political-organizational activities. Of course, and as numerous commentators have noted (see Lewis, 2002a: 225–38), global movements and interactions have been a feature of human activity from prehistory to modernity. During the post-Second World War period, however, these global interactions have accelerated and been supplemented by rapid advances in communications technology. Clearly, the most recent phase of globalization involves cultural transformations at the local, national, transnational and global levels – where 'global' implies the transcending and dissolving of national borders.

Mike Featherstone (2002) reinforces the point made originally by Appadurai that globalization is processual and involves the movement and flow of cultural elements toward and out of global and local spaces. For Featherstone, though, globalization exists in the popular imaginary as a fundamentally economic force, one that is characterized by 'marketization' and, at the level of the nation-state, 'social, cultural and political deregulation and disintegration'. The decline of socialism and the social welfare state is in many respects part of a globalization process which seeks to integrate all national economies into a single, market-based trading system that is unconstrained by local regulations, cultural specificities or political nuances. Debates about the effects of globalization on the 'home' culture have evolved from concerns over the homogenization of local subjects and cultures into a discussion about cultural appropriation. That is, current discussions frequently focus on the capacity of the local to re-appropriate and hybridize globally distributed ideas, products and text, reshaping them into new cultural forms (see Lewis, 2002a: 334–5). Moreover, and as Featherstone (2002) explains, global capitalism has encouraged new modes of decentralized, flexible and post-Fordist production and niche marketing, both of which generate new cultural idioms and specificities. Simon During (1999) has explained this process in terms of global media texts and networks, which he divides into two general categories: the global popular, which are consciously formulaic texts designed for mass international markets; and cultural globalization, which are texts generated through specific cultural formations but which penetrate global markets, creating hybrid forms and meanings. Thus, while Hollywood films and CNN are self-consciously global in their focus and marketing, local texts can 'unselfconsciously' stimulate international interest through the processes of globalization. For example, the Qatari news network al-Jazeera has become internationally renowned for its reporting on the Iraq invasion. Contrasting with CNN and the US Fox network, al-Jazeera's tell-all philosophy has enabled it to break many stories and penetrate significant layers of western news consumption.

For Featherstone, though, such distinctions between a formulaic and incidental global mediation are less important than the overall trajectory of global marketization and the inevitable compromise of national sovereignty. The impact of the World Trade Organization policies, free trade agreements, and the inevitable flow of capital to localities with deregulated labour markets and low labour costs contribute to a dubious hierarchy of economies which is not formed strictly around national boundaries. Transnational corporations like Microsoft, for example, have a larger economy than many Third World nations. These multinational corporations, along with development banks, donor organizations and 'interested' First World governments, are able to exert enormous pressure on Third World governments, forcing them to adopt policies which satisfy the interests of global economic hegemonies. Deregulated market and labour structures, reduction in social welfare and infrastructure spending, tax breaks for foreign investors, and zero tariffs – are all part of the international global policy framework that is necessary for commercial and development investment. Aid funds, especially from the United

States, are being increasingly tagged to marketization policies and support for the donor country's foreign policy interests.

As we will discuss in subsequent chapters, this dimension of globalization has direct relevance in the Middle East and other parts of the Islamic world where radical Islamicism is evolving as a response to faltering economic modernization and the more aggressive conscription of the oil nations into the global marketplace. The poverty and suffering that are accompanying this economic faltering are important aspects of the rise of radical Islam in the Middle East, Pakistan and Indonesia. As we will also discuss, trade policy in and aid from the US, the UK and Australia have become increasingly tied to security strategies and the foreign policy objectives of the donor nations, including the war on terror. In 2004, for example, the US denied aid to nations which criticized its rejection of the international war crimes treaty, a treaty which would allow signatories to be prosecuted for breaches of international regulations on war and the deployment of weapons (Traynor, 2003).

The widespread protests against the WTO and other global trade conferences over the past decade have refocused attention on the exploitative and inequitable nature of global free trade policies. Western cultural imperialism, Third World debt, global environmental damage and the uneven distribution of wealth and power within developing nations themselves were all highlighted by protests in Seattle, Davos and Melbourne. In many respects, the idea that globalization is primarily an economic force somewhat overrides the multi-flowing cultural impacts of increasing global contiguity. The positive and negative effects of cultural globalization in fact are reduced to a negative account by commentators like Noam Chomsky (2001, 2003a, 2003b) who define it purely in terms of American hegemony, Americanization or cultural imperialism. The attacks of September 11 seemed to quell the acidity of these protests, impelling anti-globalization critics, like Chomsky (2001), to distance themselves from the violence of Islamic terrorism. Even so, and as I have argued elsewhere (Lewis 2002b, 2003), there is clearly some continuity between the grievances of the anti-globalization movement and political Islamicism, most particularly as they centre on US cultural, economic and military hegemony. Jean Baudrillard (2002a) argues quite specifically that the 'spirit' of terrorism is located within the spirit of globalization. Baudrillard's ideas are distinguished from many other commentaries, however, since he argues that the progress of globalization is characterized by the parallel advance of good and evil. This is an idea we will take seriously as we explore the cultural politics of globalization and its role in the language wars of terrorism and political violence.

GOVERNMENT, DEMOCRACY AND THE MEDIASPHERE

Globalization, therefore – most particularly as it is conducted through trade, finance, development, cultural interaction and the mediasphere – is a critical part of the language wars of political violence. As we have noted above, warfare, terrorism and political violence are shaped in terms of global media networks, where the media is to be understood as a set of relationships that are discursively formed through a cultural and governmental context. This governmental context is perhaps best rendered in relation to Michel Foucault's (1991) concept of 'governmentality'. Referring not merely to 'the government', governmentality covers a broad range of social management processes and practices, including the distribution of discourses of public authority. The media, in fact, is a principal agent in the interaction between this public authority and private interests – corporate, community and individual. The government, therefore, asserts its interests and authority through these processes of governmentality and the exercise of 'power'.

Power, most particularly as it attaches itself to meaning and meaning-making, however, is neither unitary nor absolute. As Foucault also explains, power is multiply flowing, self-contradictory and highly unstable. This book is directly engaged, therefore, in debates around the exercise of power and the ways in which it flows toward and against governments, media corporations and other hegemonies such as the military. It is not assumed, however, that hegemony is absolute; the capacity of individuals, communities and audiences to exercise their own power is of central importance to this study. Within the context of global terrorism and political violence, the whole notion of government and governmentality, in fact, becomes problematized, not the least because various forms of militancy assault directly the ideals which inform a given culture's political imaginary. In this sense, the September 11 attacks on Washington and New York constituted a radical irruption for America's sense of political and cultural inviolability. Through much of the apocalyptic discourses which surrounded the attacks, the US and other 'western' governments were forced to reassert the legitimacy of the democratic state, reaffirming their own values and ideology over the iniquity and 'evil' of 'terrorists'.

Indeed, George Bush's war on terror has been forged around the specific discourses of western statehood, most particularly through an aggressive re-inscription of key political tropes – 'freedom', 'democracy', 'civil society' and 'rule of law'. The invocation of these tropes by the US government and its allies in the war on terror is designed to distinguish the legitimacy of the 'just war' against the iniquity of radical militancy, especially Islamic militancy. To this extent, the 100,000 civilians who have been killed during the invasion and occupation of Iraq are subsumed within the ideological imperatives of US self-defence and the unswervable project of democracy, modernization and global integration. As we have indicated, however, the hegemony of these discourses is challenged by external and internal forces. Thus, while the US State Department suggests very directly that 'terrorism' is fundamentally opposed to democratic government and the legitimacy of democratic authority, militant groups like al-Qa'ida frequently invoke a politics of liberation against the oppression of US international imperialism. Moreover, America's response to the 9/11 attacks has been more broadly challenged within the democratic nations themselves where protestors frequently point to the 'undemocratic' and aggressive demeanour with which the US has treated the people of the Middle East and indeed its own citizens.

These language wars are conducted specifically through various forms of mass media, creating discourses of dispute within various gradients of the national and global polis. Danilo Zolo (1992, 1997) has suggested very specifically that this polis – a cosmopolis – is formed through new modes of historical and cultural complexity. While Zolo has marked the escalation of political complexity in terms of events like the fall of Soviet Communism and the first Gulf War (1990–91), the combative force of language wars within a 'global polis' has undoubtedly been further intensified by 9/11 and its aftermath. The attacks on America, in fact, amplified the divisional contingencies of 'culture', creating the discursive conditions which are generating a new east–west divide. This divide, of course, is populated by historical polemics which, as we will explore in detail throughout this book, are shaped by a seemingly inexhaustible propensity for suspicion, hatred and violence. Yet while this violence might seem to be random or sporadic, it is constructed around the deeper problematics of language wars which are fused to the broadening political context of a hierarchical and profoundly inequitable global economic and social system. The media and culture, as we are defining them here, are critically bound to this system and to the complexity of a discourse of democratic modernization, most particularly as it is played out through the matrix of governmentality.

The politics of the media, therefore, cannot be simply reduced to autonomous zones of corporatization, ownership or political bias. Important as these issues are, they cannot be substantively disengaged from the ways in which the media operates as a meaning-making facility and conduit within a complex public sphere. The rise of broadcast and interactive media forms, in fact, has contributed significantly to the transformation of this public sphere, most particularly in terms of the discourse of democracy. The emergence of a televisual mediasphere, therefore, implicates audiences in the cultural politics of language. Within this mediasphere significant disputes emerge over the meaning of global terror and political violence. The war *on* terror may thus be distinguished as a war *of* terror, as global participants in the mediasphere struggle to convey and evince their specific political imaginary.

Within this war, however, I can think of nothing more terrible than the forfeit of a child's life. The mass killings at Beslan are almost incomprehensible to those of us who have been conditioned by a belief in the sacred value of all life, especially the lives of the young. But the response of the Beslan killers to the accusation of inhumanity is to point back to the tens of thousands of deaths in Chechnya, Ingushetia and Afghanistan for which, they believe, the Russian and Soviet states are responsible. Osama bin Laden said something similar in his declaration of war on the US, arguing that western history is replete with the inhumane slaughter of Arabic men, women and children. The cycle of violence in the disputed territories of Israel and Palestine has each side accusing the other of acts of terrorism and the brutal slaying of innocent people. My aim in this book is to unpack these language wars by situating them within the context of a globalizing mediasphere. Through the deployment of this strategy, we would hope to facilitate a cultural politics which may contribute to social progress and to a reconciliation that may shield us somewhat from the excesses of political violence, terror and despair.

STRUCTURE AND METHODS

The idea that the world radically changed after 9/11 has become something of a mantra for social and political commentary. A brief survey of the post-9/11 world might seem to confirm this prescience, especially as the US continues to assert its global primacy over those whom it regards as enemies. The reprisal attacks on Afghanistan and Iraq, new and quite draconian restrictions on civil and human rights, the marginalization of the United Nations and the unheralded flush of new discourses of terror and globally oriented divisiveness have all contributed to a sense of historical departure. While citizens within the Coalition countries have become increasingly disapproving of the invasion and occupation of Iraq, the re-election of incumbent governments in the US, the UK and Australia during 2004 and 2005 might seem to suggest that the Anglophonic polis is at best ambivalent about international security and the threat of global terrorism. At worst, the killing of so many innocent people in New York, Bali, Madrid, Beslan and London has contributed to a tolerance for authoritarian modes of First World political violence, which are justified through resurgent discourses of historical and cultural division. The current book, while taking account of the historical density of these language wars, focuses on the 9/11 period in order to elucidate more fully the ways in which the world has come to experience this new age of terror.

Chapter 1 focuses specifically on the media and its role in global terror and political violence. Expanding on a number of the issues raised in this Introduction, the chapter addresses directly the ways in which political violence is shaped through mediation. Chapter 2 extends these discussions through a more direct analysis of the concept of culture. While the chapter examines directly Samuel Huntington's (1993) now (in)famous 'clash of civilizations' thesis, it offers a more detailed account of 'culture', one which situates the current language wars within the evolving context of televisualization and globalization. Chapters 3 to 6 examine the role of media and culture in specific sites of global terror and political violence. Each chapter analyses these sites through the lens of those democratic discourses we have outlined above – freedom, democracy, civil society and rule of law.

Andrew Milner (2002) has suggested that 'cultural theory' constitutes its own heuristic methodology. While I have some sympathy with this position, the current book deploys a range of analytical tools to support and generate its discussions. These tools include the exposition of critical concepts and theory, various forms of textual analysis and some direct empirical interview-based research. The book examines a range of texts which are contributing to the language wars – news texts, Internet bulletins and blogs, political discourses, photographs and government reports. Chapter 5, which examines the impact of the Bali bombings, draws specifically on empirical research conducted in Indonesia and Bali. In many respects, all these modes of 'data' are cultural artefacts or texts, and all are available to a deconstructive critique which seeks to expose underlying assumptions within a specific cultural and political context.

KEY CONCEPTS

Language wars

Language wars are disputes over meaning that are more or less systematic and historically constituted. In contemporary culture language wars are frequently conducted through the mass media and may involve groups with markedly uneven access to the resources of culture and expressivity. At their most critical, these language wars may erupt into actual physical violence.

The mediasphere

The mediasphere evolves out of the democratic public sphere and represents the convergence of public and private interests. It is the site where media organizations, governments, texts and audiences 'converge' in a cultural politics which may be described as 'broadcast democracy'.

Writing democracy/Broadcast democracy

Writing democracy emerged out of the Enlightenment. It is what we have traditionally called 'democracy' and involves certain logical forms such as constitutions, electoral systems, divisions of power, parliaments, legislation and rule of law. Writing democracy evolved around the logical and linear patterns of writing, which is its critical communications medium.

Broadcast democracy does not replace writing democracy but evolves in relation to the rise of broadcast, especially visual, technologies. Broadcast democracy engages citizens in various modes of political activity and expression, including the personal creativity and pleasures associated with media consumption.

Signs and Signifiers

For the purposes of this book 'sign' refers to any meaning-making artefact within a meaning-making system; the concept of 'language' (discourse) refers to any meaning-making system (writing, speaking, images, music, etc.). The sign, according to classical semiology (the study of signs), has two constituent parts: the signifier is the material sign (written words, photographic image, stop sign, etc.); and the signified is the 'meaning' or mental concept that is associated with the signifier (red illumination on a traffic light [signifier] = *stop*). Meanings are generated through the association of signifiers and signifieds.

Dissociating signifiers

This is a process of meaning disruption where the material sign (symbol, concept, word, text) deviates from standardized or imposed cultural meanings. Dissociation is the process which enables standardized meanings to be challenged or new meanings to be generated.

Intertextuality/Supplementarity

These concepts are adapted essentially from the work of Jacques Derrida. Intertextuality refers to the interconnectedness of all texts and meaning-making systems. All meaning relies on prior or future knowledge which is itself derived from other texts. In this sense, all meanings must be deferred or 'supplemented' by other texts. Since the process of supplementarity is infinite, meaning is always constrained by its own internal deficits and momentum.

Hyperreality/Televisual Culture

Hyperreality derives largely from Umberto Eco and Jean Baudrillard. It refers to the reality that is constituted in relation to the mass media, especially televisual texts. Baudrillard insists that there is only one reality, which suggests that hyperreality is pervasive. Contemporary culture is dominated by mass mediation, especially the electronic image, so it may usefully be described as a 'televisual culture'.

Cultural imaginary

Culture is the process by which a given social group engages in meaning-making. While the principal resource of meaning-making is language (all symbolic systems), the collective consciousness of the social group may be called the cultural imaginary. The imaginary brings together the rational, creative and emotional–psychological dimensions of individuals and communities; the aggregation of these experiences contributes to the formation of the collective of cultural imaginary. Like culture, the cultural imaginary is dynamic, open and unstable.

1
Mediated Terror and the Politics of Representation

TERROR

According to the Centre for the Study of Terrorism and Political Violence at St Andrew's University, international terrorism kills around 350 people each year. While they are exceptional, events like 9/11, the Bali bombings, and the Beslan school massacre create a spectacle of horror which inscribes itself into the cultural imaginary of the international community. The mediated visions of a chaotic and terrible death, of burning and shattered bodies, and of the destruction of our towering symbols of progress and social order have become etched into a new consciousness, a new fear, that is both pessimistic and strangely ennobled by the imperatives of a heroic defence. 'Terrorism' becomes the rubric for an insidious and darkly imagined power – the risk conditions of an annihilation which randomly assaults the integrity of our history, institutions, community and being. Out of the shadows of a cosmopolitan and democratic order, these forces condemn us, attacking the foundations of our culture and the values which separate good from evil, the innocent from the guilty, the civilized from the barbaric. In many respects, terrorism, as it is infused through the spectacle of media discourses, becomes the antithesis of our modern project, creating a new threat, a new disorder, that challenges the trajectory of a global political and social harmony.

Some commentators suggest that the level of community fear is somewhat disproportionate to the actual risk posed by global terrorism (see Wilkinson, 1997). This view, however, tends to parenthesize the symbolic amplitude of terrorism and the ways in which the media and public discourse constitute a social imaginary that re-presents the world of phenomena as social knowledge. The danger and likelihood of physical attack are shaped through a cultural imaginary that draws upon the deep expressivities of history and a pre-existing social knowledge which operates through institutional discourses and the broader resources of culture. In telling their stories, governments, the media and publics engage in the limitless dynamics of language and meaning which reconstitute or represent experience in terms not only of what is known, but what can be known. As we noted in the Introduction to this book, the media is thoroughly implicated in the formation of social knowledge, most particularly through the broadcasting of televisual information. We can only know the events of 9/11, Bali and Beslan – we can only share in the agony and grief of the victims – through a vicarious system of experiential representation. Our understanding and experience of terrorism must be forged, therefore, through an understanding of the media and the ways in which our culture creates its meanings through the discourses of political violence.

In fact, there are significant disagreements over the definition and character of this specific form of violence. George W. Bush's own invocation of legislative authority which declared a 'war on terror' referenced a specific definition which distinguishes the legitimacy of 'war' against the illegitimacy of 'terrorism'. To this end, US law defines terrorism as 'premeditated, politically motivated violence against noncombatant targets by sub-national groups or clandestine agents' (22, USCA, 2656 [d]). This definition privileges 'the state', which is legitimized by the citizenry and rule of law, and which is protected by military and paramilitary agents who conduct 'policing' and 'war' in order to maintain order. The US Department of Defense expands the definition slightly, suggesting that this 'calculated use of violence or threat of violence against individuals or property' is an act of terrorism when it is designed 'to inculcate fear, intended to coerce or intimidate government or societies in the pursuit of goals that are political, ideological or religious' (DOD, 1986: 15).

Combined, these definitions specifically exempt the state from terrorist action. Moreover, they suggest that the motivation for terrorism cannot be random or criminal in the sense that the violence is not specifically or exclusively designed to obtain property or engender some intrinsic pleasure. Rather, the terrorist action is politically motivated, though politics in this sense might include ideological or religious motivation. Not surprisingly, a number of commentators have questioned this dichotomy of legitimacy, noting in particular that rulers throughout history have threatened and perpetrated incredible atrocities against conquered peoples and indeed their own citizens. Annamarie Olivero, for example, suggests that definitions, like those offered by the US government, marshal the concept of 'terrorism' for the specific ideological interests of the state. In these terms, terrorism

> contains its own rhetoric, which has been transformed throughout history by different states. By claiming to be defining a type of violence, i.e., one that threatened the site of legitimate violence (the state), it is clear that this term is reserved for the art of statecraft. (Olivero, 1998: 142)

In other words, the accusation of terrorism becomes a tool in the management and durability of state-based hegemony.

It is clearly for this reason that organizations like the Irish Republican Army (IRA) refer to themselves as an 'army' which is fighting a 'civil war' against an imperial force; for the British authorities, however, the IRA's attacks on noncombatants and their sub-national status condemn them as 'terrorists'. Critics such as Robert Fisk, Edward Herman and Noam Chomsky (see *Znet*.com) argue, similarly, that the whole notion of a 'war on terror' serves merely to legitimate the military and discursive hegemony of the US over its opponents and their political claims. The dichotomy between a legitimate, state-sponsored 'war' and an illegitimate act of 'terror' is blurred, these critics argue, when the state acts brutally or unjustly or when rebels act with just cause. Noam Chomsky claims, moreover, that America's own official strategy of 'low intensity warfare', which is explained in various military manuals and in the 'US Code' (2001: 57), in many ways parallels the strategies of sub-national militant groups. The low intensity strategy of the US military code includes, for example, the 'coercion of civilians' which may result in death and the destruction of social and material infrastructure such as transportation lines, communications, hospitals and so on. As Chomsky points out, this is precisely the strategy adopted by those who destroyed the World Trade Center.

Equally, the targeting of citizens and infrastructure by clandestine paramilitary organizations like the Central Intelligence Agency (CIA) would fit within many definitional boundaries of terrorism. The CIA's assaults on state agencies and involvement in the political processes of Nicaragua, the Sudan and various parts of the Middle East are not entirely dissimilar to the activities of national and international terrorist organizations that have been sponsored by specific states such as Libya, Taliban Afghanistan and Saudi Arabia. In his seminal work on the formation and operations of modern terrorism, Walter Laqueur argues that terrorism can, in fact, be perpetrated by the state and state agencies. Laqueur distinguishes between top-down and bottom-up terrorism, both of which are characterized by a long and widely dispersed history of systematic political brutality. Thus, while '[n]o definition of terrorism can possibly cover all the varieties of terrorism that have appeared throughout history' (Laqueur, 1987: 11), the strategies and tactics of terror are common to all modes of politically motivated violence. To this end, terrorism 'aims to induce a state of fear in the victim that is ruthless, and does not conform to humanitarian rules … [P]ublicity is an essential factor in the terrorist strategy' (1987: 143). Laqueur and other more recent analysts of terrorism argue that the notion of 'victim' or 'target' needs to be widely interpreted. While the terrorist act will produce 'corporeal' victims of the specific act of assault, the violence of terrorism has its repercussive effects on those who witness the event. The publicity to which Laqueur refers is the central strategy of a violence which is specifically rhetorical (Tuman, 2003). Nareen Chitty (2003) argues, in fact, that terrorism is effectively 'anti-democratic' since it adopts strategies that lie beyond the borders of humanitarian values. Subjects seek to influence opinion through a form of violent 'theater':

> Terrorist acts are often deliberately spectacular, designed to rattle and influence a wide audience, beyond the victims of the violence itself. The point is to use the psychological impact of the violence or of the threat of violence to effect political change. As the terrorism expert Brian Jenkins bluntly put it in 1974, 'Terrorism is theater'. (Chitty, 2003: x)

Alex Schmid suggested some time ago that terrorism is essentially a communicational act by which 'the immediate human victims of violence are chosen randomly (targets of opportunity) or selectively (symbolic or representative targets) from a target population, and serve as message generators' (1983: 70). The messages produced may seek to elicit a range of responses in the broader audience, including fear, increased awareness or sympathy about an issue, or even change in government policy. Whether this use of the media by terrorists to publicize their interests and create fear is 'anti-democratic' is a question we will return to later. What is clear, however, is that the strategy of engaging distant publics through the spectacle of violence is effective inasmuch as global media networks seem thoroughly absorbed by the current phase of political violence. At the simplest level, the September 11 attacks on America generated a dramatic increase in media coverage of Islamicism and issues pertaining to the Middle East. Brigitte Nacos (2002) demonstrates that the issues raised by Osama bin Laden's 9/11 video – the Palestine–Israeli issue in particular – achieved significant penetration in media and public discussion. Sandra Silberstein (2002), Joseph Tuman (2003), Pippa Norris et al. (2003) and Stephen Hess and Martin Kalb (2003) have all shown, in fact, that the terrorist attacks on New York and Washington have significantly raised the profile of, and interest in, al-Qa'ida and America's role in the Middle East.

Nacos (2002) argues specifically that communication is the central element of terrorism and anti-terrorism (see also Lewis, J. & Lewis, B. 2004a). Indeed, it might be suggested further that the relationship between terrorism and the media has become more or less symbiotic over the past decades. Following Sissela Bok's (1999) examination of media violence as crime-based entertainment, Nacos claims that terrorist organizations have employed critical marketing strategies designed to meet the demands of media networks' interests, style and scheduling. Citing 9/11 as the most dramatic and sophisticated example of this strategy, Nacos argues that al-Qa'ida timed the attacks in order to achieve maximum television coverage, most particularly through presentations on the evening news bulletins. A violence-obsessed media could do little else but be entranced by the narrative and horror of the attacks, repeating over and again the spectacle of falling bodies and the collapsing towers.

In this way, the victims of the attacks on New York and Washington were only conduits to a broader audience. The terrorists are neither arbitrary nor motivated by petty material gain; rather, they seek to communicate specific messages through the mass mediation of brutal and frightening details (Nacos, 2002: 10). In this way, the mass media is absolutely implicated in the political activities of the terrorist organization: 'The starting point is the notion of mass mediated terrorism and its definition as political violence against noncombatant/innocents that is committed with the intention to publicize the deed, to gain publicity and thereby public and government attention' (Nacos, 2002: 17). This emphasis on the media acknowledges the substantive link between the material and discursive dimensions of political violence in the exercise of power. It is reasonable to suggest, in fact, that terrorism is critically bound to the contemporary world's compulsive communicationalism, a drive to 'expressivity' which constitutes the very fabric of the culture (Deleuze & Guattari, 1987). In this sense, the terrorists' use of the media might be understood as a response to their enemies' communicational power – most particularly the capacity of hegemonic social groups, like governments, the military and multinational corporations, to generate and broadly disseminate their own interests, perspectives and ideologies. Paradoxically, though, it might also represent the integration of the dissident groups into the world of symbolic warfare and symbolic exchange: that is, the world in which language and persuasion are principal tools in creating, ordering and contesting community and culture.

At this level, terrorism becomes another element in the broadening sphere of public discourse. While many may be offended by the suggestion, terrorism may participate in the democratic field, at least inasmuch as it opens discussion on the problematics of electoral and textual representation, persuasion and participation from the margins. This question returns the definition of terrorism to the dichotomy of state and sub-state legitimacy. By restricting the definition of terrorism to sub-state organizations, the 'nation' clearly condones its own strategies of violence, even as they are perpetrated against 'noncombatants' and 'innocents'. If marginalized groups are excluded from the democratic process and have a global governance system merely imposed upon them by greater and alien powers, they are condemned to seek other means of political expressivity, persuasion or resistance.

It is certainly for this reason that many commentators have included the possibility of a state-sponsored terrorism in their taxonomies of political violence. Totalitarian regimes, in particular, have most obviously perpetrated acts of terror against their own and other citizens. But as we suggest, even democratic states have employed various terrorist tactics which may quite explicitly seek the submission of domestic or alien populations to a particular government policy or interest. For our purposes, we would identify this violence in terms of strategies and operations, rather than fixing it to a specific human category, social group or political perspective. That is, rather than speak of 'terrorists', this approach will identify specific kinds of groups – transnational and sub-national militant organizations, government-sponsored agencies, governments and their armed forces – who engage in specific kinds of politically motivated violence. In this way, some of the complexities of terrorism might be more fully elucidated, most particularly as they are generated through culture, meaning-making and the media. The approach permits, for example, the exposition of the relationship between terrorism and counter-terrorism as contingent rather than privileged or hierarchical. This strategy may also allow us more clearly to articulate the perspectives of the antagonists and the ways in which the language wars of the current phase of terrorism and political violence are being waged.

We might understand, as we noted in the Introduction, how it is that the 100,000 civilian deaths that have occurred during the invasion and occupation of Iraq (Roberts et al., 2004) have been symbolically subsumed by the discursive strategies of the Coalition government and media, while the deaths of several thousand Americans in the twin towers effectively 'changed the world'. In given circumstances, therefore, the state, including the democratic state, may be prone to the deployment of 'terrorist' tactics, including the infusion of a communicational violence which is designed to publicize its interests and intimidate, coerce and persuade its audiences. As we shall see through the course of this book, this predisposition raises again substantive questions about freedom, democracy and the legitimacy of culture within a hierarchically forming global context.

To this extent, our definition of politics is also expansive. Following Michel Foucault's disarmingly simple mantra which claims that 'politics is everything and everywhere', we are particularly interested in a 'cultural politics' which is constructed around semiotic or discursive processes. While this will be already clear, the current study is modelled on the work of people like Foucault (1977a, 1981, 1991) and Ernesto Laclau (1991) who have sought to examine the trajectory of modern history and culture in terms of a broadly dispersed discursive dissemination and exchange model. To this extent, power is considered a dynamic and precarious contingency of human relationships; power may be exercised through specific social institutions such as the military and government, but it is not grounded or fixed in ways that are unalterable or incapable of exchange. Moreover, and as Foucault insists, while power is exercised and exchanged through the facility of discourse or language, it is inevitably experienced at the level of the individual body. Terrorism is conveyed through various symbolic and discursive channels, but it is ultimately experienced through the biology, psychology and emotions of the body. The body feels its fear and pain and these responses are simultaneously generated as a message to other bodies in other contexts.

By focusing on the strategies and attributes of terrorism, our notion of 'global terror and political violence' is inclusive and not constrained by a strict legal or operational definition, nor by the caricature of specific 'terrorist' organizations. The primary interest of this book, in fact, centres on the ways in which the characteristics of terrorism are mediated within the complex relationships of globalizing culture. The focus, therefore, is drawn toward those zones of terrorism that are emanating out of the rising discourse of east–west divide. These attributes can be summarized in the following terms:

1. Terrorism exists in a contingent relationship with the global media networks. As has been argued, modern terrorism is fundamentally communicational; it could not exist without the network of communicational channels that convey its impact and message to broad audiences across the globe. As a cultural form, terrorism is a violence that has its semiotic roots in the culture of the modern media. This contingency of violence, however, becomes a facility or strategy which is available to governments, as well as sub-national and transnational militant groups. The strategy of silence or censorship, in this sense, constitutes a form of representation, a media strategy which is designed to shape meanings and social knowledge. Thus, the strategy of imposed silence (censorship) is as much a manifestation of the contingent relationship between violence, power and mediation, as is the release of specific messages (public relations). As we have seen in Russia and the United States, governments may typically invoke the rubric of security in order to justify the management and control of information surrounding terrorism and terrorist events.

    While a number of commentators have acknowledged the importance of the media for modern terrorism, they have tended to treat the process involved as one of simple message delivery. When we remind ourselves that the media is formed through a set of relationships – producer, text, audience – within a cultural and governmental context, it becomes obvious that the predisposition toward violence is reflexive and somewhat paradoxical. Violence generally, and political violence in particular, are major revenue generators for the media industries: violence, through its various permutations, is part of the fiscal and semiotic foundations of the modern media. Media audiences, who are also the polis, the community and the public, seem also to be implicated in this reflexive contingency of violence.

2. Terrorism is a category of political violence which is intended to influence foreign, occupying and domestic–home governments, as well as communities. As many commentators have noted, terrorism uses its immediate victims and material targets for semiotic and

symbolic purposes. Attacks may be designed to create fear or a sense of threat. As in Beslan and occupied Iraq, hostages may be used as bargaining tools with foreign governments. Successful attacks may be used to promote causes and attract new recruits. It is certainly true that the 9/11 attacks were critical to the survival of al-Qa'ida.

3. To this extent, terrorism is both material and highly abstract. Its meanings are thus shaped by culture's immanent complexities and tensions – its language wars. The current wave of terrorism and political violence is bound, therefore, by ethnic, religious, discursive and political differences which are being shaped by a resurgence of an historical east–west divide. This cultural politics of difference manifests itself in terms of equally problematic disputes over territory and economic resources, especially oil. However, these resource wars are themselves the predicate of a globalizing culture which implicates differentials of power and the uneven distribution of discursive resources. The east–west divide is the abstract manifestation of cultural disputes which use violence to maintain or subvert this global hierarchical order.

   In fact, the whole notion of a 'war on terror' signifies the level of abstraction that is driving the highest level of policy-making and legislative–military authority in the developed world. The enemy of this new 'war' is a concept, a metaphor, that fills the heart and mind with dread – not merely because it is insidious but because it can never be seen other than through the lens of a highly politicized cultural imaginary. Culture, therefore, is an absolutely critical feature of terrorism.

4. Terrorism tends also to focus its violence against non-military or civilian targets and infrastructure. Attacks like 9/11, Bali, Madrid, Beslan and London are clear examples of this strategy. The carpet bombing of Afghanistan and Iraq by American-led forces is less clear – even though innumerable civilians have been killed and maimed in the attacks. Whether this sort of 'collateral damage' can be seen as a form of terrorism pivots upon the issues of intentionality, military strategy and morality. US military strategists claim that these bombings were focused on military or 'strategic' targets and civilian death and injury are largely unintentional or accidental. The smart bomb technology, proven to be a fraud in the first Gulf War, has nevertheless been designed to minimize civilian casualties.

Certainly for many Iraqi and Afghani citizens, the invasion and occupation of their countries by American-led forces constitute a form of political violence which is both brutal and oppressive. The US forces deliberately destroyed water, electricity and sewerage infrastructure in Baghdad, for example, leading to the suspension of hospital facilities and the spread of water-based diseases. Along with the continuing violence, the destruction of infrastructure is creating considerable risk of disease and death for many non-military Iraqis.

The use by US forces of scatter and percussion bombs, which are designed to inflict maximum damage and death to personnel, if nothing else, suggests an astonishingly careless approach to the lives of noncombatants and non-military infrastructure; the UK and Australian forces refused to support this weaponry precisely for this reason. For the US authorities, however, it is the issue of 'targeting' which exempts them from the accusation of terrorism. For our purposes, however, this question of incidental or intended target seems less important than the corporeal and symbolic effects of the military strategy. Certainly, there are many commentators who believe that the aggressive military response to Islamic insurgency by America and its allies, particularly Israel, is actually contributing to the forward spiral of global violence, oppression and human rights abuse – especially in the Middle East. To this extent, we include this ambiguous category of government and military assault on civilians within our general taxonomy of global terror and political violence.

Clearly, this list of attributes is somewhat more complex and controversial than the accounts provided by other texts. In particular, the reference to culture, censorship and the possibility of a violence which may incidentally as well as deliberately target civilians provides a basis by which the strategies and activities of democratic states, governments and their military can be examined within the broad rubric of terrorism and political violence. This is not to suggest that there is an equivalence between a militant extremist organization and a democratically elected government; rather, this approach seeks to expose the politics of violence as a communicational and cultural strategy. Underpinning this violence is a faithfulness and ideology which continues to privilege 'democracy' as a cultural and political norm. The objective, therefore, is to deconstruct the privilege, exposing its underlying assumptions to re-examination and ultimately reconstruction.

TELEVISUAL MEDIA AND THE BROADCAST OF VIOLENCE

Persuasion and propaganda have long been important tools in politics, social management and war (Laqueur, 1987, 2003). The ascendancy of a televisual mediasphere, however, creates new conditions for persuasion, appending to the Enlightenment political and social institutions that were constructed around the primary medium of writing (the *logos*) a new mode of visual and screen-based communication. While there are a range of continuities and overlapping strategies that bridge the *logos* and broadcast culture, there are also some very important differences and tensions (see Lewis, J., 2003). If we are to appreciate more fully the ways in which political violence is shaped through mediation, then we need to examine these continuities and differences, most particularly as they are engaged through the formation of certain kinds of social and cultural knowledge. Recalling once more that we are defining the media as a set of relationships – text, producers, audiences, government – we are able to see that the cultural and cognitive shaping of political violence is constituted through a *process* of semiotic interaction. This interaction is itself defined by the notion of 'representation' – that is, the process by which the experiential or phenomenal world is transformed as text (discourse, image, language).

An act of terrorism is, of course, immediately phenomenal, but it is also and inevitably a discourse which is available to the broader expressivities of representation. As text, the act becomes engaged in the amplitude of communicative dissemination and culture (including economic and political context). The emergence of broadcast technologies and networks has clearly accelerated this process, creating conditions for the proliferation of image-based information and televisual populism. This new cultural condition does not necessarily imply the obliteration of Enlightenment writing technology or the condition of the *logos*. Rather, modern cultures have created new social and semiotic spaces in which the various communicational media – interpersonal, oral, written and broadcast – function through, within and on occasions against one another. Broadcast media, in fact, has integrated the immediacy of oral communication with the representational facilities of writing through a new visual dynamic (Lewis & Best, 2002). At this point, we would also argue that the new interactive digital technologies – the Internet in particular – combine a number of communicational functions, including writing, telecommunications, broadcast and narrowcast imaging; while the Internet will be discussed specifically during the course of this book, its general functionality will be included within the ambit of broadcast televisualization, along with television, cinema, photography, video-DVD and digital games technology. In this sense, the Internet may operate as a narrowcast or targeted communications medium, like art house cinema or public broadcasting television, within the general spectrum of the mass media.

The televisual mode, in fact, accentuates the seemingly opposite effects of immediacy and representation through a highly unstable and hybrid cultural compound. As Martin Heidegger noted in his analysis of early-twentieth-century media, the visualizing technologies of photography and cinema actually contributed to the transformation of modern consciousness: according to Heidegger, all things are transmogrified into 'a world as picture', a seeming presence which is fabricated from what is actually absent (Heidegger, 1977, Lewis, J., 2003). James Carey (1991) corroborates this idea, arguing that the new broadcast technologies and media forms that emerged in the early part of the twentieth century contributed significantly to the establishment of new communications cultures with new standards, codes and expressive etiquettes.

While we need to avoid a determinist conception of these transformations, it is nevertheless important to recognize that the televisualization of communications culture significantly affected the consciousness and social knowledge (*episteme*) of the contemporary world. Writing and the *logos* remain significant for the *episteme* of contemporary culture; however, televisualization, with its proliferation of signs, images and informational ephemera, contributes to the destabilization of meaning in the formation of what Umberto Eco and Jean Baudrillard have called a state of 'hyperreality'. This hyperreal consciousness, in fact, enables particular conceptions of the 'real', including the sense in which knowledge may be visually constituted. As Fredric Jameson (1991) has famously noted in his discussions of postmodernism, the essential qualities of time and space are radically re-imagined in a culture that is bound to the visualization of its reality. Paul Virilio claims that this new conflux of dynamic mediation and static resolution constitutes a form of 'polar inertia', a context in which all time is surrendered to the televisual image:

As on stage, all things are concentrated on the spot, everything is played out in the privileged instant of the act, the immeasurable instant that replaces extension and protracted periods of time. No longer a golf course but a 'video performance', no longer a road circuit but a track simulator: *space no longer stretches out ahead; the moment of inertia replaces constant movement.* (2000: 17)

The image, that is, like the culture it helps create and from which it draws, has become increasingly destabilized by this concentration of opposite effects.

It isn't possible, of course, to disengage televisualization from other social-historical trends which have contributed to semiotic destabilization. However, we can see that the electronic artefact itself carries specific qualities which predispose it to various kinds of semiotic volatility. As we have already noted, for example, the electronic artefact integrates the immediacy and ephemera of the human voice with the extemporizing effects of representation. This conflux of immediacy and durability inverts the spatial separation of lived and representational experience, most particularly as the electronic text becomes part of the mass production system and is broadly accessible to significant numbers of people. Thus, the proliferation of visual information challenges the informational status of lived experience, blurring boundaries as it renders the exceptional familiar and the familiar exceptional. In an informational environment where representations and experiences flow so rapidly and convulsively between one another, texts and meanings invariably clash and seek allegiances with corroborating or affiliated knowledge.

In this sense, the semiotic values of violence and politics impregnate the *episteme* which governs public perceptions and public opinion. The audience–elector becomes enmeshed in the unceasing wash of televisual information within the mediasphere. The perpetually unfolding web of hyperreality entraps the audience–public in a particular conception of hyperreal violence, including political violence. Adapting and developing Julia Kristeva's (1984) concept, Jacques Derrida (1974) has dubbed this semiotic momentum 'intertextuality', a process by which words and texts seek 'supplements' in order to generate meaning. While Derrida is discussing the specific qualities of writing, the process is in fact accentuated in an information-dense televisual culture. The absent–present compound, which underwrites all modes of textual representation, is even more acutely destabilized through the rapid generation of images and signs; meanings are perpetually deferred as the signifiers encounter their supplements, alternatives and preternatural emptiness (non-meaning). The pervasive image and voice of the human subject, along with televisualization's more accessible and less rarefied context of 'viewing' (as opposed to reading words), mediate a new sensibility of subject-oriented community. Televisualization's capacity for rendering the familiar exceptional and the exceptional familiar enables viewing subjects to be bonded through the mediational presence of textualized subjects. This mediational community of subjects, however, is immediate and 'real', but also profoundly deceptive. The immediacy of the imaged subject is not housed in a durable context of lived experience, but is duplicitously evanescent and intensely abstract – a seeming presence which is merely conditional; a life that has no depth-presence, nor resonance beyond a memory which is also and inevitably a counter-memory (Foucault, 1977b).

As we will discuss in detail in Chapter 3, this sense of a mediational community was most spectacularly evident in the events of 9/11. The horror and shock of the attacks created precisely the semiotic void we have been discussing. In a sense, the image of the conflagration and collapsing towers, and of people pitching themselves out of windows to certain death, formed a new dissociation, a semiotic space in which audiences, journalists and public authorities struggled for adhesion and meaning. The initially incidental, but powerfully wrought, concept of a 'war on terror' provided for many a reference for the construction of new meanings. A flush of patriotism gathered around the seeming omnipresence of characters like the US President and the New York Mayor, creating a mediational community which shared the emotions of disgust, outrage, grief and nationalism. Each new pronouncement from the government, each new bulletin, interview or image served to propel further the narrative of communicational patriotism and a sense of national memory which could be personified in the character of the President.

But as a narrative, these stories existed by the subtle interchange of absence and presence, and the momentum of the deferral of meaning. Within the global industrial economy deferred meanings are integrated into a complex of semiotic and commercial deficits. Each media pronouncement or text is shaped through a deferral narrative in which the meaning of the story is linked in perpetuity to its supplement – the next news bulletin, episode, CD release, film, PR campaign or advertisement. Each new discourse or text is gestant, that is, with its own arrival and departure, and with the generational connection to past and future texts. This system of connectedness creates a fiscal and semiotic debt which can only be redeemed through the exigency of the next instalment, the next great event, the next epiphanal spectacle. In order to support this semiotic exigency, media organizations within the industrial complex must invest in new technologies, strategies, productions and personnel. Everything must be the newest and the latest: ratings, market data, advertising contracts, licences, boards of directors, shareholders, parliamentary hearings, audiences and creditors – all contribute to a sense of informational volition for media professionals. This 'imperative for information' drives journalists and editors, with an accelerating momentum, toward an ever greater level of production and productivity in an increasingly vigorous and contested semiotic and financial environment.

In many respects, this environment is impossible for media professionals who must serve the informational and ideological needs of a complex democratic social system while satisfying the specific interests of private capital. The news media, in particular, incurs a further 'social' debt in relation to specific Enlightenment and democratic ideals. As a foundational component of mass writing culture, the news media created the civic and informational bridge between the state and its citizenry. Thomas Carlyle makes explicit the link between the news and democracy, arguing that the 'truth' which journalists generate (in their role as the Fourth Estate) enables democratic institutions to function effectively: 'Printing, which comes out of writing, I say often, is equivalent to Democracy: invent writing, invent Democracy' (1905: 349). And indeed, while the rise of the professional media and mass writing may have promised a new plurality of ideas and ideals for modernizing, democratic societies (Gouldner, 1979), this plurality is critically stifled as informational oligarchs generate increasing financial debt-loads around a process of centralization and control (see Habermas, 1989, MacKay & O'Sullivan, 1999, Rantahen, 2005). In their zeal for standardization and mass market unity, corporate media organizations are necessarily threatened by an excess of diversity in public ideas, tastes and preferences.

One of the significant paradoxes of terrorism reporting, in fact, relates to the huge increase in media revenues following a major event: violence sells. The dramatic events of 9/11 and the invasions of Afghanistan and Iraq continue to generate texts and public interest. Media companies have invested significant sums in network technologies, professional labour and media space – all of which are designed to generate textual supplements and advertising income that will help override the massive debts that corporations necessarily carry. Like the medical profession, which aspires to human benefice but which thrives on human suffering, journalism is fundamentally paradoxical; the message-bearing capacity of media texts is perpetually undermined by these contradictory impulses toward public good and private interest.

To this extent, accusations that the mass–corporate media are the servants of conservative political interests tend to overstate the effectiveness of message delivery systems and the capacity of a given message to overcome these competing intensities. While there will be more to say about this issue later, it should be noted here that these systems are themselves subject to reflexive semiotic and financial deficiencies which surrender messages to the whirring uncertainty of a complex and often contradictory culture. Messages are subsumed, therefore, within a radical textual and cultural momentum, a momentum which frequently confounds the meanings that professional communicators seek to inscribe in their production. Thus, while media professionals might seek sincerely to resolve the classical tension between private capital and public good, their efforts will always be frustrated by the evolution of a communicational culture which is moving beyond the textual acuity of the Enlightenment toward the proliferation of meanings and their contention.

This is especially the case where 'meaning' is charged with the discourse of economy and the viewer–audience is perpetually aggregated as a more or less unreliable 'market'. The fragmentary and emotional power of the image, in fact, appends itself to the culture of mass consumption; news becomes info-tainment and the professional journalist becomes celebrity. The lived experience of the viewer and the lived experience of the generated image converge in a powerful remixing of consciousness. In this way, the political status of the citizen and his/her relationship with the state are dramatically transformed. The conduit of mediated truth and information which connects the state to the citizen becomes a complex matrix of economic, ideological and textual interplays. A politician no longer simply represents the interests of an electorate; s/he becomes a media representation by which the consumer/elector and the media text are transposed and become increasingly indistinguishable. In a politics of the hyperreal, in which the momentum of representation is perpetually seeking to overcome its semiotic and fiscal deficits, the televisual media becomes the new public sphere – the mediasphere

– where knowledge and judgement are perpetually undermined by their own self-referencing and exigent contingencies. The military strategies and notional 'public consent' that have evolved around the war on terror are only comprehensible, that is, through an analysis of this mediasphere.

REPRESENTATION AND VIOLENCE

With all this in mind, it is important to emphasize that the media is both element and conduit in the matrix of social, political and cultural relationships; these relationships are themselves conditioned by the predominance of the image and the imperatives of fiscal, semiotic and ideological deficit. In modern, western-style capitalist economies where the social nexus is forged around various permutations of hierarchy and the uneven distribution of wealth, the media generates an uncertain subliminal effect. The effect is never complete since it is a contingency of the fiscal, semiotic and ideological deficits which necessarily frustrate any attempt to fix meaning as an absolute social referent. The social knowledge that is generated by the fictional and news-based media remains unstable since it's created through the volatile mixing of a textual and subject consciousness which has neither centre nor substance. Thus, even the ideological power of organizations like the Fox media network, which unashamedly promotes the interests and policies of the Bush Republican administration, can never be absolute or unassailable since it must confront its own internal and external deficits. The 'power' of the media, therefore, is actualized only inasmuch as it is a momentum within the broad cultural trajectory of unstable semiosis – that is, media power is a force that is not 'controlled', but like fissile material threatens at any point to erupt into unexpected and unmanageable language wars.

This is precisely what Martin Heidegger has in mind when he describes the televisualized world as having the appearance of the gigantic – 'The gigantic presses forward in a way that seems to make it disappear' (Heidegger, 1977: 135). When vision becomes fragmented and enlarged as 'spectacle', Heidegger explains, the complexity of life and the living subject begin to disappear. Visual technology, thereby, creates a context of 'subjectivism' which for Heidegger refers to an obsessive individualism. Even so, Heidegger makes clear that the formation of the world as picture is an outcome of 'man's' separation from his essential nature: that is the separation of the subject from his world of objects. The slide to subjectivism, or obsessive individualism, results from man's efforts to position himself at the centre of all things. The world as picture is not merely a representation, therefore, but a centralizing process whereby 'Man becomes that being upon which all that is, is grounded as regards the manner of its Being and its truth' (Heidegger, 1977: 128). The subjectivism of such a world implicates the technology of representation by which the oscillation of 'bringing forth and setting before' generates its own mass logics, its own mass effects. In Heidegger's broader philosophy, then, the question emerges:

> Only where man is essentially already subject does there exist the possibility of his slipping into the aberration of subjectivism in the sense of individualism. But also, only where man *remains* subject does the positive struggle against individualism and for the community as the sphere of those goals that govern all achievements and usefulness have any meaning. (1977: 133)

A world which is 'conceived and grasped as picture' (Heidegger, 1977: 129) distinguishes itself in terms of the conflux of absence in seeming presence. What appears to be present as the essence of the modern age, Heidegger tells us, is precisely what is missing. The pictorialization of the vastness of the world actually reduces detail, events and texture into a conforming whole which is at once enormous and enormously reduced. If we substitute the notion of 'world' for the more contemporary concept of 'culture', we can sense a profound resonance in Heidegger's anxiety over 'Americanization' by which representations only resemble themselves, avoiding at all points the possibility of 'calculation' or measured understanding. This process of 'becoming incalculable' constitutes an invisible shadow that is cast around all things everywhere as 'man has been transformed into *subiectum* and the world into picture' (Heidegger, 1977: 135). Extending the perspectives in *Being and Time* (1952) and 'The question concerning technology' (1977), Heidegger makes clear that this transformation of the world into picture defines the 'essence of the modern age' (1977: 130). The modern era is not to be delineated in terms of the binary set, reality–signification; rather, the world is actually a picture, a consciousness that is slipping into an absolute and homogeneous subjectivism. The spectacle of violence, in particular, seems to have been a central and defining quality of screen culture virtually since its inception. Like the spectacle of sexual romance, most particularly as it is manifest in the female body, the vision of masculine violence has been an essential motif for image-based media.

This is not to suggest that violence is entirely absent from writing culture. It is rather to argue that the coding of the *logos* subdues the emotional and psychological impact of violence. Indeed, this capacity of representation to transform the phenomenal world was recognized by the Enlightenment, most particularly as it aestheticized and resolved the excesses of human 'passions'. The Romantic writers and philosophers, in particular, claimed a unique power for writing (especially poetry) which, as Coleridge claims in *On Imagination*, could release the higher virtues of human reason and creativity from the degradation of technology and history. Like Carlyle, Jacques Derrida identifies the critical importance of writing for the formation of the modern, democratic state: 'In opposition to the autocratic cities of Antiquity, which were their own centers and conversed in the living voice, the modern capital is always a monopoly of writing; it commands by written laws, decrees and literature' (1974: 302). There can be little doubt that the transformation of western political culture through the period of modernity is inevitably implicated in the rise of writing and print technology. Historians such as Walter Ong (1982), Elizabeth Eisenstein (1983), Benedict Anderson (1991) and Michel Foucault (1972, 1974) have explained how printed writing facilitated the capacity of the state to administer, socialize, educate, discipline and manage mass populations. This record-keeping capacity, however, is also associated with a significant transformation of 'consciousness', most particularly as the individual subject is reshaped in terms of the abstract nature of mass society and the representational processing of writing itself.

In this sense, representation in writing is paralleled by representation in the politics of democracy. Authority is delegated (supplemented) through polis, government and state; meanings are delegated through writer, reader and text. The object and the subject of political authority are separated or 'divided off', leading to a problematization of power, responsibility and transferral; democratic representation creates, that is, a dynamic of concentration and deferral, presence and absence: 'Political decentralisation, dispersion, and de-centering of sovereignty call, paradoxically, for the existence of a capital, a center of usurpation and of substitution' (Derrida, 1974: 302).

The profound achievement of writing and writing democracy, then, centres on their capacity to mobilize the absent–present of conflict and violence through idealized discursive forms. The ideals of progress and reconciliation, in particular, are coded within the political designs of 'democracy' in order to neutralize the negative effects of mass society (massification) and the potential dangers associated with capitalist hierarchy and the rise of individualism. Heidegger's preference for this idealization is echoed in the writing of recent political scientists like John Keane (2004), who argues that the institutions of democracy have, at least in the 'mature democratic state', the capacity to deploy violence in a measured and rational manner. In this sense, the establishment of parliamentary systems, public education and print news media constitutes the significant legacy of the first three hundred years of the Enlightenment.

Michel Foucault (1977a, 1991) argues, in fact, that the discourses of violence become captive to the interests and capacities of statecraft and governmentality. In order to manage mass populations, the state and the broad matrix of its agencies transform coercive violence into various forms of 'violent' discourses – that is, legitimated modes of expression which confirm the authority of the state over the citizen. While assuring us that the power that is inculcated in discourse is widely distributed, Foucault nevertheless focuses his historical studies on the managerial and surveillance capacity of the state and its 'technologies of power' (1977a). The threat and discourse of violence remain infused in government, law, policing and defence; the legitimacy of the state discourses of violence is thus contrasted against the illegitimacy of violence perpetrated by the citizenry, especially as it is expressed through sedition and various forms of crime. Of course, where the state requires the citizenry to act violently on its behalf – as military, police or penal agents – the state delegates its legitimacy and authority, under strict provisions, to particular members of the community. In most cases, these particular members of the community are the most expendable, based on class, ethnicity, gender, education levels and wealth-generating capacity.

The state and the citizen, in fact, are bound within a fundamental nexus of violence (Lewis, J. & Lewis, B., 2004a). While this nexus will be explored in greater detail in subsequent chapters, it is worth noting here that the ideal of reconciliation inscribed in democracy is simply and paradoxically the predicate of the specific discursive strategies we have just outlined. More generally, though, the state itself is a contingency of the violence of the citizenry; the threat of violent sedition, civil conflict or the rejection of state legitimacy perpetually *underwrites* the violence of the state. The codings of democracy, therefore, *overwrite* these contingencies through an imaginary of grounded and referential authority. In effect, the language wars that have given rise to the modern democratic state, the incendiary of violence which created the need for a democratic discourse, have not been expunged by the rise of writing and the parliamentary system – they have merely been re-coded and placed within parentheses.

Nor indeed, have these codes dissolved the violence that exists within publics and communities that are contained within democratic states. Violence and threat continue to be legitimate and quasi-legitimate activities and discourses within social groups and various cultural forms. While numerous sociologists have recognized this point, especially as it relates to codes of masculinity within marginal and criminal subclasses, there is a sense in which violence and conflict are more broadly inscribed in everyday practices of family management, sexuality, sport, news, information and entertainment. It is certainly around this final point that the rise of screen culture is profoundly implicated.

We have suggested that televisual culture, especially television, has become enormously pervasive; it has the remarkable capacity to render exceptional events and phenomena familiar, and familiar events and phenomena exceptional. We have also suggested that the emergence of a hyperreality removes the clear delineations that separate the phenomenal from the representational. This is certainly the case with violence where the more subdued dimensions of 'writing' conflict are released through various gradients of visually explicit detail (Sontag, 2003). The image, in fact, creates precisely that sense of 'the gigantic', as Heidegger calls it, liberating the more subliminal codings of writing to the extremes of human emotion and sensate response. More generally, of course, the transformation of violence into televisual codes also marks an entry into the broad industrial economy of broadcast media and symbolic exchange. The emergence and elevated profile of this new era of apocalyptic terrorism, along with its antithetical 'war on terror', engage immediately with an economy of signs in which violence is already an ascendant motif.

To this extent, the instances of political violence in America, the Middle East and other parts of the world are both commodities and semiotic values which are 'supplements' to, and interact with, pre-existing discourses of violence: the meanings of these events are constituted in terms of this broad history and lexicon of physical harm. The perpetrators of the violence (military and militant) are as much bound to these intertextualities as are the media professionals, audiences and governments who seek to comprehend and explain the actions of the perpetrators – and their own responses. Thus, the 'reading' of a violent act engages audiences in the process of cultural renderings; these responses form part of a politics of violence that reaches beyond the framework of the *logos* and democratic discourses into the broader personal and social lexicon of televisual violence. While this issue will be explored in later chapters, it is noted here that the rise of broadcast technologies has brought with it a cultural politics which appends itself to the Enlightenment discourses of writing-based democracy. This new broadcast-based politics, manifest in the current phase of global terror and violence, works through, against and around the conventions of *logos* and its specific mode of governmentality.

In modern, televisual societies, therefore, legitimate, quasi-legitimate and latent discourses of violence are contained within an ideal of democracy which seeks to neutralize and reconcile difference without recourse to actual physical conflict. The moral and ideological inviolability of responsible government and 'rule of law' is nevertheless compromised, if not directly challenged, by the codes and motifs of televisual violence, heroic masculinity, militantism and, especially in the United States, 'gun culture'. This televisual violence is not simply a force that exists as aberration or at a distance; nor does it provoke a singular or easily estimable response of repugnance or adulation. Rather, it exists as an already composed and gestant image which works through various public conduits and texts, infiltrating the private domiciles and consciousness of the individual citizen. While Jean Baudrillard (1990, 1994) has described this power of mediated infiltration in terms of a sexualized simulacra which arouses an indefinable and insatiable desire in viewers, televisual violence seems to provoke a similar response. Drawing together the private and public domains, the televisualization of violence confronts viewers with a miasma of emotional and psychological effects within a familiar narrative of moral–ideological conflict. The viewer, entranced by the horror and excitement of the drama, is inevitably seduced by the possibility of heroic restoration, the conquest of good over evil, order over chaos. Yet in the process of seduction, the viewer also confirms the validity of violence and violent coercion, reaffirming the violence that underpins the seeming order of contemporary democratic politics and the authority of the state. Like the amorphousness of sexual desire provoked by televisual imagery, the violent arousal experienced by the viewer has no substance or focus. Whether generated through news or fictional texts, this violence seems symptomatic of a culture which, like a scorpion, is stinging itself with its own relentless and uncontrollable pathology.

THE FIRST CASUALTY: WAR AND TRUTH

We have established through the course of this chapter that contemporary terrorism is a form of political violence which exists in a contingent relationship with culture and the media. Political violence, it has been suggested, is formed through the process that has been defined as 'representation'. This process is itself the predicate of a complex interaction between the cultural politics of writing and broadcast, televisual communications. In particular, it has been argued that political violence emerges through a multitude of sources, including the discourses of citizenship, state authority and the more broadly dispersed violence in broadcast media texts and everyday culture. It remains for us to address more directly the question as to how the media might be conscripted into the service of the antagonists in this current incarnation of political violence constituted around a re-emergent east–west divide. As we have noted several times already, there are many commentators, public figures and military/militant strategists who believe that the resources of the media can (and should or should not) be deployed for the promotion of particular ideas, ideals and ideologies. While I have argued against the idea that the media and a message can *determine* an absolute effect on audiences, it needs to be asked whether it is possible for propagandists, journalists and PR professionals to exert an *influence* over the political perspective of audiences within the polis – most particularly through the manipulation of the language wars of political violence and terrorism.

The neo-Marxists and social control theorists are entirely unambiguous on this issue. According to commentators like Edward Herman and Noam Chomsky, the media is simply the servant of the government and other social elites. While the news media manipulates the truth, the narrative media create conditions for the rise of the pseudo-individual, the 'citizen' who is entirely distracted from real politics by the saccharin and materialist optimism of melodrama and other modes of popular culture (Postman, 1987, Adorno, 1994). Expanding on Althusser's notion of ideology, these views have been frequently adopted by anti-American protestors who argue that US cultural product distracts the public from important political decision-making, leading to an indifference towards or public consent for policies like Third World exploitation and the war on terror. As suggested above, however, these views take too little account of the complex interactions that form around politics, the media, violence and audiences. Herman, Chomsky and others fail to appreciate fully the instabilities that have evolved through televisual politics, in particular, and the ways in which meanings are constituted and dispersed within an hyperreal culture. In many respects the 'gigantic', to which Heidegger refers, is both to be feared and welcomed since it delimits the potential of meaning, consensus and communication as effected by the hegemonic interests of semiotic authority. That is, the emotional and psychological impact of the image releases meaning from the simple and singular control of the text producer. The 'gigantic' unleashes itself through the potential of the audience's own interests and psycho-cultural predispositions.

Governments and other elites, of course, recognize this potential, and hence a fear of the citizenry is marked through a fear of the media. So, while citizens may fear the capacity of elites to access and deploy textual resources, the elites in turn are afraid of the people's intrinsic creativity and capacity for resistance, indifference or rejection of authority and privilege. The regulatory power of governments, of course, enables the exercise of significant managerial techniques, but this is not tantamount to the exercise of direct control. The slippage of meaning, the complexity of culture, and the nature of mass mediation – especially the mediation of violence – combine with the intrinsic creativities of individuals and communities to unsettle the effectiveness of managerial intentions. For this reason, perhaps, the framework of 'instrumental rationality' by which modern governments claim to construct policy and law may be challenged by the problematics of communication and the often irrational, emotive or semiotically precarious demands of communication management. This struggle between policy and communicational imperatives illustrates more than anything else the ways in which the gigantic has infiltrated the formation of social knowledge and governmentality.

Slavoj Žižek concedes as much in his discussion of the US government's reaction to 9/11, especially its policies on Iraq. The war on terror, which is largely a discursive war propagated for the engagement of the media and various global publics, is shaped, according to Žižek, by an artful but erroneous logic: 'Only the twisted logic of dreams can explain why the United States thinks that the aggressive pursuit of contradictory goals – promoting democracy, reaffirming US hegemony, and ensuring stable energy supplies – will produce success' (2004: 1). These contradictory goals reflect, as much as anything else, the underpinnings of a contradictory media-based culture in which terrorism and war compete for legitimacy and the approval of a complex social polis. Governments of democratic states, in particular, must reconcile the contending imperatives of communication and economic–military action.

Critics like Žižek suggest, in fact, that governments obscure or distort the conditions of communication in order to deceive their electorates. In *Forbidden Truth* Jean-Charles Brisard and Guilliame Dasquié (2002) contend, for example, that the US government's real motivation for attacking and occupying Afghanistan relates to the failure of secret diplomacy which would have permitted the establishment of an oil pipeline across the territory for western consumption. This form of secret diplomacy and other types of government-sponsored clandestine activities are frequently justified in terms of 'national security'. However, as Sheldon Rampton and John Stauber (2003) argue, there is a clear tendency among governments of all declensions, including democratically elected governments, to manipulate their authority through the exclusion of significant portions of their citizenry. Under a system of 'expert knowledge', governments construct a value-based policy framework which is mandated by the processes of representation. Thus, while governments might tell us, through their expert system, what is 'good for us', these decisions are usually based on ideology and the interests of elite constituent groups (Stauber, 1995). Truth, honesty and transparency in government are immediately surrendered, Rampton and Stauber (2003) claim, when governments believe their elite interests and the perspective of the broader electorate might be in contention. The war on terror was declared, various critics suggest, because citizens are more likely to indulge the government's obfuscation in the name of national interest. As Rampton and Stauber argue in *Weapons of Mass Deception*, the complicated web of meanings that led to the American war on Iraq confounds the tension between transparency and information:

> Reality is messy, of course, especially in the aftermath of war, and these developments do not necessarily imply that disaster looms on the horizon as the United States tries to juggle the tension between occupying Iraq militarily and acting as its liberator. They do, however, suggest that the situation is more complicated than the images of victory that looked so unambiguously

inspiring on American television. It is important, therefore, that we ask ourselves what lies behind those images, how they have been constructed, and what they may be hiding. (2003: 7)

A more benign account of national interest in times of political violence and war, however, is offered by Young and Jesser (1997). In their assessment of the media and the military, Young and Jesser claim that the successful waging of a 'just' war is critically dependent on the capacity of the state to communicate necessary information to its citizenry. National security, Young and Jesser argue, must subsume all other governmental responsibilities during times of direct threat. Information must therefore be strategically managed in order to maximize military advantage and minimize social disquiet or anxiety. Governments must effectively communicate their perspectives in order to persuade the citizenry of the 'justness' of any specific strategy or action. To a certain degree, these processes of information management include the tactical release and withholding of information in order to optimize communicative effects. As Pinsdorf (1994) has noted in relation to the first Gulf War, military and government authorities deploy similar strategies as are used by advertising and public relations agencies, deftly manipulating public emotions and promoting interest in their ideas and 'products'.

Phillip Taylor (1992) argues, in fact, that the military's management of the media in the first Gulf War ensured that the horrors of military engagement were kept at a distance from America's domestic citizenry and indeed from the citizenry of the entire world. Carruthers (2000) explains the management of information in terms of a two-tier system. Privileged journalists were located within military bases and were provided with strategically packaged information, including televisual imagery, by the authorities. In a war which was fought largely through aerial bombardment, journalists were not able to record directly the events of engagement. In this way, they became dependent on military briefings and particular data packages in order to prepare their stories for domestic televisual consumption. Governments, thereby, were able to sidestep much of the critical and interpretative interpolation of the media and speak directly to the domestic citizenry. As Taylor notes:

[P]erhaps the most important lesson to be learned from the Gulf War is the need to redefine the relationship between the media and their audience. When the authorities can speak directly to the audience via live television rather than indirectly via the interpretations with which journalists have rationally informed their readers and viewers of what was going on, the gap between government and governed is narrowed substantially. What role is therefore left for the media? (1992: 272)

In Taylor's view, this role might best be defined in terms of 'facilitation' – as a conduit that engages the state with its citizenry. As we will discuss in Chapter 4, the embedding of journalists during the 2003 Iraq invasion extends this strategy, ensuring that the action of the invasion (and the heroism of the 'liberating forces') is presented through the prism of national interest.

Eric Luow (2001) argues similarly that the first Gulf War marked a moment of transformation for the western media. The very direct interventionism and censorship strategies that governments had evolved during the World Wars seemed less suitable for advanced media cultures of the late twentieth century; equally, however, a more open-access strategy had failed to satisfy the interests of government authorities during the Indo-China wars. During the 1990–91 Gulf War, therefore, US authorities deployed a more sophisticated and complex information strategy, one which was formed around a coalition of private media interests, public relations companies and the intelligence machinery of the military. America's 'stunning victory' in the Gulf is frequently measured in terms of the precision, brevity and intensity of its assaults on Iraq and the 'liberation' of Kuwait. The lingering memory of the '100-hour War' centres on the technological mastery of the United States, both in terms of its missile accuracy and the computerized representations of its assaults. In this sense, the aesthetics of the war were shaped by a particular kind of *scientica abstaractacus*, a disinterest which pivoted victory around an efficient and precise technological discourse. While US audiences were exposed nightly to a series of narrativized military miracles, the Iraqi soldiers and citizenry were mercilessly bombarded in a campaign that was designed, as much as anything else, to terrify them into submission and an ignominious retreat. Significant parts of Baghdad were razed. The enemy troops were annihilated as they flooded out of Kuwait and across the borders into Iraq.

The vast numbers of Iraqis who were slaughtered during the campaign (40–200,000) were kept from our eyes. Similarly, the 150 or so allied dead were deftly camouflaged in stories of heroic self-sacrifice or tragic misadventure. Of course, even before the killing, the American people had been softened up by a brilliantly conceived public relations campaign which had the daughter of the Kuwaiti ambassador posing as a hospital worker and telling stories of Iraqi atrocities in the invasion of Kuwait (MacArthur, 2004). This now infamous PR campaign paid for by the Kuwaiti royal family and conducted by CFK/H&K presented a range of false reports to the American Congressional Committee, including stories of Iraqi troops switching off infant incubators and committing vicious assaults against women and the infirm. Of course, these conflagrational events added an emotional intensity to the rational arguments about democracy, freedom, oil and commerce. Once engaged, the PR machinery turned its creative energies toward the maintenance of public support; the Gulf War became pre-presented as a war without death, bloodshed, pain or trauma. It became a war of miraculous and relentless western superiority. It was a clinical war in which justice was swift and precisely calculated.

Phillip Taylor (1992) argues, in fact, that the US-led victory in the first Gulf War remains 'stunning' because state and military information managers were able to construct the war as an event taking place 'at distance'. This 'distance', Taylor suggests, was created both through the effects of media management and the intrinsic nature of the strategy of 'saturation bombing' – a Second World War strategy that had been developed by the Americans in order to destroy the infrastructure and morale of the enemy with minimum direct ground combat. The medium of television confirmed this distance for home audiences, reinforcing the idea that a war can be articulated in a sort of virtual space (see also Luow, 2001: 181–4); televisualization ensured that the audience was kept at a distance from the details and conditions of actual warfare. Paul Virilio (1989, 2000) extends these arguments, suggesting that modern warfare is itself constructed around the technologies of distance – cinematic and 'telescopic' technologies which allow the military of advanced nations to attack their enemy from vast distances without any sense that they are dealing with human biology or human presence.

In fact, these notions of distance only partly explain the problematics of media representations of war as a mode of political violence. Physical space is transmogrified as it is 'mediated' and drawn closer to the viewing subject; this representational process creates the oscillating effect of distance–proximity. While Virilio speaks of the absence of human forms in telescopic or oracular warfare, in fact, these human forms are merely trans*formed* and re-articulated in the process of representation: they become forms of the absent–present, as we have outlined it in the earlier part of this chapter. Extending Martin Heidegger's notions of representation, we might see clearly that the televisualization of an event will simultaneously bring it closer and re-fix it within a new subject-defined reality. This contradictory engagement of distance and proximity parallels the absent–present of textual representation – the text and its constituent elements might seem to be present and near, but this proximity can only ever be 'apparent' and can only ever obscure the other dimensions of its constituent absence and distance. This unstable compound of opposing effects creates a televisual geography which can only be defined culturally, that is, in terms of cultural imagining.

Thus, America's 'stunning' victories in the first and second Gulf wars are not merely an expression of military competence and the effective construction or re-ordering of truth; they are equally and more definitively an evocation of the texture of cultural minds that are embedded in a televisual context. Taylor conceives of a distance which is effectively produced by a well-managed confluence of interests; Luow, like Noam Chomsky, attacks the American authorities and the co-opted media institutions for their falsification of the facts of war. But beyond these explanations is a forging of social knowledge that is extraordinarily adaptable and volatile, and hence susceptible to the rapidly evolving and devolving imaginings of a 'stunning victory'. As in Afghanistan and the 2003 invasion of Iraq, the first Gulf War demonstrated how the 'distance' of these modes of political violence defies its geography and enters the hyperreal consciousness of First World mediation. As governments engage in their communications and military strategies, they are encountering a profoundly volatile semiosis – a condition in which the truth is as elusive for governments and their PR machinery, as it is for the electorates who watch within their own domestic imaginaries.

Jean Baudrillard's (1995) argument that *The Gulf War Did Not Take Place* has been savagely criticized by a number of commentators who regard the claim as a piece of offensive, postmodernist sophistry. Christopher Norris, for example, complains that Baudrillard treats the War as a predigested and predetermined television event, one which left little more than an 'endless charade, a kind of phony war in which the stakes had to do with the management of public opinion, itself nothing more than a reflex response to the images, the rhetoric and PR machinery which create the illusion of consensus support by supplying the right answers and attitudes in advance' (1992: 11). The essence of Norris's complaint, a complaint echoed by the broad field of rationalist and materialist critique of postmodernist theory, is Baudrillard's belief that the whole notion of truth – and hence untruth – has been overwhelmed by the proliferation of signifying product in a televisual cultural context. This notion of an impossible truth, Norris argues, simplifies excessively the substantial and material facts of existence, leaving open the possibility of an unrestrained human infamy, one in which justice and injustice are indistinguishable and where public opinion can never be swayed or influenced by informed, substantive and reasonable argument. Thus, in Norris's view (see also Kellner, 1989, McGuigan, 1996, 1997) Baudrillard surrenders the world to those forces most able to manipulate this semiotic decay in order to suit their own iniquitous and hierarchical ends.

No doubt, most commentators on the current military activities in Muslim Asia would be equally contemptuous of claims such as 'the Afghan War or the Iraq invasion did not take place'. Indeed, the parallels are clear enough: the saturation bombing, the highly managed media, the demonization of the enemy, a stunningly brief, precise and intense military victory resulting in the 'liberation' of Afghanistan and Iraq. Claims that the military PR machinery and a co-opted media are manipulating public opinion are hauntingly similar to those registered during the past decade – in the Persian Gulf, the Sudan, Serbia and Kosovo. And, though complaints about the fatalism and pessimism of Baudrillard's perspective continue, the issue of a constituted televisual or 'hyper' reality emerges as pertinent in the current context. For example, Baudrillard argues in his analysis of the Gulf War that the virtual absence of fatalities on the American-led side suggests a radical re-inscription of the whole meaning of warfare. The Gulf War composes itself as a war without death: 'Strangely, a war without victims does not seem like a real war but rather the prefiguration of an experimental, blank war, or rather a war that is even more inhuman because it is a war without human losses' (Baudrillard, 1995: 73). In many ways, the first Gulf War provided a template for the US authorities, who in the more recent Iraq invasion and occupation have prohibited the publication of images of American deaths, including depictions of American coffins. Major media networks like Fox have also sponsored a war without mortality; as the most viewed information service covering the 2003 Iraq invasion, Fox adopted a policy of excluding graphic depictions of the violence, injuries and death.

In Jean-François Lyotard's terms (1991, see also Lewis, 1997) the reference to the 'inhuman' is not merely a manifestation of extreme brutality; the absence of death represents the suspension of humanist values. It is a double-play, an absurd rendering of an event which the government and its PR machinery would claim to be something entirely different. But if it is not a war involving brutal and terrible tactics, then what is it? The distance–absence that is created around the war and the information that frames it, remains peculiarly poised within this suspension of values – within the hyperreal which creates a domesticated, TV 'presence' out of something that is called a war but which only resembles its absence. For audiences, in fact, this remains an ineluctable violence, a mode of human tragedy which, like an accident on the highway, insists on being viewed. Within the mediasphere, this semblance of a war invokes a cultural memory that situates the visualized conflict within the history of other violent narratives, narratives which reassure the public–audience that the American hero–victim must ultimately prevail and confirm the ideals of humanist and liberal democracy. As Baudrillard argues, however, this 'resolution' is never quite released because the values that drive it can only exist within the dramatic suspense and suspension of truth that are forged through a hyperreal consciousness. That is, the expectation of restored humanist values exists only within a 'representation' from which it can never actually escape.

While Norris and others reject Baudrillard's questioning of the ontological and epistemological status of 'truth', there can be little doubt that the whole process of televisualization, the transformation of experience into representational image, intrinsically problematizes the concept and nature of truth. This does not render the war less terrible, as Norris and others might claim, but returns terrorism and war to the culture that creates them: it makes the conflict and threat more hideous because it suspends the viewer between the higher ideals of a non-violent democratic resolution of difference, and the pervasive codes of coercion and physical violence by which the media conditions our consciousness. Caught within the narrative of violence and suspended values, the viewer has no greater reference than the absence of the war that is not, and the culture that arouses without gratification. It is not, therefore, that the viewer believes the narrative of a war without death, but that s/he is poised within the deferral, perpetually awaiting the denouement of a meaning that the text promises though never seems to reveal. The viewer is trapped, that is, within the process of meaning deferral and supplementarity, as we have outlined it above.

What is perhaps most devastating about this condition, however, is that the state and its governments, those most charged with the responsibility for protecting truth and the humanist values of writing democracy, have contributed so substantially to their disintegration. Even a democratic government's claim to moral and ideological authority seems to unravel under the pressure of the truth. When the American troops entered Baghdad in 2003, this contradiction revealed itself as US tanks opened fire on the Palestine Hotel, killing a number of Reuters and al-Jazeera journalists. As Robert Fisk (2003) noted, there was no strategic reason for the attack, other than to punish those who had been reporting the war from 'behind enemy lines'. The al-Jazeera journalists, in particular, had adopted an open information policy, recording and publishing the events of the invasion in as much detail as 'the truth' could possibly bear. While the al-Jazeera reports were primarily broadcast through the Middle East, their information seeped into the western global networks, especially through the Internet. When the American tanks opened fire on the journalists, they were in a sense assaulting the premise of their own history and the ideals that had guided the path to democracy. Their fear of al-Jazeera mirrors the fear and loathing they carry for their own citizenry and the 'responsibilities' that democracy and freedom bear them.

Like the destruction of bridges in Kosovo, the killing of journalists in Iraq expresses a deep anxiety about the unruly and potentially subversive power of culture and communications. The ancient bridges in Kosovo represented community, communications, transportation and a powerful link to the region's history and culture; their destruction was an act of a delinquent terror, a fear that people might be capable of running their lives outside the force and brutal vision of government, the state and the genealogy of military elites. Similarly, the Reuters and al-Jazeera journalists were murdered because the government and its military fear the mediasphere they seek so vigorously to control. Just as Plato banned poets from his ideal Republic, the US authorities seem determined to obliterate the free flow of information and ideas, as well as any journalist who cannot fully subscribe to their strategies and ideals. The slaughter of the al-Jazeera and Reuters journalists, like that of so many others, is part of a state-sponsored terrorism that is as formidable and appalling as the deaths of children in Beslan or workers in the twin towers of New York.

CONCLUSIONS

There are several conclusions we can draw from the discussion in this chapter:

1. The label of 'terrorist' is used by adversaries in a violent conflict to demonize their enemies. Terrorism is a form of violent assault which targets civilians and civilian infrastructure in order to create fear and insecurity in enemy populations and governments. Terrorism is politically motivated and is designed to communicate the cause of the perpetrators to their enemies and potential affiliates. It is a form of political violence which may be exercised by governments, government agents, sub-national and transnational organizations.

2. As a cultural conduit and bearer of information, the global networked media is profoundly implicated in modern terrorism.

3. Media messages do not produce or determine specific effects. The process of 'representation' transforms lived experience into mediated text, creating a sense of 'presence' out of what is actually 'absent'. This process has proliferated in contemporary televisual culture, contributing to the broad transformation of social knowledge and consciousness. This includes the political consciousness which is evolving through the new public sphere which might be termed the mediasphere.

4. Within this mediasphere media organizations and their professional journalists must work within a context of semiotic (meaning) and financial deficit. This deficit drives the momentum of media production and consumption.

5. Violence is a central and defining quality in contemporary televisual culture. Violence is critical to the semiotic and financial momentum of contemporary media organizations. In this context, journalists and other text producers are caught between the demands of public good and private–commercial interests.

6. The nexus between the state and the citizenry is founded on violence. Democracy, at least ideally, has been designed to reconcile diversity and difference without recourse to physical conflict and coercion.

7. Individual governments seek to assert their interests through the control of the mediasphere. While messages never produce direct effects, government participation in the mediasphere and

in the processes of representation (including the representation of violence) 'influences' the public–viewer in various ways. At least part of the impact of this participation contributes to the insecurity and uncertainty of the polis. Governments, including democratic governments, inevitably compromise their own ideological and moral authority through an engagement in the mediasphere which suspends humanist values.

2
Conflict and Culture: Civilization, History, Identity

CULTURE AND ISLAM

In Chapter 1 contemporary terrorism was defined in terms of media and representation. It was argued that modern terrorism is essentially a communicational act, involving new forms of political expression within a televisual culture. While a general definition of culture was sketched out in the Introduction to this book, it is necessary to elaborate on this definition in order to appreciate fully the role of culture in the current phase of global terror. In particular, and this is the essential aim of the current chapter, it is necessary to locate and describe the relationship between global terror and culture in terms of critical concepts of civilization, history and identity. This chapter, therefore, examines the ways in which the concept of culture has been mobilized by antagonists in the current language wars on terror and political violence. The chapter begins with a study of those 'western' academic, public and media discourses which are contributing to a revitalized Islam–west divide. The chapter then examines the ways in which Islamic identity itself has been forged by members of the Muslim faith; the study includes an examination of the historical conditions which have contributed to the formation of a radical Islamic militantism. These discussions are finally situated within a general analysis of modernization, globalization and the processes of identity–subject formation.

'Culture', in fact, is a particularly efficacious term with a complex etymological history (see Lewis, 2002a, Milner, 2002, Williams, 1981). Enlightenment and Romantic philosophers and poets adopted the term into English to describe the more refined and transcendent states of human expression: high art and advanced civilization are manifestations of the cultured mind. The propinquity of the term 'culture' to a normative notion of 'civilization' seems to have provided a semantic bridge for anthropologists wishing to describe the more symbolic dimensions of human social groups. In this way, 'culture' has been adapted for the description of pre-modern (pre-civilized) groups who were unified through complex rituals and invisible 'webs of significance', as Max Weber and later Clifford Geertz described it. It is through these webs of meaning that humans are able to bring system, purpose, cohesion and order to their social and natural worlds. For anthropology, culture describes the more abstract and binding language and symbolic systems which identify a given social group from all other groups.

While never entirely shedding its more aesthetic application, 'culture' has been adapted as a more generic descriptor for a specific 'way of life' – a descriptor which emphasizes the symbolic, ritualistic and belief patterns of a given social group. While such a definition might be useful for empirical research on relatively closed and cohesive pre-modern societies, the concept is also being adopted for the study of complex, mass, modern societies. Studies from various areas of the social sciences, in fact, have applied a mode of 'cultural analysis' which seeks to identify and explain the 'symbolic order' of social formations or communities; these communities range from highly localized social subgroups such as 'ethnic minorities' through to national and transnational groupings such as 'Islam' or 'the west'. The object of these studies is not dissimilar to that of the earlier anthropological studies: that is, to locate the symbolic order or web of meaning that informs and sustains a particular social group and its 'way of life'.

This approach to culture is somewhat problematic on at least two counts. First, there has been a tendency in these studies to understate the importance of language and meaning gaps, particularly as they have been described by theorists like Jacques Derrida. Language is an imperfect tool and meanings are subject to the unceasing dynamic of what Derrida calls supplementarity – the process by which meanings are always attached to other meanings provided by other texts. This is not merely the polysemy that writers from Wittgenstein through Nietzsche and Barthes have acknowledged. It indicates, rather, that meanings are never complete but exist in a state of perpetual deferral and instability (see Chapter 1). As I have developed at length elsewhere (Lewis, 2000, 2002a, 2002b, 2003), this instability is actually exacerbated by political pressure. As institutions seek to fix meaning to a particular political perspective in order to create 'ideology', that meaning becomes necessarily separated from the everyday meaning-making practices of ordinary citizens (de Certeau, 1984, 1988, Laclau, 1991). This separation exposes the signifier to the radical contestation and re-ascription of meaning by those individuals and communities over whom the ideology is imposed. Under these conditions, new meanings and political perspectives will necessarily emerge out of the gaps created by the processes of deferral and signifier dissociation. These meaning gaps contribute to various forms of social change and historical discontinuities, as they are described by Michel Foucault.

The second problem with an homogenized 'way of life' approach to culture centres on the actual diversity and complexity of contemporary societies. The great diversity of lifestyles and their symbolic 'spheres of reference' problematize a model which assumes cohesion and structural integrity. In this sense, an individual may belong to, or participate in, a range of different cultures within various social boundaries. This may include cultures that are constructed around work, family, ethnicity, neighbourhood, religion, class, recreational activities, political allegiances, gender and sexuality. While boundaries may be drawn around political and legal institutions of 'nation', there may be enormous variations in values, rituals, customs, language and expressive practices. Central to these formations is a mode of 'identity' and a cultural imaginary by which the individual understands and explains the social and natural worlds. Thus, within a national 'cultural' framework, there may be cultural constituencies which overlap, complement, interact, contend or even seek to destroy one another through the various shapings and effects of historical and contemporary language wars. A social group's 'web of meaning', therefore, might be better understood as a mixing tide of flows and counterflows, a sea of meaning which may be described geographically or elementally but which can never be precisely contained or easily bordered.

Contemporary culture, which is comprised of these complex community and semiotic formations, is therefore highly dynamic and unstable. With multiple spheres of reference, culture is complex and often difficult to describe and identify. However, it has a very strong presence in public and scholarly discourse, providing a rubric for the more ineffable dimensions of human social activities, including political activities and the construction of social identities. Within the field of global terror and political violence, culture has become pivotal for the analysis of conflicts within a broad historical framing; this is particularly true for the major antagonists who are creating, or at least refurbishing, the polemic of an east–west divide. The notion of a cultural imaginary is valuable here since it acknowledges the interaction of a reasoned politics of social organization with the more abstruse dimensions of language and meaning-making processes. It also acknowledges the twists and contradictions that may underpin a cultural constituency, and the ways in which individuals may construct an identity and a perspective which emerges out of the broad assembly of contending historical, experiential and mediated cultural elements. Our task in this chapter is to explain more precisely how these elements are formed in terms of current discussions on global terror and political violence.

We need to begin this analysis, however, with the clarification of some key concepts. In particular, it is important to distinguish between 'Muslim', which is a mode of religious belief, and 'Islam', which links that faith to specific political ideals. Islam, in fact, might best be understood as the ideal 'state' which integrates the spiritual dimensions of the Muslim faith with the practical functions of law and social governance: that is, it brings together a transcendent with an earthly utopia. While many commentators treat Muslim and Islam as synonymous, this practice risks compounding all Muslim peoples and the diversity of faith within a unitary political framework. To this extent, the concept of Islam will be treated as *political* Islam. Of course, there are various gradients of political Islam expressed by various followers of the Muslim faith. Individuals, communities and governments which support the faith might thereby subscribe to or impose a more or less rigorous interpretation of *shari'ah* (Islamic law) and *fiqh* (theological knowledge of the law). Countries like Turkey are generally secularist; others like Saudi Arabia, Iran and Taliban Afghanistan are distinctly Islamic states, imposing a strict regime of Islamic law. Similarly, political organizations which support the Muslim faith may be more or less radical, and more or less militant in their approach to Islamicism and the imposition of its governmental regime. In fact, the term 'militant Islamicism' will be applied to distinguish those radical Islamicists who sponsor and employ violent means to bring about social and political change.

THE CLASH OF CIVILIZATIONS THESIS

It is difficult to discuss the formation of the new east–west divide without reference to Samuel Huntington's (1993) widely read essay, 'The clash of civilizations'. Amid the euphoria that accompanied the collapse of Soviet communism, Huntington's thesis expressed a more cautious prescience than the idealism expressed in Francis Fukayama's 'end of history' or George Bush senior's notion of a 'new world order'. According to Huntington, history is shaped by conflict, and the next major phase of warfare will be waged over 'culture' rather than ideology or economics. While nation-states will remain the most powerful entities in global politics, war will be waged through broad cultural alliances and divisions which Huntington calls 'civilizations': 'A civilization is thus the highest cultural grouping of people and the broadest level of cultural identity people have short of that which distinguishes humans from other species' (Huntington, 1993: 21). For Huntington these civilizations are characterized by shared language, history, religion, customs, values and institutions and a distinct mode of self-identification. Huntington adapts the 'web of meaning' approach to culture, arguing that these large and distinctive human social groupings would ultimately form around a shared and relatively well-integrated semiotic superstructure. In a definitively pessimistic teleology Huntington outlines the reasons why civilizations will clash, focusing primarily on the issue of fundamental and irreducible cultural differences. These differences are experienced within a context of increasing international competition for economic resources, and a deepening religiosity and resistance against the primacy of the west.

Huntington is particularly interested in the deep historical antagonism between the west and the Muslim east. Invoking Bernard Lewis's equally polemical account of 'The roots of Muslim rage' (1990), Huntington makes vigorous claims about the inevitability of Muslim hostility toward the west. With the likelihood of a Confucian–Muslim military alliance against the west, Huntington claims, it is incumbent upon western governments to limit intra-civilizational conflicts in order to unite their resources against non-western rivals. To this extent western authorities and policy-makers must seek 'to limit the expansion of the military strength of Confucian and Islamic states' and 'strengthen international institutions that reflect and legitimate Western interests and values' (Huntington, 1993: 38). Foreign policy, including aid, development and security policy, should be focused around self-preservation and civilizational goals. The primacy of the west is not to be taken for granted, but needs to be seen as a precarious and historically legitimate condition which must be protected at all costs against those who might seek to destroy it.

The events of 9/11 seemed to revitalize interest in Huntington's prescience. Those neoconservatives in the US administration known as the 'hawks' have been vocal in their re-rendering of Huntington's idea that the US and its allies should seek to limit the expansion of Islamic influence. Supported by academics like Bernard Lewis, the

Bush administration has constructed a raft of policies which seem to satisfy Huntington's appeals. Bernard Lewis, in fact, has suggested in his own analysis of September 11 that history is the central issue for contemporary policy-making. While claiming to acknowledge the great diversity within the Muslim faith, Lewis nevertheless aggregates the peoples and history of the Middle East, creating a sense that all Muslims are politically predisposed to the formation of an Islamic state. Hearkening back as far as the Crusades, Lewis reads the current pronouncements of Islamic radicals like Osama bin Laden as elemental reverberations of earlier jihad. The 'crisis' of Islam, Lewis claims, is being brought about because of the intrinsic nature of the Islamic state and of a religion which is ultimately incongruent with modernization, most particularly a modernization which insists on the separation of the state and religion. Like Huntington, Lewis points to the incompatibility of specific kinds of political values and the processes of a capitalist transformation. Using Christianity and Christian civilization as a reference, Lewis identifies the specific characteristics which distinguish Islamic modes of worship, epistemology, law and political authority which are incommensurate with a modern capitalist state. According to Lewis, 'Muslim' knowledge is entirely embedded in holy law and theocratic authority. In this sense, the *ulema* or 'clergy' are the keepers and protectors of knowledge, history, culture and law. Their authority in the spiritual world can never be disengaged from their authority in the material world: within Islam the two are simply co-extensive.

It is in this context that the attacks of September 11 need to be understood, Lewis urges. While accepting the possibility of diverse interpretations of the Qur'an, Lewis nevertheless warns that religion is a central platform for the political actions of many Muslims, including extremists and fundamentalists like Osama bin Laden. Lewis tracks bin Laden's jihad against the United States as an exercise in historical revelation. Lewis cites bin Laden's famous declaration of war against the United States, noting that bin Laden frequently invokes the more militant passages of the Qur'an, matching them against the various infidel incursions into the holy territories of the Arabic world. It is through bin Laden's 'Declaration of War against Jews and Crusaders' (1998), that Lewis finds the essence of Islamic terrorism:

> After citing some further relevant Qur'an verses, the document continues: 'By God's leave, we call on every Muslim who believes in God and hopes for reward to obey God's command to kill the Americans and plunder their

possessions wherever he finds them and whenever he can. Likewise we call on the Muslim ulema and leaders and youth and soldiers to launch attacks against the armies of the American devils and against those who are allied with them from among the helpers of Satan.' The declaration and the fatwa conclude with a series of further questions from the scriptures. (Lewis, B., 2003: xxvii)

If we are to believe Huntington and Lewis, then, the crisis of Islam is not merely an aberration of a fundamentalist minority but the expression of a cultural condition which embraces the extremes within the general context of Islam and its 'fourteen centuries of history [and] a billion and a third people' (Lewis, B., 2003: 1). America and its allies must do everything they can, Lewis urges, to protect themselves against this vision and its inevitable aggression.

Michiko Kakutani (2003) has suggested that this sort of cultural polemic has significantly influenced America's neoconservative perspective of Middle East politics. According to Kakutani, many in the current White House administration support the arguments of scholars, like Bernard Lewis, who believe that Islam is fundamentally constituted around the overthrow of all other religions, most especially Judaeo-Christianity with which it has been at war for a millennium. Kakutani also notes that this community of conservative scholars – Lewis, Eliot Cohen, Victor Hanson, Robert Kagan and William Kristol – has made significant contributions to the ideas and ideals of the Project for the New American Century, a highly influential think tank which urges a more 'muscular military posture' against those peoples and regimes 'hostile to our interests and values'. Eliot Cohen, for example, argues that these values – democracy, freedom, capitalist economics – cannot be divorced from America's responsibility as the world's primary power. America must defend its moral and material interests through the assertion of 'supreme command': through the moral and ideological authority of 'democracy', the US president must assert his will over the nation and the entire globe.

In a more general context, in fact, the New American Century urges the US government to assert its economic and military primacy in world affairs. As the only superpower, the US has the opportunity to shape globalism for its own advantage – and by implication the betterment of humankind (see Kaplan & Kristol, 2003). Robert Kagan and William Kristol make explicit, for example, their support for an interventionist American policy in the Middle East, claiming that the defeat and occupation of Iraq send a clear signal to the whole of the region:

> It is also becoming clear that the battle of Iraq has been an important victory in the broader war in which we are engaged, a war against terror, against weapons proliferation, and for a new Middle East. Already, other terror-implicated regimes that were developing weapons of mass destruction are feeling pressure, and some are beginning to move in the right direction ... From Iran to Saudi Arabia liberal forces seem to have been encouraged. We are paying a real price in blood and treasure in Iraq. But we believe it is already clear – as clear as such things get in the real world – that the price of the liberation of Iraq has been worth it. (Kagan & Kristol, 2004a: 13)

America's willingness to assert its power in the global politics, most particularly against the sponsors of terror, contrasts dramatically with the old European states (Kagan, 2002). Railing against the reluctance of France and Germany to deviate from United Nations' processes around Iraq and the Middle East generally, Kagan locates a distinct paradox in the European position. The evolution to a European Union and a 'post-history' perspective, which prefers 'peacekeeping' to the assertion of military power for just causes, have left Europe and its civilization entirely vulnerable:

> Most Europeans do not see the great paradox: that their passage into post-history has depended on the United States not making the same passage. Because Europe has neither the will nor the ability to guard its own paradise and keep it from being overrun, spiritually as well as physically, by a world that is yet to accept the rule of 'moral consciousness', it has become dependent on America's willingness to use its military might to deter or defeat those around the world who still believe in power politics. (Kagan, 2002: 11)

Against threat by the world's uncivilized peoples, the ideals of moral consciousness and rule of law are thus provided by American military power. The core Anglophonic members of the Coalition of the Willing, the US, the UK and Australia, appear to have understood the force of these arguments. By following the US into a pre-emptive war on Iraq, the UK and Australia committed themselves to a civilizational alliance with a superpower that seems to be discounting the ideals of the United Nations and international community collaboration. The willingness of continental European powers, especially Germany, to support America's most recent belligerence toward Iran and its

Islamic theocracy might also affirm US global primacy and the force of Huntington's civilizational argument.

THE MEDIA AND CULTURAL DIVISION

Just prior to the September 11 attacks, Karim Karim (2000a, 2000b) released a study which examined the ways in which 'Islam' and Muslim societies were being represented in the Canadian print media. According to Karim, the Canadian 'mass media share with the mass media of other Northern countries the myths of modern technological society, which provide the primary fields of meanings for the interpretation of events taking place in the world' (2000a: 15). These myths are part of a nation-state's 'propaganda' machinery designed to create consensus around critical matters: 'these can include the right of holding power by certain individuals or groups, the legitimacy of uses of violence by the state, and the illegitimacy of certain kinds of opposition to the nation-state' (Karim, 2000a: 15). It is also used, Karim argues, to generate cohesion and consensus within specific groups, enabling the maintenance of intra and international hierarchies. These hierarchies are embedded in forms of social order to which media industries subscribe.

Within this framework, Canada's mass media is entirely bound to the perspective of the United States. As a global and regional minnow, Canada is dependent on the US, not merely because of America's economic–military primacy, but because of its capacity to generate information and 'cultural knowledge'. In particular, the Canadian print media and its perceptions of 'Islam' remain heavily dependent on the global information networks dominated by the UK and the United States. This is particularly evident when powerful nations are confronted by oppositional forces that are prepared to use the tactics of violence against their hegemonic foes:

> When the powers are involved in confrontations with southern entities, the transnational media agencies – based in the North – largely align themselves with the hegemonic position. This has led to the growth of a global media narrative in which civilized nation states led by the U.S. are besieged by 'Terrorism International'. (Karim, 2000a: 30)

Karim's empirical analysis of the Canadian print media goes on to demonstrate that the multiplicity and diversity of Muslim peoples, cultures and societies are radically reduced by these interests and perspectives, which create them as a monolith of 'mythic Islam'. Following the Althusserian notions of dominant ideology, most particularly as they are translated through recent postcolonial theory, Karim criticizes the mainstream media's tendency to identify Muslim diversity with a radical and fundamentalist Islam that is intent on deposing Northern social values through jihad and terrorist assault:

> While some Northern discourses do attempt to impart alternative views on Muslim societies, much of the mainstream reporting is laden with formulaic references. 'Islam' becomes a composite entity, with little distinction made between its diverse followers and their respective beliefs, cultures and actions. Since setting off a bomb in a skyscraper is portrayed as being 'Islamic' then the act of Islamic prayer becomes evidence of radical militancy. Time and space lose all meaning when talking about this 'Islam' – ideological genealogies of 'Islamic terrorists' going all the way back to the time of Muhammad are drawn up by Orientalists and reproduced by the mass media ... Such essentialist views of the religion's adherents reinforce the idea that they are inherently unable to rise above their supposedly savage state. (Karim, 2000a: 176)

Significantly, this media-constituted 'Islam', which represents radical difference, is not to be trusted. This homogenizing of Muslim diversities within and outside the province of the nation-states of the North, Karim concludes, reflects the propensity of the modern globalized media to reconfirm the interests of dominant groups. As Althusser had explained, these dominant groups have the ability to convince the populace that their own interests are actually the shared values of the entire society: the ideology of the elites is the consensus view of the mass.

Ross Perigoe (2005) has adapted Karim's research model for his study of the reporting of 9/11 in two major Canadian daily newspapers. His results show, similarly, that the terrorist attacks have been constructed in terms of civilizational and cultural disputes. 'Islam' and 'Muslim' become conflated as epithets within a news system that privileges the perspective of the victim and the home culture against the pervasive sense of 'alien' threat. These empirical studies suggest that the global networked media, dominated by the US, are generating conceptions of culture and civilization which are similar to those of conservative scholars like Huntington, Lewis and Kagan. Mahmood Mumdani (2002) fears that the whole notion of 'culture' may be counterproductive for effective analysis of issues of global politics and power, especially around the Middle East. Mumdani warns that a fixation on the concept of 'culture' can lead to the sort of 'culture talk' which is impeding our understanding of Muslim peoples, politics and global security:

> Rather than see contemporary Islamic politics as the outcome of an archaic culture, I suggest we see neither culture nor politics as archaic but both as very contemporary outcomes of equally contemporary conditions, relations and conflicts ... [T]errorism is a modern construction. Even when it harnesses one or another aspect of tradition and culture, the result is a modern ensemble at the service of a modern project. (Mumdani, 2002: 46)

Mumdani is particularly concerned about commentaries like Huntington's which tend to collapse the complex details of history into simple cultural polemics. By embedding culture and cultural difference within deep history, Mumdani contends, the media and conservative scholars are reinforcing the idea of intractable conflict and the inevitability of war. This strategy of 'essentializing' culture reaffirms the idea of a military imperative and the right of one group to dominate another.

Mumdani's rejection of culture treats the concept as a synonym of 'civilization'; Mumdani is particularly hostile to the pejorative implications which the western media and neoconservative commentators attach to the category of Islam or Islamic culture. John Docker, for his part, is less concerned about neoconservative appropriations than with the failure of contemporary humanities analysis to understand the profound links between history and modern culture. Docker bemoans the inadequacy of specific kinds of cultural analyses which are not only 'determinedly secular but also blindly and contentedly recent-minded' (2002: 74). For Docker, therefore, it is not the engagement of culture and 'deep' history which is a problem for effective analysis of conflicts around the Middle East and Islam, but rather its limited scope. Like the neoconservatives, Docker returns to the Crusades and the complex relationships between tribes and religions in order to explain the culture(s) and politics of the Middle East. Unlike the neoconservatives, however, Docker does not attach negative qualities to the category of Islam; nor indeed does he seek an excessively simplistic framing for the history of the region.

As Edward Said frequently demonstrated, in fact, our understanding of the peoples, cultures and politics of the Middle East is not bound by either history or contemporary circumstances, but is a conflation of both (see also Chan, 2005). Said persistently sought to remind commentators and advocates that the complex relationships and ethnic–religious divisions and associations in the Middle East are far from monolithic. In his unapologetically strident rejoinder to Huntington, Said argued that culture and power are intricately woven through history, and must never be excluded from contemporary policy-making. As a long-time critic of American foreign policy, especially in the Middle East, Said claimed that consecutive US administrations had overlooked the details of Arabic culture. In particular, Said warned both the George Bush senior and George W. Bush administrations against an invasion of Iraq, which would further destabilize the precarious ethnic relationships between various Muslim groups. While in no way approving of Saddam's brutal regime, Said believed that a US invasion would unleash a complex inter-communal rivalry that would have resonance across the whole Arabic region.

Fred Halliday (2002) makes a similar point in his survey of recent literature on Islamicism and Islamophobia. According to Halliday, many scholars, journalists and public officials are guilty of essentializing the differences between the Muslim and western spheres. While the experience of being Muslim may provide overlapping sensibilities in identity, religious practice and politics, this is not 'the whole story':

> Islam may, in some contexts, be the prime form of political and social identity, but it is never the sole form, and it is often not the primary one. Within Muslim societies, divisions of ethnicity matter much and often more than a shared religious identity, and this is equally so in emigration. There is no lack of division between genders and classes, between those with power and wealth and those without. No-one can understand the politics of, say, Turkey, Pakistan or Indonesia, on the basis of Islam alone. Despite the rhetoric, Islam explains very little of what happens in those countries. (Halliday, 2002: 21)

Halliday cites the work of postcolonial writer Bobby Said, who extends this argument, claiming that the impulse to Islamophobia in the west derives less from an excess of power and hegemony than from a fear which is symptomatic of diminishing influence. This tendency by the western media and its Orientalist overlords betrays a deep sense of threat, a sense of losing control of the globalist agenda generally and the Middle East in particular. According to Bobby Said, a powerful resistance to US global capitalism has evolved through Islam and Islamic nationalism. With the collapse of Soviet communism, Islam appears to be the only genuine source of resistance, a site in which a powerful and powerfully united community has been able to say no to American domination. In this sense Eurocentrism (or more specifically Euro-Americanism) is a cultural fortress being created by the west in order to protect itself from the actualities of historical decline. Eurocentricism, Said insists, is a manifestation of weakness rather than power.

DIVISION AND IDENTITY POLITICS

Our discussion so far has focused on the ways in which the notion of Islam has been discussed and culturally created, particularly by western-based media and commentary. The discussion demonstrates that 'Islam' and the 'west' are cultural constructions designed to serve particular political and economic interests. At their more extreme, these political interests shape cultural differences as intractable conditions of deep history. For neoconservatives such differences necessitate pre-emptive assertions of self-preservation by a US-dominated 'civilization'. While emerging from the other end of the polemic, similar civilizational arguments have been invoked by radical Islamicists themselves in order to unify the forces of resistance against their oppressors – the Judaeo-Christian civilization, especially articulated in the states of Israel and America. It is also evident that 'Islam' is of interest to western political and cultural reformers, like Bobby Said, who are interested in identity as a radical politics of resistance. Thus, while many western social commentators welcome the rising pluralism and relativism of contemporary, globalizing culture, there remains a somewhat contradictory satisfaction among reformers like Bobby Said in the capacity of Islam to resist American hegemony. Said himself, in fact, impugns those commentaries which demean the force of Islamic nationalism as a form of western mimicry. For Said, Islam is a genuine and deeply sourced mode of political resistance against western imperialism and the appropriation of all peoples, cultures and resources into the global capitalist web. Said's position, of course, aligns him with the broadening cultural politics of postcolonialism or 'de-colonization', a politics which tends to imbue formerly colonized peoples with an ontological power that inspires the politics of opposition.

Interestingly, however, the work of Edward Said (esp. 1978, 1993), who is often seen as a canonical figure in postcolonial studies, might on the surface appear to avoid the essentialism which characterizes a good deal of postcolonial rhetoric. As we have seen, while neoconservative scholars reach into history in order to explain fundamental differences between the west and the east, Edward Said examines historical texts in order to explain the ways in which history is itself shaped by discourse. Said distinguishes between 'colonialism', which is the material management of conquered territories by an alien nation, and 'imperialism', which is the discursive and ideological supplement to coercive administration. The invasion and colonial administration of the Arabic territories by European powers are supported by various forms of imperialist, cultural imaginings. These imaginings reflect more about the European writers and their home cultures than they do about those peoples and cultures they were forming into text and ideology.

As Said explains in *Culture and Imperialism* (1993), the material aspirations and cultural fantasies of the colonial overlords are imposed on the 'otherness' of the vanquished peoples through various narrative and scholarly texts. This form of cultural appropriation serves not merely to vindicate the conquest, but provides an aesthetic and imaginary space for the expressivities of the conquerors. It becomes a semiotic site in which the imperialists can experiment and explore their own identity by attributing specific cultural qualities to the alien others. Said's work is framed by an intense politicism which on occasions returns his analysis to a form of essentialism. While demonstrating that culture and identity are largely constructed by those with greater access to informational and narrative resources, Said is lured into normative descriptions of Muslim culture and history. Against the deficiencies of American foreign policy, Muslim culture is distinguished as rich and complex – which it very clearly is. Despite his best intentions, however, Said restores a polemical structure to global politics, defining the world in terms of the east–west divide he has so valiantly sought to deconstruct.

The paradox for postcolonial politics is simply this – oppressed peoples have had to rally around their sense of difference in order to transcend the identity of difference that has been imposed upon them by more powerful nations. Thus, the peoples of the Middle East who have had the character of Orient or the boundaries of nation imposed upon them by European colonists have used the European category of nation and nationalism to dispute their oppression.

Islamic militants have adapted a form of 'difference', as well as the technologies provided by western nations, in order to challenge the categorization that has been forced upon them. The resistance in Iraq to American occupation, for example, is the predicate of various forms of nationalism, ethnicism, Islamicism and regionalism – all of which are 'united' by their shared antagonism toward the United States and its imposed administration. As they are based on resistance, the cultural category and implicit identity become a contingency of the imposed order. In other words, the identity that is to be dissolved by resistance tends, in effect, to be re-articulated (even in a modified form) by the very act of resistance. This is what Jacques Lacan has called a 'double entry matrix' – identity is forged around the interdependence of perspective, even where the perspective is forged through conflict or hatred. As in the Israeli–Palestinian dispute, there seems to be no way of breaking the cycle of hatred and violence since the modes of control and resistance are being constantly re-aggravated through the affirmation of categories of national and religious difference.

The same, of course, is true within the broader context of contemporary global terror; the antagonists have deepened the conflicts through their persistent reaffirmation of categories of difference – most particularly as they are articulated through religious and cosmological conditions of good and evil. In his book entitled *The Clash of Fundamentalisms* (2002), Tariq Ali makes the basic point that the antagonists in this war of terror have each invested their violence in ontological modes which resonate with the horrors of a holy war. Within their cultural borders, each side is fixing their sense of identity within a Manichean structure that distinguishes the virtue of the self against the Satanism of the other. Yet, even without this cosmological dimension, the antagonists seem to be constructing themselves and their mission as a form of resistant heroic: the sense of self is consolidated through conflict, violence and the imaginary of conquest.

Manuel Castells (1997) has offered a relatively straightforward explanation for the geo-politics of identity-building. For Castells there are three modes of identity-building. The first refers to 'legitimizing identity', a process whereby major institutions reinforce the inherited social knowledge about subjectivity and authority. In the case of the east–west divide, this mode reinforces the privilege – and superiority – of western cultures and subjectivity by identifying (and stereotyping) the deficiencies of the non-west. The second mode is 'resistance building' generated by those individuals and groups who are in conditions and cultures devalued by the dominant culture. According to Castells, this may be 'the most important' mode of identity-building since it creates the circumstances for social change: 'It constructs forms of collective resistance against otherwise unbearable oppression, usually on the basis of identities that were, apparently, clearly defined by history, geography or biology, making it easier to essentialize the boundaries of resistance' (Castells, 1997: 9). With the example of feminism's shift toward institutional change, the third mode of identity-building refers to a gradual re-assignation of interests, practices and subjective attributes. In the emergence of a networked, global society, Castells argues, these processes of identity-building become increasingly disjunctive and complicated since 'the network society is based on the systemic disjunction between the local and the global for most individuals and social groups' (Castells, 1997: 11). With the disruption to national boundaries by various forms of media networks, social change becomes articulated through a 'prolongation of communal resistance' rather than through the project of civil society:

> Under such condition civil societies shrink and disarticulate since there is no longer continuity between the logic of power-making in the global network and the logic of association and representation in specific societies and cultures. The search for meaning takes place then in the reconstruction of defensive identities around communal principles. (Castells, 1997: 11)

For Castells, in fact, the current historical conditions, promulgated through the new global media networks, change the way identity (and, by implication, culture) is formed. The new network formations do not necessarily expunge the political and economic integrity of nation, nor the ideological force of nationalism; they do, however, situate nation within a broadening context of identity and community formation.

Castells' concept of civil society in many ways approximates what I have called 'writing democracy' in Chapter 1. Against Castells' view, however, the notion of a writing democracy doesn't imply that civil society is shrinking so much as it is being integrated into new cultural conditions constituted around broadcast media networks and their relatively unstable expressive spaces – that is, within an expanding mediasphere. As we explored in Chapter 1, broadcast representation, which is characterized by the absent–present, distance–proximity compounds, is creating new forms of cultural contiguity and new spaces for the proliferation of signs and meanings. The hyperreal space, while centred around First World interests, is nevertheless creating an unstable rendering of meanings and culture, creating new opportunities for alternative semiosis, fragmentation and an uneven but expanding cosmopolis of discourses and expressivities. To this extent, a re-essentialized mode of identity politics appears to be invading or laying siege to the global mediasphere, seeking to transform its available spaces into a more acute and sharply focused language war. With the failure of various forms of writing democracy in the Middle East, Islamicists have turned to the broadcast media in order to play out their politics, including for some the politics of violence. Thus, against the tide of global, hyperreal political relativism, the polemical divide that separates the identity politics of dominant and resistant groups becomes engaged in the narrative forms of the broadcast mediasphere.

In a sense, this relativism constitutes a third force within the language wars of oppression and resistance. It may be that resistance politics, including radical Islamicism, is reacting against the modernizing conditions of this relativism, as much as against the forces of US-sponsored global hegemony. Radical Islamicism's own rendering of the east–west divide is forged in terms of a deep history of oppression and a modern context of discursive and political relativism. This is not to suggest that the new cultural relativism being facilitated by globalization and the networked media is a cause of radical militantism and its grounded identity politicism; nor that it is the cause of a First World neoconservatism. Rather, it is to suggest that the formation of these agonistic and essentialized identities and their cultural perspectives is in some respects responding to the predominant conditions of a cultural and moral pluralism. These 'relativist' conditions are as much a part of the global hyperreal and mediasphere as the polemicism which is seeking to overthrow them. As we noted in the previous chapter, this tension between semiotic slippage and political hegemony is replete with opportunity for the construction of new meanings and imaginaries – as we have seen during the period of the US occupation of Iraq, resistant forces, including those espousing a form of essentialized Islamic identity, have been invading these spaces with new and horrific expressivities of violence and resistance.

There is, of course, something paradoxical in the liberational and expressive potential of the new cultural conditions of globalism and its mediasphere, most particularly as it is being appropriated for a politics of essentialism and radical traditionalism. That is, while radical Islamicism may well reject various aspects of modernism and globalism, it is clearly not averse to the appropriation of specific elements of the things it claims to abhor: it reacts against modern relativism, but uses its spaces, cultural potential and technologies in the service of its own interests. In many respects, this is precisely the paradox confronted by Jean-François Lyotard (1984) as he attempts to explain the postmodern condition. Lyotard recognizes the liberational and transformative potential of a new cultural relativism, but he is also forced to acknowledge the oppressive potential of a politics which is removed from referentiality – that is, a politics which is self-reflexive and which seeks to transcend the limits of democratic and liberal humanism. This 'inhuman' (Lyotard, 1991) seeks to move beyond the constraints and values of humanism which constructs its politics around an ideal of inclusiveness. Beyond the universal applicability of humanist values, the postmodern inhuman exists as an open space which carries a liberational potential that is constituted around alternative subjectivities. Within a relativist context, emancipation can be shaped around ethnicity, gender, sexuality and other modes of self-expression which dissolve the borders of the nation-state and civil society (see also Giddens, 1994, Held, 1995, Held et al., 1999). However, and as Lyotard himself concedes, this potential liberation based on the expression of difference carries the alternative possibility of a brutal and violent rupture, a 'difference' which promotes radical self-interest and a brutal indifference toward, or actual assault on, the rights and interests of all others. This inhuman relativism or celebratory 'difference' would not and could not of itself protect individuals and communities through the invocation of universal human rights, national or international law.

These paradoxes have, in fact, been tragically exposed by the events of 9/11 and their aftermath. In particular, 9/11 and the war on terror have demonstrated how the politics of culture can be conscripted into various forms of historical and contemporary agonism. To this extent, the claim made by Mahmood Mumdani (2002) that 'terrorism' is not part of (deep) culture or history but is essentially a modern phenomenon is only partly correct. The actions of global terror and political violence surrounding 9/11 and the invasions of Afghanistan and Iraq are demonstrably connected to contemporary televisual culture; as we have outlined in the current and previous chapters, the contemporary engagements of terror are constituted as fundamentally communicational and representational events. However, it is also clear that history and the formation of essentialized identity and cultures are deployed through the various communicational strategies as part of the ongoing articulation of language war. The communication of the event is as important as the event itself. History is available to the warring parties: it contributes to the density of the agonism and to the intensity of the war. More broadly, however, the violence that underscores the state and writing democracy is regenerated through the formations of a relativized cultural context which is delimiting the boundaries of agonistic expression. Out of the relativism, the warring parties have sought to create a clear but seemingly irreconcilable polemic, one which may, as even George Bush concedes, have no capacity for conclusion.

HISTORY AND THE ROOTS OF ISLAM

The point here, of course, is that the construction of Islam is multilayered. Islam is deployed through the political strategies of Orientalist and neoconservative politics; it is also a central trope for the construction of an identity-based politics of resistance, including resistant militantism. We have made the point that the whole notion of 'Islam' remains highly contestable and somewhat underdeveloped, even by those, like Bernard Lewis (2003), who claim to understand its intricacies and historical foundations. There is a distinct sense, as Karim Karim (2000a, 2000b, 2002) indicates, that the western imaginary is constructing notions of Islam around a politics of violent and irrational primitivism which becomes concentrated through notions of religious fundamentalism. The representations of Islam by First World media and political commentaries frequently, in fact, reduce the complexity of Muslim histories and cultures to a typically far–near formation where a terrorist event like 9/11 comes to epitomize all that is alien (distant) to our understanding within a core of contiguous threat.

Thus, while US President George Bush claimed in his 2004 address to the United Nations Assembly that 'there is no clash of civilizations when it comes to freedom', this rhetoric largely obscures the density and depth of polemical language wars which distinguish the antagonists. In many respects, and as we will discuss in more detail in subsequent chapters, the reinvigoration of the east–west divide pivots around the different approaches to the concept of freedom itself. Bush and many others in the White House seem to conceive of freedom in a very limited and unidimensional way; the same, of course, may be said of militant Islamicists whose strategies of violence are predicated entirely upon the prospect of social, economic and cultural liberation from western and other Judaeo-Christian oppressors. As we have frequently noted, these militant Islamicists need to be distinguished from the broad community of Muslim peoples and cultures across the world, including those (radical-political) Islamicists who may wish to inculcate the state with *shari'ah* law and modes of social governance, but whose strategies do not include violent struggle and terrorism.

Thus, while all Islamicists are Muslim, not all Muslims are Islamicist in the ways we are defining it here. Many Muslims are content to separate state and religious functions; others would seek to raise the profile and influence of Islamic law through democratic institutions; others seek to create an Islamic state by violent means, if necessary. Each of these three categories – Muslim, radical-political Islamicist and militant Islamicist – is engaged in various forms of identity and cultural politics. However, the group which is clearly most active in the current phase of global terror and political violence is militant. Emerging out of the more radical end of political Islam, this group is seeking, by violent means, to impose an Islamic theocratic state over the whole of the Muslim world in the first instance and ultimately the whole of the globe. To this extent, the Islamic governments in Iran and Saudi Arabia and formerly in Taliban Afghanistan are models for a broadly based mode of social management that doesn't distinguish between the secular state and religious practice. The Qur'an becomes the paradigm of virtue, social practice and religious law. Forms of social coercion are supplemented by the discourses of *fatwa* (death sentence) and *jihad* (struggle in the service of Allah), which become translated more broadly in terms of holy justice and holy war.

In fact, holy war is also the primary determinant of foreign policy for the Islamic state. This jihad may be focused on secular Muslim states (for example, Iran against Iraq), former colonial masters, traitors to the faith, multinational corporations, the United States, Christians, Jews and the west in general. For the founder of the Sunni revivalist organization Muslim Brotherhood Association, Hassan al-Banna, the Qur'an, the *shari'ah* and Allah are the centre of all political and legal activities and modes of knowledge: 'The Qur'an is our constitution, the Prophet is our Guide, death for the glory of Allah is our greatest ambition' (cited in Castells, 1997: 15). For al-Banna, the integration of the Muslim and non-Muslim worlds is the ultimate objective of the Islamic project. Maulana Syed Abul A'ia Maududi expands on this idea, explaining why an Islamic state is necessary for the elevation of all Muslims:

> The Qur'an not only lays down principles on morality and ethics, but also gives guidance in the political, social and economic fields. It prescribes punishment for certain crimes and enunciates principles of monetary and fiscal policy. These cannot be translated into practice unless there is a State to enforce them. (1967: 175)

Thus, while 'Islam' may be loosely translated as 'submission to Allah', it is the degree, character and interpretation of this submission which will determine the political and theological perspective of various Muslim communities. Tribal, regional and the broader historical influences of the Shi'a and Sunni traditions have contributed to the dramatically different political and social evolutions of Muslim communities in the Middle East and elsewhere across the globe. These influences have worked through the experience of European colonization, decolonization and modernization to create an extremely diverse community of Muslim-dominated nation-states. We can see clear evidence of this diversity, even with a brief glance at nations like Turkey, Iran, Pakistan, Indonesia and Kosovo. Even within the Islamicist trajectory, there are significant differences between, for example, the House of Saud and the radical perspectives of writers like Maududi and Sayyid Qutb.

Many commentators, including Manuel Castells, locate the source of political and militant Islamicism in the 1970s when the modernization programmes of numerous Arabic states began seriously to falter. During this period, it is certainly true that the idea of an Islamic state, one which included all Muslims in the Middle East, had begun to gather favour among radical thinkers and political activists in the region. However, the idea of a unified Islamic 'nation' had been mooted much earlier. In fact, in medieval times, Mohammed had envisaged a unified Muslim dominion that would ensure grace through the submission of the faithful to holy law and the ideal of Allah. This vision was fractured, of course, during the period of Ottoman and European colonialism, though paradoxically the imposition of external administration provided a focus for resistance, discourses of unity and resurgent modes of Arabic identity construction. Colonization created administrative and epistemological frameworks for the construction of new ways of seeing the region and the world generally. These 'modernizing' frameworks, in fact, contributed to the transformation of a tribal consciousness into a national, Arabic and regional consciousness – which included new ways of thinking about politics and power.

From the early twentieth century a number of leaders in the region began discussing seriously the possibility of ejecting the colonial overlords and installing a pan-Arabic state. The establishment of Palestinian newspapers such as *al-Karmil*, for example, provided opportunities for the promotion of a form of pan-Arabic liberation and 'nationalism' that was part of an emerging project of modernization and identity-building. This notion of a broadly based Arabic state, however, was forced to contend with the rise of specific forms of Arabic nationalism and the competing commercial and political interests of European colonizers operating within specific geo-political boundaries in the Middle East. The collapse of the Ottoman Empire, in fact, provided a free hand for the colonial cartographers to dissect and parcel the region according to their own national and eco-political interests. At the Paris conference in 1919 the hopes of many pan-Arabists were forced to confront the realities of European power and self-interest. This was particularly the case as Shi'a and Sunni Muslims found themselves in contiguous political structures that bore little resemblance to their historic and cultural roots. Thus, new nation-kingdoms like Iraq (1932) were being forged within an alchemic context of competing French and British oil interests. The discussions around the establishment of Iraq paid little attention to the complex and precarious community structures that had been forged over millennia and which had achieved a level of balance through the intricate divisions and management of territory and kinship.

This volatile regional politics, set against the background of two European-based world wars, was further exacerbated by the uncertain presence of the Kurdish people and the Jews. While the Kurds were largely divided and shunted between various Arabic nations, the Jews were gaining increasing support from Britain and the US for the establishment of a regional homeland. These issues made it even more difficult for the supporters of a pan-Arabic state to override the increasingly chauvinistic and self-interested claims of many nationalist Arabic leaders. Even so, there was a sense in which anti-colonialist sentiment could work through both a nationalist and pan-Arabic politics of resistance. In Egypt, for example, Hassan al-Banna founded the Muslim Brotherhood in 1928. While the Brotherhood was formed initially to protect the Muslim faith from the modernizing and secularizing effects that were evident under Mustafa Kemal's rule in Turkey, the organization quickly developed a vision of pan-Arabic religious politicism. In order to spread the faith and raise the profile of Islam, al-Banna established youth and sports clubs, built mosques and embarked on a fiery education programme designed to ensure the exposure of young people to their prospects of salvation. Not satisfied with this missionary work, the Brotherhood evolved, during the 1930s, into a more radical and politicized organization. A military wing alternatively called the 'special unit' or 'secret apparatus' was established during this period; its activities included the acquisition of arms and recruits, especially among the police and military, and political assassinations. During the Second World War, the Brotherhood rejected British appeals for help and, in fact, turned their violence directly against the colonialists and eventually the Jews. The Brotherhood conducted a campaign of terror against modernists and pro-Europeans within Egypt, while maintaining a profound rage against the influences of secularism. Before his own assassination in 1949, al-Banna wrote an open letter to the leaders of all Arabic states, declaring that the west was not only tyrannical and oppressive but its people were morally and spiritually decadent and weak.

This theme was taken up by the highly influential theologian Sayyid Qutb whose prison writings continue to influence much of today's radical Islamicism, including the followers of al-Qa'ida. Qutb, like al-Banna, developed a profound and stinging hatred for the west, especially the United States, which he visited in 1948–50. Appalled by the materialism, faithlessness and decadence of America, Qutb became a fundamentalist and joined the Muslim Brotherhood. Qutb concluded that there could never be peace with the west because the battle was over truth, rather than territory. The Arabic states had won their freedom but the world remained a place besieged by untruth and unholy action. The United States and other western countries were actually afraid of Islam and the faithful because they were spiritually destitute and incapable of illumination. They simply had to be destroyed.

Qutb's vision, however, was far from universally embraced, and his early books were actually banned as apostate by al-Azhar, the leading religious studies centre in the Muslim world. Having no formal theological training, Qutb was prepared to excommunicate all Muslims, and existing Islamic states and their leaders because they were not fulfilling the literal requirements of the Qur'an. Islam, in

Qutb's view, demanded the expansion of holy law and jihad across the entire world. A true Muslim must engage in jihad – holy war – if s/he is to truly submit to Allah and achieve grace. Only when the entire world is united under the rule of Allah can there exist a truly holy state of Islam.

While the Brotherhood was active in Egypt, other parts of the Arabic world were seeking somewhat more pragmatic solutions to the territorial dissection of the region and of Arabic peoples. Throughout the Second World War, in fact, with the destabilizing effects of German and Italian incursion, the dual thrust of independence/nationalism and transnational Islamicism drove much of the political discourse in the Middle East. Key leaders such as Nuri al-Sa'id and King Abdullah I (Abdullah bin Husayh) developed a model for the unification of Transjordan, Palestine, Iraq, Lebanon and Saudi Arabia. Known as the 'Fertile Crescent', this imagined territory was never realized and a more modest scheme was developed for collaborative responsibility in defence and foreign affairs. Even in this modulated form, the idea stimulated suspicion among many Saudis who believed it to be a clandestine strategy to increase Hasimite power across the region. The Arabic League, proposed by Egyptian President Nahhas and established in 1946, was an assembly of Arabic leaders with more modest aspirations for collaboration.

During the post-Second World War period, nationalism and transnationalism were operating through and against one another within a somewhat uneven process of modernization. Oil, of course, was central to this process, particularly for Iraq, Iran, Saudi Arabia and the Gulf states, which were becoming increasingly enmeshed in the geo-politics of economic globalization and the Cold War. In 1946, for example, significant tensions emerged over the Iranian city of Azerbaijan which, the Americans believed, was tempting Soviet aspirations of annexation (see Heinberg, 2003). More recently, oil has been central to a raft of American activities in the Middle East, including support for Saddam Hussein and Iraq against an increasingly anti-American and oil-rich Iran, continuing support for the royal family in Saudi Arabia, the first Gulf War, and the recent invasion and occupation of Iraq. Thus, while oil was not evenly distributed across the Middle East, the complex alignment of nations, cultures and transnational interests, intensified the volatility of the region and its position within international oil-politics. The establishment of the state of Israel in 1948 and the completion of the Suez Canal project further complicated the geo-politics of the region, enhancing the importance of Egypt, in particular, but also Jordan, Lebanon and Syria. The question of Palestine continues as a central problem for peace and stability in the region. And while Islamicist organizations like the Brotherhood have directed themselves over recent decades toward community and civil participation (without necessarily relinquishing the option of violence), new militant groups are continually emerging under the pressure of failing economic and social conditions.

Taken together, the problems associated with modernization and global integration reached a crisis level in the late 1960s and early 1970s. It may be that the comprehensive victories of Israel in 1956, 1967 and 1973 demonstrated for many Muslims in the region that the status of their own project of modernization needed critical re-examination. The rapidity of the victories and the overwhelming military superiority of the Israeli forces, however, were only part of the humiliation. The annexation of the West Bank, the Gaza Strip, East Jerusalem and the Golan Heights represented a kind of moral and ideological prescience – a sense in which the whole project of Islam could be challenged and even overthrown by a nascent and externally sponsored interloper who had no respect for history and the dignity of the Arabic peoples in the region.

Thus, the material and military superiority of Israel and the United States, along with their aggressive indifference to Palestinian aspirations for statehood, provided even further opportunities for the escalation of pan-Arabic chauvinism. During the 1990s into the 2000s, the emergence from the Palestine Liberation Organization of radical warrior groups like Hamas can only be explained in terms of the continued failure of the US, Europe and the UN to produce an ideological, cultural and diplomatic framework that matches the rhetoric of their democratic invocations. George Bush's 'Roadmap to Peace' is exposing itself as a cynical and vacuous peace effort which has merely deepened the despair on both sides. With the death of Yasser Arafat, the erstwhile leader of the PLO, the second Bush administration is claiming that a 'two state' solution may yet prove feasible – though such optimistic plans are as common as their failure.

MODERNIZATION AND CIVIL SOCIETY IN THE MIDDLE EAST

The attacks of September 11, as much as anything else, mark this failure. The continued activity of the former colonial powers in the region, along with the newer force of American-dominated globalization, seem not to be able to neutralize the disastrous and continuing impact of colonialism. The complex and volatile mix of traditional Muslim cultures, Islamicism, regionalism, nationalism and postcolonization discourses have produced a modernization (and anti-modernization) which is both uneven and disjunctive. The blessing of oil resources has paradoxically rendered the region vulnerable to further western exploitation and the agonisms of a global geo-politics, economics and consumer capitalism which create deep social divisions and quite destructive forms of inequity. The complex social hierarchies that have evolved through various social traditions in the region have become amplified through the hierarchies implicit in modern statehood and global capital integration.

With the notable exception of Turkey, most Middle Eastern nations have struggled to manage or reconcile these agonisms; the social and political infrastructure they have inherited from the former colonial administrators has not, it seems, been adequate in the conditions created by modernization. The mix of modern, secularist political institutions with more traditional modes of governance and the Muslim faith have produced a range of outcomes across the region. It is possible, in fact, to identify three relatively distinct styles of nation-state governance in the Middle East: Islamic, secular and transitional. The House of Saud, which draws its legitimacy from Islamicism and holy law, forms a royal dynasty in Saudi Arabia, which is a clear example of an Islamic state. The *shari'ah* forms an integral part of the governmental and legislative structure in Saudi Arabia, as it does in Iran. Turkey is a distinctly secular state with no direct requirement that the head of state be a Muslim or that secular law be referred through the Qur'an. The confluence of nationalism and secularism marked the revolutionary overthrow of the monarchical systems in Egypt, Iraq, Syria and Libya. The assassination in 1970 of Gamal Abdel Nasar, the socialist leader of Egypt, in some ways reflects the instability of these institutions – as does the excessive brutality of military leaders like Saddam Hussein. Each of these states has had to deal internally or externally with the rising force of Islamicism, a force which conquered Iran and Afghanistan, and continues to threaten the governments of many Middle Eastern states, including Iraq, where the interim election strongly favoured the Shi'a religious parties over the US-sponsored secularists. Countries like Libya and Syria have had militarist leaders and have been known to sponsor anti-American and anti-Israeli terrorism. Turkey, however, remains strongly connected to the ideals of liberal democracy and is often placed in the invidious position of having to align itself with the west in conflicts with neighbouring Arabic states.

The third group of Muslim-dominated states in the Middle East are 'transitional'. Many of these nations have struggled to modernize their economies and adopt western political institutions. They retain strong links with the Muslim faith but have not entirely integrated their legislative or judicial systems with the *shari'ah*. Very often, however, there will be a requirement in the constitution that the head of state be a Muslim and that the *shari'ah* have the status of law, existing in parallel with other legislative structures. In many respects, these nations seem poised to move in one or other direction, depending on how successfully their governments manage the transitions, the impact of globalization and the vigorous politics of Islamicism itself. According to Richard Crockatt (2003), this third group, more so than the secularist states, is vulnerable to the force of revolutionary Islam. Whether this is the case or not, it is very clear that a more publicly extant and militant form of Islamicism has emerged from the 1970s with the objective, and in come cases the capacity, to invade the vacant and weaker spaces of modernization. The success of the Taliban in Afghanistan clearly marks the failure of the forces of modernization in that country, most particularly as it had been ensnared in the impotent and destructive global geo-politics of the Cold War. The protracted revolutionary war against the Soviet Union left the country exposed and vulnerable to the ideals of an Islamic utopia. And once installed, the revolutionary politics of the Taliban provided a haven for numerous militant Islamic groups who began to believe that the Arabic jihad was imminent. As Walter Laqueur points out, these jihadists believed:

> that it only might take another decade to overthrow the present Arab and Muslim governments and yet another few years to defeat America and the West. For at long last, as they saw it, the young generation in the Muslim world was coming out of its stupor. In the heady days after the Soviet withdrawal (1989), almost anything seemed possible. (2003: 49)

The rise of these aspirations is linked to the social and economic problems issuing from the uneven effects of modernization. While it is not accurate to speak of a 'failed modernization', as Manuel Castells (1997) does, it is certainly clear that Islamicism has been able to engage the populations of many Middle Eastern states through the clashes of modern and traditional institutions, religious and secular discourses, local and global cultural texts. Through these engagements, the Islamicists, whether by peaceful or violent means, have been able to identify and attack their enemies as the sources of insecurity, economic decline and historical humiliations. In the late 1960s and 1970s it became evident that the vision of economic growth, generated by the discourses of modernization and nationalism, was rapidly fading. Increasing population growth, low school retention rates, rural dislocation and urbanization were adding to high levels of unemployment. Traditional welfare infrastructure, based largely on the family and local community, was also collapsing. Without work or ongoing school or training opportunities, young people who gathered in the cities were being constantly tempted by crime and the material allure of western lifestyles. Islamicism provided an explanation for, and alternative to, this indignity, most particularly as it railed against the inequities and moral degeneration of western lifestyles. These lifestyles challenged the deep history of the Arabic world and the Muslim faith, creating a new generation of envy, social dislocation and poverty.

Thus, while the Muslim religion was never very far from the surface of Arabic culture and social life, radical Islamicism offered a shield against the negative impact of modernization – including the possibility of a degenerated Muslim faith. The ideal of a unified Islam, in particular, seemed to mollify the complex, material hierarchies and social dislocation that modernization was bringing to the region. In this way, political Islam seemed to transcend class borders, drawing many of its leaders from the educated classes, its funds from the aristocratic families like the Sauds, and its supporters and foot soldiers from the suffering masses. From the 1970s, in fact, Islamicism offered an alternative dignity, one which wasn't a contingency of material and consumer wealth, nor a set of values which seem necessarily alien to many people in the Muslim world. And while there is no sense in which the violence of extreme Islamicism is, or ever has been, popularly accepted, there is increasing evidence that Islamic political discourses are providing a history and identity for Muslim subjects which 'resist' the imposed order and identities of colonialism and US-dominated globalization. As Castells argues, the processes of identity deconstruction and reconstruction are the essential phases of social transformation: political Islam provided, and continues to provide, a facility for the renewal of a unified self which is not the predicate of US-dominated consumer capitalism.

One very important, but under-discussed, aspect of this reintegration of the Muslim self is related to gender. In the west, masculinity and femininity are structured around various forms of commodity and symbolic consumption (Bourdieu, 1984), situating individuals in terms of a hierarchy of sexual–discursive appeal. As a significant dimension of broadcast culture, the sexualized body becomes inscribed with commodity symbolism (see Lewis, 2002a: 294–330). Islamicism offers an alternative to this mode of hierarchical discrimination, restoring the traditions of masculine and feminine value which are based around family roles and responsibilities. The masculinity that is diminished by western modes of measurement – materialism, individualism – is restored to the Arabic man by Islamicism and a hatred for the things that cannot be attained. The permissive sexualities of the west, especially as they are 'represented' around the image of the female body, are rejected in favour of traditional roles and modes of masculine–feminine expressivity. The subject positions defined by Islamic governments in Iran, Saudi Arabia and Taliban Afghanistan have thus been constructed around a specific textuality, one that is created from notions of devoutness and patriarchal ideology. Islamicism, that is, offers a more integrated and uncontested subjectivity, a being in the world that seeks to replace insecurity with the certainty of moral authority, spiritual grace and the certitudes offered by God and the Qur'an.

PALESTINE AND THE 'JEWISH QUESTION'

US support for the state of Israel was one of several reasons cited by Osama bin Laden for the 9/11 attacks. We can never be sure whether the Palestinian cause was a central issue for al-Qa'ida, or merely a strategic appendage to Islamic zealotry and global jihad, as some commentators have argued. It is clearly the case, however, that the ongoing warfare between Palestinians and Jews personifies the repercussive effects of a history that is marked by oppression, exploitation, instability and often ineffectual colonial administration. Even before the establishment of the state of Israel in May 1948, the fundamental issues were being ventilated through Europe and the United States, issues that persist despite numerous attempts by recent American administrations in particular to interrupt the perpetually deepening cycle of violence and vengeance. The British Foreign Secretary, Jack Straw, was moved by his own visit to the region in late September 2001, noting 'I understand that one of the factors that helps breed terrorism is the anger that many people feel at events over the years in Palestine.' Against the outrage of the Israeli government and Zionist lobby, George W. Bush also identified the Palestinian homeland question as an issue for his war on terror. While little progress was to be made on the issue, Bush nevertheless understood that something needed to be done:

> In the Middle East, there can be no peace for either side without freedom for both sides. America stands committed to an independent and democratic Palestine, living side by side with Israel in peace and security. Like all other people, Palestinians deserve a government that serves their interests and listens to their voices. My nation will continue to encourage all parties to step up to their responsibilities as we seek just and comprehensive settlement to the conflict. (Address to the General Assembly of the United Nations, September 12, 2002)

While these sentiments may well be genuine, they seem somewhat impotent against a history of savagery and political chauvinism which marks the modern era. The Camp David Accord and the more recent Roadmap to Peace have both unravelled under the pressure of Zionist and Palestinian violence. Forged from the 1948 establishment war, Israel ultimately refused to readmit into its new sovereign state all of those Palestinians who fled the violence into Lebanon, Syria, the West Bank and Gaza. This new diaspora seems to have been generated, at least in part, by a form of ethnic and cultural vengeance, as though the centuries of homelessness that the Jewish people themselves had suffered could be wreaked upon the descendants of ancient enemies: an eye for an eye, a diaspora for a diaspora. Through this historical cauldron of violence and the modern conditions of colonialism and its aftermath, a new or at least resurgent identity was being forged for Israeli Jews and the homeless Palestinians.

As outlined above, subsequent wars in 1956, 1967 and 1973 were conducted without a peace or reconciliation treaty, deepening the tensions through what remains effectively a war of attrition, a cold war, in which the cycle of hatred seems merely to worsen with every military assault and every suicide bombing. The 1967 war, in particular, which led to the annexation of Gaza, the Golan Heights, East Jerusalem and the West Bank, confirmed for many Arabic peoples and nations in the region that Israel is an expansionist state that is being underwritten by the Zionists of America and parts of western Europe.

Of course, there are some commentators who would place this issue within the context of the 'clash of civilizations' thesis (Huntington 1993, also Laqueur, 2003) which claims that the conflicts are irresolvable, since they are embedded within a deep and unbridgeable historical difference. The deficiencies of their arguments have already been outlined, most particularly in terms of the specificities of cultural politics, the force of language and the provision of particular policy strategy. And indeed, as much as there are differences between these two warring peoples – or at least specific communities within the peoples – considerable cultural, religious and ethnic similarities also exist. The imaginary which forges the history and culture of the antagonists, combined with a brutal competition for territory and resources, clearly creates the conditions which facilitate the ascent of warrior elites and a warrior mode of governmentality (Virilio, 2000). Authorities within the Israeli state and the global Zionist movement encourage an essentialization of the Jewish character, most particularly as it shapes the hero–victim consciousness of the nation. An identity constructed around Palestinian diaspora and radical Islam is also being forged within the consciousness of statehood and the establishment of a Palestinian homeland.

Karl Marx suggests in his essays *On the Jewish Question* (1843) that a dangerous link may be forged between the foundations of modern statehood – 'civil society' – and ethnic–religious identity. Responding to Bruno Bauer's thoughts on 'the Jewish question', Marx explains that, while he sympathizes with the aspiration of subclass citizens to cast off their oppression, he is not convinced that admission to 'civil society' is the appropriate strategy. An individual's liberation and emancipation is not to be found in a capitalist-bound class context, since even the bourgeoisie are slaves to capital, money, markets and the stock exchange. Thus, 'political emancipation' to full citizenship in modern society represents only a partial self-realization because it has not revealed to the individual the worst aspects of one's own humanity: that is, a myopic egoism by which an individual loses his or her awareness of all other individuals. Participation in civil society within a liberal democratic context provides the facility of self-actualization without the reciprocal appreciation for the plight of other people. Without a recognition of, and care for, others – the totality of humankind – the individual remains trapped by ego and self-interest. Marx, himself a Jew, speaks specifically about the tendency of Jews to project and encourage egoism.

While many commentators have seen this essay as a rather stereotypical attack on Jewish identity, especially in terms of bourgeois commercialism, the more general and relevant point of the essay for our interests resides in the idea of a political emancipation that would free Jewish people from what Marx sees as a community obsession with civil (capitalist–material) success. To translate this into the terms of our current study, Marx is encouraging a decentring of identity, one which resists the move to essentializations. In ways that anticipate more recent debates about the value and force of identity politics, Marx is recommending the release of the ego from capitalist obsession on the one hand, and prescriptive ethnicity on the other. While not sponsoring a humanist frame of reference, Marx is certainly encouraging a more generalized liberation, one which would not distinguish Jewish from Palestinian emancipation.

Marx's mode of freedom, like Hegel's, diverges from the strictly conventional apparatus of the state and democratic institutions. While these issues will be analysed in considerable detail in the next chapter, it remains for us to interrogate further the question of identity politics in the Middle East. While the Israeli–Palestinian issue is politically complex, there is certainly a strong sense in which the formation of the ego – the self – constitutes a critical dimension of the cultural politics of the east–west divide. The 'body' becomes centralized in these investigations, since identity is largely a form of cultural inscription over the human biology. It is, as Michel Foucault (1977a, 1981) has demonstrated, the primary site in which power is exercised and experienced.

THE BODY POLITIC: INTERFACE WITH GLOBALIZATION

It is important to remind ourselves that the rise of Islamicism and its correlative increase in religious observance are not of themselves tantamount to an increase in politically motivated violence in the Middle East. As we have noted, the notion of Islamicism and Islamic fundamentalism represents a congregation of many factors, strategies and diverse perspectives. It is arguable, in fact, that the rise of Islamicism in the Middle East and through other parts of the Muslim world, including South and South-East Asia, has been accompanied by some significant refurbishments in cultural identity, practice and meaning-making. 'Fundamentalism' represents a specific way of characterizing the belief systems of radical Islamicists, most particularly in terms of a supposedly 'literal' reading of the Qur'an.

This 'reading' of the Qur'an text, however, is neither literal nor 'fundamental'; it is rather a reading by a given community which is historically located within specific cultural and political conditions. That is, the meanings that are generated through this reading are part of the group's cultural politics, interests and strategic ambit. The text is linked, thereby, to a range of pre-existing discourses which reincarnate the Qur'an in terms of a volition of meaning. This intertextuality, as we have called it, supplements the Qur'an with particular kinds of semiotic and political values drawn very specifically from contemporary conditions. While frequently called 'traditional', these readings are entirely engaged in contemporary politics and the formation of a contemporary '*episteme*' or mode of social knowledge.

The question therefore is not whether this *episteme* is formed through traditional values and beliefs, as Bernard Lewis (2003) claims, or whether it is entirely contemporary, as Mahmood Mumdani (2002) believes. Rather, the mode of knowledge that constitutes Islamicism is, like all *episteme*, an outcome of ongoing historical language wars, a manifestation of history's engagement with the present. Equally, the violence that is arising through this new congregation of cultural attributes is not a feature of Islamicism itself, but rather a complex conflation of the conditions that have been outlined above. Islamicism is not the source of the new waves of terrorism and political violence, but another manifestation of the source – the underlying social, political and economic conditions of the region and its interface with globalization. The political perspectives and belligerent posturing of some Islamicist groups pose a distinct threat to local as well as international interests and political entities; in the context of intense language wars, this threat becomes a catalyst for further violence.

Islamicism provides the cultural, linguistic and ideological framework for a new expressivity of global cultural politics. Clearly, the Muslim faith is not of itself predisposed to violence; innumerable Islamic theologians and scholars have denounced Sayyid Qutb's 'interpretation' of the Qur'an and the concept of jihad which commands the violent overthrow of infidel empires. Moreover, many of the warrior leaders and 'terrorists' of the Middle East are not Islamicists or particularly devout in any way. Saddam Hussein, who was once favoured by the US authorities in their dispute with Islamicist Iran, became a terrorist when the US authorities deemed him to be one. While the Bush administration has tried to link

Saddam with the attacks of 9/11 and the Taliban, the evidence shows clearly that Saddam's terrorism is entirely secular. It was reportedly a great surprise to Saddam when his American allies found cause to turn against him and later link him with the Islamicist attacks of 9/11.

It is, perhaps, the spectacular nature of this new kind of political violence, embedded as it is in Islamicist rhetoric, which is so unnerving western leaders and communities. It is impossible to know, ultimately, whether Islamic political militias such as al-Qa'ida, Jamaah Islamiyah or Hamas are motivated primarily by a genuine religiosity, or by a more pragmatic and professional power politics which merely *uses* the discourse of Islam to mobilize support from across Muslim societies and peoples. What is clear, however, is that this discourse inscribes on the body of the faithful, especially for those who die in the service of Allah, a compound of meanings that not only elevates the bearer to eternal grace, but confronts the nominal enemy with a terrifying semiotic assault.

In many respects, the body and its lexical inscriptions represent the interface between the various forces of globalization. The ontology of the Islamic body collapses the rationalist dualisms generated through European Enlightenment. The body is not, as in the European tradition, distinguished from or opposed to the mind and spirit; rather the body is generated purely as spirit and hence incapable of actual damage. The reintegration of secular and religious authority – and hence politics – is reproduced in the body politic. The body is pure servant to the will of a cosmologically refined discourse. Suicide bombers are the most extreme example of the Islamic servant–body since biology and mortality are subsumed within the broader integration of God (spirit) and self (matter). The representation of God's word, therefore, seeks to restore the 'absence' of God to the presence of biological body interacting with the Scriptures as defined and directed by theologian and radical Islamicist leaders. It is the cultural imaginary of this integration which allows the Islamicist to sacrifice the body and its biology for the greater grace of eternal blessing. The Islamicist, suicide body, as it is read by the western enemy, however, is an absurd and dangerous entity (as discourse) which menaces the rationality of fear and moral orderliness. The body of the western warrior is forged through the ideal of rationalized statehood and the possibility of survival, rather than the certitude of destruction. The western warrior body is shaped, therefore, by a radically different ideology, rationality and discourse; the suicide bomber, who has now become the scourge of occupied Iraq and occupying Israel, is motivated by a spiritual ascent which subsumes the despair that is propagated by modernization and political oppression.

As we noted above, these differences are particularly evident in the cultural formation of the female body. Quite evidently, Islamicism rejects those modes of western representation that are broadly generated through popular culture and the media. Images of sexual permissiveness, bodily display, vocational equality and the contraction of the family and the maternal role are vehemently rejected by traditional Islamic theology. Reciprocally, the images of Taliban austerity and the oppression of women in Afghanistan generated considerable anxiety for the west, including those liberal feminists who had committed themselves to the political values of cultural pluralism and relativism. While opposing the war on terror generally, and the reprisal attacks on Afghanistan, many feminists in the west nevertheless feel gratified by the liberation of women that appears to be taking place in Kabul under US-led occupation. This critical ambivalence reflects the deeper problems for political liberalism which struggles to reconcile the western model of emancipation with a tolerance for, if not active celebration of, cultural independence and pluralist values. The sight of Saudi, Taliban and Iranian women wearing the chadoor and veil, and walking several paces behind their husbands alerts western feminists to the deep questions of bodily oppression that lie at the centre of these language wars. If the liberation of women is a universal ideology, then it is difficult for western feminists to accept a mode of liberationism which accepts cultural practices like polygamy, the compulsory wearing of the hijab and the exclusion of women from full public life. Over the past two decades there have been numerous occasions when feminists from the Middle East have accused western feminists of a mode of intellectual and cultural imperialism, particularly when western feminists criticize practices that are acceptable to Muslim women but offensive to westerners.

While this issue will be discussed in considerable detail in Chapter 6, the events at Abu Ghraib prison in Baghdad illustrate how western feminism has become implicated in clashes over the body in zones of global terror. Thus, as western feminism celebrates the professional opportunities afforded women, including the opportunities for participation and leadership in the armed services, the activities of female GIs at Abu Ghraib lead to specific questions about the ways in which liberation is being expressed. Certainly, one of the most confronting images in the Abu Ghraib album features Private Lynndie

England holding a naked male Iraqi detainee by a leash. This image of western–US-sponsored female emancipation contrasts radically with the sort of liberational aspirations and values expressed by many Muslim feminists, including those in Iraq. While many western feminists have shared the Bush administration's condemnation of the prison guards, casting them as aberrant and perverse, others, such as Wendy McElroy (2003), have suggested that western feminism needs to take account of itself and the liberation it exhorts. For McElroy, the activities of the female GIs, while aberrant in many respects, highlight the radical difference between the sexual aspirations of her home culture and the more familial and religious aspirations of Muslim women in the Middle East. Abu Ghraib, among many other things, illuminates this contrast, even as it exists in the humiliation of Muslim men.

INTERDEPENDENCE AND THE
FORMATION OF THE CULTURAL DIVIDE

As we noted briefly above, Jacques Lacan has characterized the interdependence of cultures and identity as a 'double entry matrix'. Lacan is suggesting by this concept a sense in which the subject is an outcome of social interdependencies and interconnections. Homi Bhabha (1987, 1994) elaborates this point, arguing that subjectivity is itself a multiply forming and abstract entity that is constituted through language and can never be integrated as claimed by Enlightenment ontology. We have suggested in this chapter that the formation of the east–west divide is also a product of language, and we have argued that the actual relationship between western and Muslim peoples has been forged through a multitude of cultural and historical interdependencies. The formation of Islamicism is related not merely to the intrinsic history and social conditions of the Middle East, but rather is constituted in terms of complex relationships with Euro-American cultures and cultural influences. In this sense, Lacan's double entry could more usefully be termed a multiple entry matrix.

As we have noted in relation to the Abu Ghraib abuse scandal, these interdependencies manifest themselves through various forms of cultural spillage. A cultural dissonance (signifier dissociation) may emerge as subjects are exposed to extreme or unfamiliar circumstances and they attempt to adapt the resources of the home culture in order to render the new situation intelligible or familiar. It is important

to recognize that, just as culture is always transitory an
are never complete, identity is also open and processual.
Abu Ghraib wardens were not able to complete the loop of Ame
hegemony, finding within the spaces of its authority various form
of spillage and semiotic double-coding. As they referred to the
familiar televisual culture and its broad lexicon of sexual expression,
the wardens, either consciously or incidentally, were engaging in
various forms of political subversion. It was not just the orderliness
of masculo-Islamic culture which the wardens were challenging; they
were creating new spaces of pleasure and inversion out of the rigid
and brutal structures of military authority.

This, of course, is the process of cultural formation and
contestation we described in the Introduction: the predicate of
all culture is instability, challenge and change. Even within the
rigidity of Islamicism, there are various kinds of subversive impulses,
disagreements and a volatile mix of opinions and perspectives. Inside
Taliban Afghanistan, for example, where various forms of western
decadence, including television, were banned, individuals and
communities devised strategies for the expression of selfhood which
could not be detected by the Islamic police. Within private homes,
for example, small groups of young women congregated, discussed
significant issues and wore make-up, which was forbidden by the
Taliban authorities. This engagement with external cultures does not
necessarily reflect a dissatisfaction with the Muslim faith, but with
the authority of a specific regime and its control over the discourses
of the body. The offence of wearing make-up creates extraordinary
allegiances with western consumer symbology and discourses of
femininity which second-wave feminism in the west was keen to
deconstruct. In this sense, the political alliance between these forms
of western feminism and the Taliban, like the expressivities of the
female wardens at Abu Ghraib, challenge directly the validity of
ideology and the clash of civilizations/cultures thesis.

The private subversion of Afghan women under the Taliban regime
parallels subversion in the Islamic state of Iran. In Iran, however, the
cinema excavates private grievances, allowing them to be explored
through a sanctioned but highly scrutinized public forum. Like
the Indonesian kulit puppetry, Iranian cinema vocalizes social and
political concerns using various gradients of metaphor and double-
coding. It may be that Iran's more mature Islamic statehood views
integration with the global economy as a necessary, if regrettable,
precondition of economic development and prosperity. It seems

...ultural products of Iranian cinema are an ...anian culture, a culture which the Islamic ...e to announce to the global community. ...nd Saudi Arabia, Iran may well be seeking to ...omic system – global capitalism – which is in ...ically repugnant but materially and practically ...m of cultural and economic interdependence is even more dra...lly evident in the Islamic state of Saudi Arabia which represents itself nominally as a 'friend to the United States', but which is clearly sponsoring many Islamic militant organizations and activities across the Middle East. The oil revenues derived from exports to the US and other western nations, that is, are being diverted to the ultimate overthrow of the imperialist countries of the west.

CONCLUSIONS

1. Theories like Huntington's 'clash of civilizations' tend to aggregate the diversity and dynamism of culture into unitary structures. These theories, along with their antitheses of Islamic liberationalism, contribute to the formation of a revitalized east–west divide.
2. An identity politics is forming around a mode of significant or essential cultural difference. Neoconservatives distinguish this difference in terms of American global primacy. This primacy is viewed as a form of aggressive hegemony by resistant forces in the Middle East and wider Muslim world.
3. The modern, global networked media contributes to the revitalized east–west divide.
4. Radical and militant Islam is not representative of all Muslim peoples, cultures, communities and individuals.
5. Culture needs to be considered in terms of transition, instability and change as well as an impulse to communicative and community stability.
6. Radical and militant Islam has a particular history in the Middle East and other parts of the Muslim world. This history is forged around the processes of colonialism, modernization and globalization. Different groups and nations within the region have responded differently to these conditions.
7. The Israeli–Palestinian question remains problematic for the resolution of complex agonisms in the region.

8. The essentialization of identity, manifest in disputes like the Palestinian–Israeli conflict, leads to the perpetuation of discourses like the clash of civilizations and radical resistance.

9. The body has been conscripted into these language wars. Various governments, scholars, militants and media professionals inscribe the warring bodies with various ideologies of 'essential' difference. These ideologies of essential difference, however, are themselves subverted by everyday practices which seek out free spaces and slippages of meaning. Such expressivities were to be found in Taliban Afghanistan where young women experimented with make-up and self-education.

10. Cultural diversity, impious expressivities and open identity may help to shield communities and individuals from the excesses of essentialization which condemn the world to a structured and inevitable mode of warfare and violence.

3
The Meaning of 9/11:
In the Midst of Infinite Justice

MEANING AND THE AESTHETICS OF TERROR

One of the most striking features of the September 11 attacks was the level of global sympathy expressed for the victims and for America generally. Whatever criticisms or misgivings the international community may have felt toward the US, they were largely subsumed by the horror of these attacks. Yet, the settling dust of Ground Zero revealed not only the massive fissure in the New York skyline, but a yawning gap in the semiotic system of 'America' itself. The US security structures had failed; thousands of Americans were dead, injured or bereaved. The seemingly unassailable American self-belief was ruptured and everyone was cast into a shadow of doubt. This was a precise moment of dissociation: the signifier 'America' had split from its signified, leaving a vacant and smouldering absence of meaning. Iconic American novelist Norman Mailer was among the first to attempt an adhesion:

> [T]he best explanation for 9/11 is that the Devil won a great battle that day. Yes, Satan as the pilot who guided those planes into that ungodly denouement ... Yes, as if part of the Devil's aesthetic acumen was to bring it off, exactly as if we were watching the same action movie we had been looking at for years. That may be at the core of the immense impact 9/11 had on America. Our movies came off the screen and chased us down the canyons of the city. (2003: 110–11)

Within the realm of cultural politics, this invocation of a religious and televisual aesthetic seeks to transform the visceral and visual shock of the collapsing towers into a comprehensible framework. For Mailer, as for many others, the spectacle of the imploding fireball and the vision of desperate people diving from windows to certain death transcend the conventions of political debate. This was all too terrible, too shocking. The world order that had been so confidently announced by George Bush senior and which had positioned America as the inviolable harbinger of justice, democracy and global governance had been utterly inverted. The screen had burst open. This was not the work of mere mortals: it was something more hideous, more unimaginable. This was the aesthetic of terror, a radical irruption of faithless and chaotic inhumanity.

There are, of course, alternative aesthetics. And while Mailer speaks for many who would seek to reconstruct a more normative American narrative around the twin towers collapse, other voices struggle to be heard. Noam Chomsky most famously identified this normative American aesthetic as a muddle of contradiction, an ideological compound which suffocates the freedom of others and suppresses the narrative of dissent wherever it arises. According to Chomsky, the shock of 9/11 is stimulated by false sensibilities, including a belief in the inviolability of American power and the justness of its actions. For the first time since 1812, Chomsky points out, the United States had received 'return fire' on its homeland from those it had exploited, assaulted and coerced. Colonialism, which was the form of globalism initiated by Europe and adapted by the US, had created a radical division of social, economic and political difference. The exceptional nature of 9/11, however, was that the victims of these foreign adventures had actually conducted their reprisals on the imperialist's soil: rarely had Europe been attacked 'by their foreign victims. England was not attacked by India, nor Belgium by Congo, nor Italy by Ethiopia, nor France by Algeria' (Chomsky, 2001: 11–12). America's victims in the Middle East, however, had found a pathway back to the perpetrators of their military, economic and cultural incarceration. As we have noted in previous chapters, the distance was overcome by the exercise of the very technologies which had been deployed against them – military and communicational.

Susan Sontag (2001) also queried the broad aesthetic by which American cultural politics constructs itself. The conception of the perpetrators of the 9/11 attacks as 'cowardly' confounded Sontag. In essence, she argued, 9/11 was not an assault on 'liberty', 'civilization' or 'the free world', but was rather a response to America's own alliances and actions in foreign territories. This perspective was also echoed in the *London Review of Books* special edition on September 11, where Mary Beard boldly suggested that 'however tactfully you dress it up, the United States had it coming'. These comments precipitated a deluge of responses, most of which attacked Beard's perspective. One American academic from Stanford University, for example, was incensed by the lack of sensitivity expressed by the British journal, claiming that she rejected the idea that America was 'to blame' for the attacks and that she would cancel her longstanding subscription to the *LRB* as a matter of protest. An equally forceful response to criticism of US policy and its corollary of disrespect for the victims of 9/11 was directed against Bill Maher, the host of US TV show *Politically Incorrect*. Explicating a point made by guest Dimesh D'Souza, Maher suggested that 'Lobbing cruise missiles from two thousand miles away, that's cowardly.' Like Sontag, Maher was savaged by the media, the public and the White House. A major sponsor cancelled its contract and Maher was abandoned by his network; the programme was cancelled several months later.

In his book, *Ground Zero* (2002), Paul Virilio suggests that these language wars are fundamentally implicated in the cultural formation of the televisual technologies themselves. This is not merely a matter of message conveyance, but of the cultural complicity of the apparatuses of war and the apparatuses of mediation. As it has been argued in Chapter 1, the meaning of terrorism is clearly bound to the global media and its context of cultural politics. Virilio elaborates on this point, claiming that the 'telescopic' or 'oracular' technologies of mediation and war now function within a single techno-sphere, a sphere shaped around the cultural effects of speed and progress:

> [W]hat is troubling about the covert state of transnational terrorism ... is its growing subordination to a techno-scientific progress which is, itself, unauthored and dependent on the development of its own audio visual media and platforms ... The scientific imagination ultimately suffers the same fate as 'e-tainment'; it comes to resemble ... that of the Islamic suicide-attackers no doubt dying happy at becoming actors in a global super-production in which reality would tip over once and for all into electronic nothingness. (2002: 68)

In contrast to Norman Mailer's cosmological aesthetic, Virilio raises the prospect that 9/11 may mean very little or nothing at all – a prospect which no doubt prompted many commentators and public officials to enter the fray and seek to fill the semiotic void created by the collapse of the twin towers. Most particularly, Americans rushed to fill the void with a form of zealot patriotism which would not, under any circumstances, tolerate criticism or vacuous nihilism. The nothingness to which Virilio refers, however, sits within the vector of televisual culture and a politics which evinces itself through the semiosis of a nascent broadcast democracy. In either case, the meaning-making that surrounds 9/11 is fundamentally bound to the meaning of 'America'. The aim of this chapter is to examine the ways in which these various commentaries have engaged their meaning-making processes in terms of 9/11 and America. In particular, the chapter seeks to elucidate the ways in which the televisual media are implicated in these various meaning-making formations and language wars.

DIVINE JUSTICE: GLOBAL ORDER

In the first few days following the 9/11 attacks, US President George W. Bush declared vengeance. In what he initially called 'Operation Infinite Justice', Bush announced a scale of retribution that would resonate throughout history and perhaps beyond. The convolution of a direct assault on ordinary people and America's unique status in the world constituted for Bush the ultimate offence, an offence against the pinnacle of civilized being, morality and social progress. On the day of the attacks Bush's public statements repeated a common theme of shock, belligerence and indignation. Bush's address to the nation, in many ways, became the foundation for much of the rhetoric of the war on terror:

> Good evening. Today, our fellow citizens, our way of life, our very freedom came under attack in a series of deliberate and deadly terrorist acts. The victims were in airplanes, or in their offices: secretaries, businessmen and women, military and federal workers, moms and dads, friends and neighbors. Thousands of lives were suddenly ended by evil, despicable acts of terror … A great people has been moved to defend a great nation. Terrorist attacks can shake the foundations of our biggest buildings, but they cannot touch the foundations of America. These acts shattered steel, but they cannot dent the steel of American resolve. America was targeted for attack because we're the brightest beacon for freedom and opportunity. And no-one will keep that light from shining. Today our nation saw evil, the very worst of human nature … This is a day when all Americans from every walk of life unite in our resolve … None of us will ever forget this day. Yet, we go forward to defend freedom and all that is good and just in the world. (Bush, 2001)

While regarded by many commentators, especially in the Internet blog community, as incompetently 'belated' (Wood & Thompson, 2003), Bush nevertheless was drawn to fill the semiotic void of 9/11 with an epiphanic polemic. An 'infinite' justice, of course, is one that marshals the divine powers against evil. Bush calls on a divine retribution in his hastily coined, but extraordinarily effective, 'war against terror'. The ritual of prayer and the interlacing of blessings on the nation, its people and its ideology punctuate the speeches on September 11. Bush attributes to the events a cosmological meaning, one which elevates the victims as heroes and condemns the perpetrators as evil, inhuman and perverted by a hatred which would 're-make the world ... imposing its radical beliefs on people everywhere'.

It is not, however, that an attack on US interests was exceptional in itself. Since the 1980s US citizens and soldiers had been targeted by terrorists, both domestically and internationally; the Trade Center itself had been bombed in 1993, killing six people and injuring around a thousand more. Against this context, moreover, various other forms of political violence over recent years have produced many more casualties than September 11 – in Rwanda, for example, around 800,000 people were killed in a campaign of ethnic cleansing, while in Serbia, Kosovo, Sierra Leone and most recently the Sudan tens of thousands of people lost their lives in politically charged ethnic and territorial disputes. The distinguishing feature of the 9/11 attacks, in fact, centres on the sudden exposure of America's vulnerability, not merely as a material and social space, but as a semiotic system.

As we have noted, the meaning of 9/11 is absolutely implicated in the meaning of America. This meaning is a contingency of substantial dispute, especially as it is situated within the context of an international media network and the processes of globalization. The attacks of 9/11 were, as much as anything else, a clear indication of the global significance of the cultural trope 'America', not merely in terms of economic and military primacy, but also through the imposing character of American global cultural ubiquity. During the immediate aftermath of the attacks, this cultural ubiquity concentrated itself through the President's discourses and especially the ideal of American life which was unrestrainedly valorized through George Bush's rhetoric. This ideal of divinely guided American values (democracy, freedom, plural humanism) is, however, shadowed by its contingent other – a pragmatic, capitalist materialism that relies ultimately on hierarchies of social order and social discrimination. Expressed within a discourse of globalization, this ideal promotes and facilitates, at its best, a cultural contiguity that advocates tolerance, respect and the exchange of ideas, values and aesthetics; in themselves, these values may generate egalitarianism, mutual advantage and a form of universal human rights that supports new forms of global governance (Zolo, 1997). At its worst, it merely confirms a hegemony that privileges US autonomy, First World primacy and a hierarchical system by which four fifths of the world are condemned to poverty and various modes of economic, military and cultural subjugation.

Tom Nairn (2002) has suggested that George Bush's primary motivation as a public official is largely directed by elite self-interest. In this sense, 'America' becomes a synonym for an ideology which packs the collective of diverse publics into a nationalist discourse; the language of the ideal becomes part of the weaponry of domestic and international authority aimed at, among many other things, winning the war of terror. For Nairn, the better parts of globalization can be phrased in terms of 'people coming together to share our common fate' (Nairn, 2002: 46). But this more elevated form of globalization, Nairn argues, is leaving the US behind. That is, while the US continues to cling to its own autonomous vision of global domination, the remainder of the world is seeking a global, cultural condition which prioritizes community over self-interested aggrandisement. To this extent, the official discourse of 'America', which continues to conceive of itself as 'the Chosen' and as marked by some unique and divine providence, exists within an incongruous material and imaginary space. While it remains a 'big country' with an enormous base of resources, including the world's largest stockpile of military hardware (Nairn, 2002: 46), America is trapped by its own ossifying self-interest:

> A ragged and confused divorce is underway, and was well underway before September 11. Since 1989 the underlying globalization process has begun to emancipate itself from a US hegemony that was initially inevitable, given the nature of the Cold War, and the way that it ended. This would have happened anyway and was already strongly underway by 2001. But it was then brusquely accelerated or shocked on by events, above all, in consciousness. (Nairn, 2002: 51)

The disjuncture Nairn identifies between a globally forming consciousness and American self-conception is not, however, a simple dichotomy. The material and semiotic force of globalization is a matter of intense dispute. Over all other things, the events of September 11 and their continuing cultural, political and military resonance demonstrate that the war of consciousness and the variant shapings of social and cultural knowledge are far from resolved.

The meaning of 9/11 is embedded within these battling modes of discourse and thought, most particularly as they are engaged through diverse social groups across the globe.

Jean Baudrillard has taken up this point, arguing that all contemporary consciousness remains largely open and indefinable, most particularly as it engages in the hyperreality being generated through contemporary global mediascapes. As we noted in Chapter 1, Baudrillard (1995) has argued famously that the Gulf War did not take place. While this claim outrages many critics (e.g. Norris, 1992), in essence Baudrillard is suggesting that the American attack on Iraq should not be called a 'war': first, because the two sides of the conflict were so unevenly matched; and second, because the official US military imaging of the 'attack' profoundly distorted the event, constituting it for world TV audiences as a 'war without death'. Following the September 11 attacks on New York, Baudrillard broadened these arguments, suggesting that American domination of the hyperreal global 'system' was of itself the essence or 'spirit' of terrorism. This global domination manifests itself through the hyperreal of media communications, but is also critically linked to American military and economic primacy – this is the essence of globalization. This is not merely to say, as Noam Chomsky (2001, 2003a) and others might, that American foreign policy contributed to the attacks on New York; it is rather to suggest that the actual existence of a single, and unitary global superpower constitutes its own predicate of violent reprisal. Michel Foucault (1977a, 1981) has said something similar, of course, in arguing that power generates its own inevitable resistance. For Baudrillard, however, it is the sheer singularity and mass of this power which cannot be directly and genuinely opposed, altered or exchanged. The terrorism which assaults the megapower of US global domination is merely reactive, an inevitable response to singularity itself:

> To a system whose very excess of power poses an insoluble challenge, the terrorists respond with a definitive act which is also not susceptible of exchange. Terrorism is the act which restores an irreducible singularity to the heart of a system of generalized exchange. All the singularities (species, individuals and cultures) that have paid with their deaths for the installation of a global circulation governed by a single power are taking their revenge today through this terroristic situational transfer. (Baudrillard, 2002a: 9)

Like particles of dust being cast up by the monster's own feet, this terrorism may assault the eyes of globalization. In this sense it is 'terror against terror' though without the density of ideas or ideology. In a hyperreal cultural condition, therefore, the triumph of globalization leads inevitably to a battle against itself. This Fourth World War, as Baudrillard defines the current agonisms, is not a battle of ideologies or a clash of civilizations (Huntington, 1993, 1996, 2004), but rather it is the world or globe battling against the inevitable flows of globalization. In other words, it is a world system in which power is both feeding on itself and attacking itself – 'if Islam dominated the world, terrorism would rise against Islam' (Baudrillard, 2002a: 12).

The spirit of terrorism, therefore, is to be found in its momentous and inclusive progression. While other commentators concern themselves with the details of political or military conflict, Baudrillard's more ontological enquiry seeks to expose the force that lies behind US globalization. In this sense, Baudrillard's ideas directly address the cosmology of President Bush and Norman Mailer; in fact, Baudrillard is in many ways confronting both the global and cosmological conception of America itself. The idea that good must prevail over evil, perhaps the most common motif of American televisual culture, is challenged by Baudrillard's conception of 9/11 and the spirit of terrorism itself. Achieving an even more theological epiphany, Baudrillard argues that good and evil work simultaneously toward the same political ends:

> We believe naively that the progress of Good, its advance in all fields (the sciences, technology, democracy, human rights), corresponds to a defeat of Evil. No-one seems to have understood that Good and Evil advance together, as part of the same movement. The triumph of the one does not eclipse the other ... Good does not conquer Evil, nor indeed does the reverse happen: they are at once both irreducible to each other and inextricably interrelated. (Baudrillard, 2002a: 13)

This meaning of America and 9/11 is constituted, therefore, in terms of this mutual advance of good and evil. Thus, while Tom Nairn applies a normative approach to the social and political reform of this power, Baudrillard pursues a form of radical scepticism which is constituted around Manichean principles, 'underlying the inseparability of good and evil, and hence the impossibility of mobilizing the one without the other' (Baudrillard, 1993: 105). According to Jonathan

Smith (2004), Baudrillard's approach distinguishes terrorism as a form of 'pure appearance' – the manifestation of what he calls in his earlier writings hyperreality. This pure appearance resembles the 'pre-consciousness' in Lacanian theory, though for Baudrillard it is the pure appearance of the 'ephemeral moment in which things take the time to appear before taking on meaning or value' (Baudrillard, 1987b: 88). It is through this state of pure appearance that humanity is exposed, Baudrillard argues, to a profound moral and spiritual ambiguity. Terrorism, which merely responds to the excess of globalization, constitutes a form of pure appearance, at least in as much as it is a functionally communicational act that has neither substance nor clarity.

Thus, while Nairn may bemoan America's flagging consciousness and Chomsky might accuse America of being an essentially 'terrorist state', Baudrillard reinterprets America as the manifestation of globalizing singularity and itself: that is, America has become a monolith of an aggregated and singular global structure to which terrorism merely *reacts*. It is important to note, however, that Baudrillard is not identifying with or directly supporting Islamic militantism against America, though some commentators seem to assume this is the case. What is especially disturbing to these commentators is the claim by Baudrillard in *Simulacra and Simulation* that 'I'm a terrorist and nihilist in theory as others are with weapons' (1994: 163). As we have noted, however, Baudrillard's claim here is shaped by his radical scepticism, itself an expression of a Manichean and Gnostic sensibility. To this extent, it is not that Baudrillard is advocating the murder of innocent people, but rather he is advancing an idea about the 'system' that prevails over global culture. The good and evil which underpin this system cannot be truncated from the history of terrorism and the formation of a paradoxical but pure evil which contributes to the illusion of reality: 'A principle of illusion – the concept of the world as the work of the devil and, at the same time, that of perfection achieved here on earth – are the two fundamental concepts of the Cathars' (Baudrillard, 1996: 82). The Cathars, a sect of French Gnosticism of which Baudrillard claims a genealogy, are 'terrorists' inasmuch as they 'based their theologies on the very negation of the real' (Baudrillard, 1987a: 44). This idea that the Gnostics were terrorists, who accepted the inevitability of evil and the illusory, encouraged Baudrillard to claim that: 'Religion in its former heretical phase was always a negation – at times a violent one of the real world, and this is what gives it strength' (1987b: 124).

A number of commentators are affronted by Baudrillard's testimonies, pointing to the simple fact that most of the people who were killed on September 11 had little or no connection with American global hegemony and were not even necessarily supporters of the current US administration. Baudrillard rejects these criticisms, claiming that the commentators who valorize the victims of terrorism are simply missing the point. In a well-publicized dispute with Susan Sontag, Baudrillard argues that those members of the post-reality, modern First World who seek to ease their own loss of reality by paying homage to victims of political violence seem merely to be 'sunning their good consciences in the warm glow of solidarity' (Baudrillard, 2002a: 46). Referring specifically to Sontag's collaborative production of *Waiting for Godot* in the besieged city of Sarajevo in the early 1990s, Baudrillard acidly rejects the whole idea of recovering our modern reality through such ridiculous gestures of good will:

[W]e have only one reality, and it has to be rescued. And rescued even with the worst of slogans: 'We have to do something. We can't just do nothing'. But doing something just because you cannot not do it has never amounted to a principle of action or freedom. Merely a form of absolution from your own impotence and compassion for your own fate. (2002a: 45)

While Sontag might accept the problematics of solidarity, she interrogates the notion of reality as 'spectacle' or hyperreality as proposed by Baudrillard and another French theorist, Guy Debord. In essence, Sontag denounces the idea of reality as 'spectacle' since it:

universalizes the viewing habits of a small educated population, living in the rich part of the world, where news has been converted to entertainment ... It assumes that everyone is a spectator ... It suggests that there is no real suffering in the world ... There are hundreds of millions of television watchers who are far from inured to what they see on television. They do not have the luxury of patronizing reality. (Sontag, 2003: 109–11)

Sontag's pronouncement places her with Nairn and to a degree Chomsky for whom reality is posed in terms of political co-ordinates and the actualities of human corpo*reality* and human suffering. In this sense, Baudrillard is treated as a sophist, one whose 'fancy rhetoric' exceeds the value of the ideas. Of course, Baudrillard's Manichean conception has never denied the actuality of human suffering; it simply identifies the causes of that suffering with an ontology of 'language'. Thus, while Baudrillard would reject Sontag's distinction between the 'reality' of suffering people and the reality of a hyperreal consciousness, there is certainly some level of agreement about the ways in which this consciousness is formed through our First World technologies and the centrality of the image. In this way, Baudrillard reflects on the events of 9/11, which appears as the 'Manhattan disaster movie', bringing together 'the twentieth century's two elements of mass fascination ... the white magic of the cinema and the black magic of terrorism' (Baudrillard, 2002a: 30).

CITIZENS, CONSENSUS AND DISSENT

One of the most notable features of 9/11 and the war against terror is the relatively high level of public support, both for the reprisal attacks against Afghanistan and for the increased security intervention in the private lives and rights of the citizenry (Gallup Poll, 2001). As a number of media analysts, including Sandra Silberstein (2002, also Hess & Kalb, 2003, Norris et al., 2003), have noted, there was a rapid and relatively uniform public adoption of official discourses during the 9/11 crisis period. Critical voices like those of Noam Chomsky, Edward Herman and Susan Sontag (see also the *London Review of Books*, October 2001) were rare during the period, as public sympathy for the victims and the semiotic shock of the event were at their peak. Global sympathy, with the exception of particularly hostile regimes, was also considerable, lending weight to Tom Nairn's suggestion that the event is something greater than America itself.

This level of global sympathy began to subside, however, as the US authorities focused their war on terror through direct attacks on the Taliban and Afghanistan. Even so, while global concerns over the Afghanistan invasion compromised the sympathy of many non-Americans, the US public, according to the majority of public opinion polls, remained more or less steadfast in their support for, and trust in, the US government. As we indicated above, the semiotic vacuum that was created by the crisis of 9/11 was being occupied by official discourses which invoked the authority of God, nation, democracy and freedom. The victims and emergency workers of 9/11 became reconfigured as national heroes within the great lineage of a noble history. The President's speeches and the reports on major news networks were replete with a sense of grand destiny. The flags, the speeches, the raw fury of New York Mayor Rudolph Giuliani – all spoke of an unswervable greatness, a collective consciousness which could not be deterred by the 'unspeakable' evil of terrorism. Clearly, the semiotic vacuum was being captured by a vigorous national conservatism which would not concede culpability or error. The neoconservatives were flapping their eagle wings.

We now know that the military responses to 9/11 were being underwritten by pre-existing concerns about the Taliban and secret oil deals which involved a border-to-border pipeline across Afghan territory. While two French journalists, Jean-Charles Brisard and Guilliame Dasquié (2002), claim that the primary motivation for the attacks on Afghanistan derives from this oil conspiracy, we can be relatively certain that there was at least some confluent 'serendipity' between the war on terror and the oil scheme. In either case, the US authorities needed to convince the American citizenry that an attack on Afghanistan was appropriate and necessary – that it constituted a 'just war'. As John Keane (2004) has pointed out, democratic states require, for their own moral and ideological survival, that the wars in which they participate are demonstrably 'just' and justifiable. In this sense, the discursive response to 9/11 was critical for the formation of a semiotic environment in which war could be undertaken.

In fact, and as Susan Carruthers (2000) argues, this confluence of state authority and public opinion has frequently been viewed as a necessary precondition of war. In the modern context, where the mass media filters and scrutinizes public affairs and where governments must submit to public judgement, citizens have to be convinced of the viability of any military campaign. In order for a war to succeed, most particularly an offshore war, publics must be convinced it is just and winnable. In their management of recent wars, therefore, the authorities have sought to enlist the support of the media power they so vehemently fear – 'this power has often been considered by the state … [a]s negative: the very act of representing war has been taken as anti-war in effect, if not in intent' (Carruthers, 2000: 9). The consensus of state and public, therefore, is critically implicated in the functions and status of the modern media.

In fact, the media is necessarily problematized in the role of interlocutor. While positioning itself as the 'fourth estate', in Carlyle's terms, a facility which scrutinizes government through the formation of disinterested social knowledge, the media nevertheless may be co-opted by, and constitutive of, various modes of institutionalized hegemony. In other words, mediated knowledge becomes 'interested' as it becomes available to the claims of particular social groups. Thus, the lesson of America's defeat in the Vietnam War was as much informational as military. The 'reality' presented to domestic audiences by journalists produced disjunctive rather than confluent effects because the knowledge of the authorities deviated quite markedly from that of the citizenry. The war vision, that is, became the subject of a broader language war and various struggles to signify. As we noted in Chapter 1, since Vietnam, First World state authorities have been far more active in media and information management, most particularly in limiting public 'exposure' to the graphic details of war. In the Falklands (1982), the Gulf War (1990–91) and the Balkans (1998–99) respective First World governments sought to balance the interests of the state and associated hegemonies against the alternative invocations of democracy, freedom of speech and the public's right to know. The success of these strategies may be measured in terms of military outcomes, 'security' and the satisfaction of the public. The public, according to Young and Jesser, have tended to applaud these strategies, preferring to compromise short-term freedoms for the sake of longer-term national security: 'opinion polls have shown overwhelming popular support for constraints on the media during recent limited conflicts' (Young & Jesser, 1997: 11). If this is so, then it appears that the state has succeeded in asserting itself over the media or at least that dimension of the media which might challenge, rather than conform to, the hegemonic impulses of state interest.

For some critics, however, these measures of success are themselves highly problematic. In his various analyses of the post-9/11 American wars, Robert Fisk (2003) claims that the US government treats the truth, the public and the independent media with contempt, engaging directly only those media like the Fox network which subscribe to its strategic interests and informational goals. Commentators like Noam Chomsky (2001, 2003a, 2003b) believe that the media is simply distorting the truth about US foreign policy and military strategies – therefore a confluence between hegemonic interests and public opinion is constructed on a false premise. For Chomsky (see also Bourdieu, 1998, Knightley, 1989, Postman, 1987, Tester, 1994) the mainstream broadcast media and its 'information professionals' create illusions about social knowledge, most particularly as it forms around American international hegemony, warfare, dominant social values and state policy. Chomsky argues (see Herman & Chomsky, 1988) that the media, rather than pose a danger to government, are most often complicit in the manufacturing of public consent. This pattern is evident in relation to Nicaragua, the Sudan, the Persian Gulf, Serbia and now Afghanistan:

> It is entirely typical for the major media, and the intellectual classes generally, to line up in support of power in a time of crisis and try to mobilize the population for the same cause. That was true, with almost hysterical intensity, at the times of the bombing of Serbia. The Gulf War was not at all unusual. (Chomsky, 2001: 30)

The American-led reprisals against bin Laden and the Taliban government of Afghanistan were shaped therefore by a coalition of interests which typically censor the opposing perspective. The mainstream media's venomous condemnation of the perpetrators of the 9/11 assaults on New York and Washington refused to concede the possibility that America's own policies might have contributed to the crimes. The *New York Times* of September 18 denied any mitigation since 'the perpetrators acted out of hatred for the values cherished in the West as freedom, tolerance, prosperity, religious pluralism and universal suffrage' (Serge Schnenann, cited in Chomsky, 2001: 31). In other words, the fourth estate was as much a target as the commercial iconography of the World Trade Center. According to Chomsky, however, it is precisely this freedom which is threatened by America's own foreign policies and by a compliant media elite which serves the interests of the state and state authority. The 9/11 atrocities and the subsequent US-led reprisals against Afghanistan were relatively straightforward manifestations of policy and its extreme expression in warfare. Public consent was achieved through a strategic disciplining of information and mediated social knowledge.

Among other critiques of America's war on terror, Chomsky's analysis rests on a fundamental distinction between the truth of American policy and the 'artifice' of a knowledge created through propaganda, censorship and limited access. Thus, while bin Laden himself might not be interested in fighting a war against global privilege or American cultural hegemony (Fisk, 1999), Chomsky's mission is to expose the real and material circumstances of America's global hegemony and in particular the policies which have led to the catastrophes of 9/11 and the Afghan invasion. Wishing not to confuse the issues of Middle East politics with First World community protests against economic globalization, Chomsky unequivocally denounces claims by various conservative commentators that 9/11 was intrinsically linked to the globalization protests in Seattle, Washington and Melbourne. Such claims, Chomsky and others argue, represent a further attempt by the ruling elite to silence criticism and the legitimacy of challenges to globalization and media imperialism.

HERO–VICTIMS

Thus, the meaning of 9/11 for Chomsky and others resides in an imperialist US demeanour which is supported by a compliant and inevitably conservative and plutocratic multinational media industry – and a public which remains ignorant to the true facts. There can be no doubt that the Bush administration were at pains to manage the 9/11 crisis and the embedding of the reprisal attacks within a pre-eminent aphorism, 'war on terror'. This intersection of discursive effects made possible a strategic initiative which, on the surface at least, seemed only tenuously linked. An assault on an entire nation in order to capture a single individual, Osama bin Laden, was nevertheless rationalized by the discourse of terrorism. Public support for the assault was compounded, it seems, by the President's strategic enlistment of the ideologies of nationalism, modernization and globalization; the values of humanism, democracy and freedom were perpetually revitalized in the official discourse and the mechanisms of mass mediated narrative. The meaning of 9/11 was strategically transfigured as the meaning of war on terror and the capture of bin Laden. The Evangelical discourse continually invoked by Bush served both to confuse the public and to elevate the project as a mission from God.

As we noted above, this is most powerfully evident in the intense and disturbing heroization of the 9/11 victims. As was the case a year later in the context of the Bali bombings, much of the official and media discourse defined the victims as both sufferer and ascendant force. This precarious balance of discursive effects largely personifies the oxymoron of nationalist imaginary where the nation – that abstract, 'imagined community' (Anderson, 1991) – becomes the material and corporeal manifestation of an ideologically defined historical trajectory. In one of his speeches on September 11, President Bush exposes the underlying absurdity of this opposite effect:

> On September 11th, enemies of freedom committed an act of war against our country. Americans have known wars – but for the past 136 years, they have been wars on foreign soil, except for one, Sunday in 1941. Americans have known the casualties of war – but not at the center of a great city on a peaceful morning. Americans have known surprise attacks, but never before on thousands of civilians. All of this was brought upon us in a single day – and night fell on a different world, a world in which freedom itself is under attack. (Address to Congress, September 20, 2001)

The rhetorical condensation of the hero–victim moves from individuals, to nation to the supreme value of freedom. Bush seems oblivious to the possibility that fighting so many wars on foreign soil might be problematic – that these forms of military engagement may be part of an offensive or aggressive posture which is expansionist and imperialist rather than defensive. These foreign excursions, it seems, are naturalized somehow into the psyche and meaning of America; the privilege of power seems to rationalize aggression when it is perpetrated by the mighty.

Bush's speeches during the few months following the 9/11 attacks all bear this same mark of self-assured belligerence and sense of self-righteous inviolability. It is, of course, difficult to know how far the citizenry was prepared to accept the timbre and effect of these discourses, and to what extent the determination and self-belief are shared by others throughout the nation and culture. What is clear is that the government and military public information campaigns were highly focused and well planned (see Rampton & Stauber, 2003, Carey, 2003). Even though its genesis as a rhetorical figure may have been relatively spontaneous, the emergence and ultimate primacy of the 'war against terror' motif for the expression of national grief and retribution were not accidental. The government and military PR machineries ensured a continual feed of highly positioned media materials, maintaining a significant supply of drama, 'talent' and suspense. For all the serious doubts the global community may have had about George W. Bush, the events of 9/11 drew together an astonishingly polished televisual political performance. Everything possible was being done in order to bring together the government, media and public perspectives of the 9/11 disaster. In terms of the triad of consensus, the preparations for an attack on Afghanistan could not have been more cleverly construed. Public opinion was being galvanized; a just war was being created as history unfolding (Blondhelm & Liebes, 2003).

According to Paul Waldman (2004), Bush's performance around 9/11 was facilitated by a media which both feared and revered the White House administration. The volley of freedom speeches which the Bush writers generated was highly strategic, providing the premise not only for the consensus of government, media and citizenry but for a specifically targeted reprisal policy that camouflaged the administration's desire to assert greater control over oil resources in hostile regions. According to Waldman, the whole notion of a 'polished media performance' from Bush was entirely propagated. The mainstream media, in the flush of patriotic fervour and compliance to White House authority, merely overlooked the familiar bumbling of the President:

> Coverage of Bush after September 11 was not simply devoid of criticism over what some might consider trivial matters like his struggle with syntax. Reporters went much further, offering glowing tributes to his strength of character, his commanding leadership, and his pure heart. They treated every word out of his mouth as a message of great import all citizens should heed. (Waldman, 2004: 123)

This 'fraud', as Waldman calls it, became the foundation of a messianic project of freedom. Along with their fear of being excluded from the information feeder, the acceptance by much of the media that Bush is a 'regular folksy guy' enabled the White House to pursue this project through some exceptionally dangerous policies and military activities. As will be discussed in detail below, the pursuit of this project seems directly to compromise the integrity of the higher ideals and values upon which it is based.

PUBLIC OPINION AND THE NOT-QUITE-REAL

The meaning of September 11 and the meaning of America might seem to be bound, therefore, to this triad of government, media and the public. While we can measure reasonably effectively the force and focus of official discourses and the general attitude of the mass media, the views of the public are somewhat more elusive. We rely on public opinion polls to tell us what the citizens' views on a specific issue may be; however, these polls are notoriously limited, most particularly in terms of the density and durability of specific views. As was outlined in the previous chapters, the relationship between the media and its audiences is far more complex than simple message-sending and 'effects' propaganda models recognize. To this extent, Noam Chomsky's notion of a 'manufactured' public consent and Paul Waldman's notion of 'fraud' are limited, not merely because the public are not passive recipients and acceptors of measurable messages, but also because public opinion is itself an astonishingly reductive concept, drawing into a quantitative frame the very complex machinations of perspective and experience which constitute an 'opinion'. This is not to deny the value of Chomsky's views, nor indeed opinion polling. It is rather to situate these social readings within the broader context of 'the media' (as a set of relationships) and the cultural imaginaries with which the media interacts.

Citizens who are also creative, 'reading' audiences, therefore, are not the dupes of a mass media machinery and the propaganda apparatuses of government and the American military. The confluence of state interest, media and citizenry is a filtration effect of innumerable discursive elements, elements which become generalized through a reality that has no greater substance than the representational particulants which constitute it as 'truth'. Thus, the compliance of the American (First World) citizenry as it is shaped in language and expressed, for example, in a media opinion poll, can never be durable, stable nor even trustworthy since it is conceived and culturally 'ennobled' through the auspices of the same representational mode that has become the fabric and rubric of our social knowledge. The opinion poll has become another media game, another mode of televisual entertainment which draws into the field of representation the 'audience' and their perspective. A little like the notion of a 'reality TV', an opinion poll creates a space for generating representation with all its fallible and complicated volatilities (see Chapter 1). Like the war itself, therefore, the agreement of the public is 'inhuman', sustainable only through the moment to moment replenishment of that knowledge – through the indices of a generated ideology and media immersion. The compound of distance–proximity, absence–presence creates the conditions of this imagined ideology and popular perspective, as well as the certainty of their inevitable uncertainty.

Thus, while we might point to particular indices of the ideology which support the American war on terror – including the US government's official discourse on globalization – we are effectively using a media construction (the opinion poll) to calculate a media effect (compliance with the ideology). Much has been written about the fallibility of objective and quantitative measurement, and we don't need to be distracted by these arguments. Rather, we are interested in the simple reflexivity of public opinion and its sources within mediated culture. To this extent, the frequently noted 'volatility' of public opinion and the electorate is not a symptom of human fallibility or fickleness, so much as it is a condition of mediated sensibility. The principal question is not whether the citizenry are merely dupes of a powerful state and its complicit media. Nor, in fact, do analysts of the media have to choose between Baudrillard's radical scepticism and Chomsky's structuralist polemic. Rather, we need to identify the various strategies that the antagonists in this language war are deploying in order to engage the media's primary elements in their meaning-making. The public, that is, are to be identified both as a collection of individuals and communities capable of creative semiotic and cultural participation, *and* as a configuration of governments and media producers. Texts may well position audiences, as Althusser suggests; but audiences are also capable of positioning texts. As we indicated in Chapter 1, this is precisely why governments fear their citizens and engage in such intensely energetic processes of information management.

Thus, the history of agonisms as we outlined it in the previous chapter is radiated through what is culturally known in order to generate the new social knowledge (which itself is distilled as 'opinion' by the media). Those who viewed the destruction of the towers, in most cases through televisual replay, were confronted by a mesmeric, terrible and strangely beautiful event – strangely beautiful because it drew on an aesthetic of destruction and human nobility, which engendered a grace that transcended the conditions of its absolute annihilation: it was beautiful, as numerous commentators have observed, because it was about the essence of the human soul and the power of mourning. Through the various processes and phases of response, the viewers drew on their resources of intertextuality: other events, other representations. Inevitably, they were drawing on the resources of the televisual culture which inscribes their individual meaning systems, as well as the collective consciousness. Innumerable witnesses reported, for example, that watching the collapse of the towers was like watching a movie, something already digested, already known. In a contribution to the *New Yorker*, novelist and eyewitness John Updike notes that 'the destruction of the World Trade Center twin towers had the false intimacy of television, on a day of perfect reception … [T]here persisted the notion, as on television, this was not quite real' (2001: 28).

THE MEANING OF AMERICA AND THE TWIN TOWERS

In a sense, Updike is referring to the hyperreal and the intersection between the immediacy of the phenomenal event and the consciousness that is perpetually generated in relation to mediated representation. When the vision of the terrorist attacks on the twin towers began to appear across the global news networks, the response was surprisingly adaptive, the shock muted by a sense that what was being witnessed was already inscribed as culture, the meanings already pre-set in film and television narrative (see Silberstein, 2002: 61–87). The shock, in fact, had already been created by the televisual culture – disaster movies, news bulletins, a raft of apocalyptic fears that American political imagining had already been imposing on the world since the end of the Second World War. Terrible as the events were, terrible as the vision of the towering conflagrations appeared, there was nevertheless already a sense in which the calamity was culturally predetermined. Like *The Towering Inferno* or other disaster movies, the arrival of the hero, bearing the jacket of the United States, was scripted and anticipated, even in the midst of horror. Perhaps for this reason, the flying of the American flag over the disaster area, the Congressional anthem, and George Bush's invocation of the Wild West and the Wanted Dead or Alive all seemed to resonate with a knowledge and reference that Hollywood had already provided. The world of good and evil had fallen into relief: the outcome would be the reassertion of American will, dignity and values. A terrible vengeance would be wreaked upon the perpetrators.

Paul Virilio (2002) claims, in fact, that many citizens of the United States believed that the images of the collapsing twin towers were part of a new action movie. As we noted at the beginning of this chapter, Virilio identifies 'Ground Zero' with the convergence and primacy of oracular technologies: that is, Virilio claims that the technologies which facilitate the waging of war from a visual distance are largely identical to the network machineries of global mediation. These oracular technologies have now encased the world, producing a mode of progress and progression which ensures that all wars – mediated and military – are wars of vision. In *War and Cinema* (1989) Virilio establishes these arguments, suggesting that wars are constituted around representation: even ancient battles were forms of highly staged costume drama where weapons were carried as much to mystify and terrorize the enemy, as they were to slay them. The history of cinematic technique, planning and technology is forged around visualization and the staging of effect; this is precisely the evolution characterized by modern warfare, a history which leads ultimately to the command centre for the Iraq war being based in Florida, thousands of kilometres from the battlefields of the Middle East. September 11 represents an invasion by the Islamic militants into the virtual spaces of global media networks and hence the consciousness of the global polis.

In a war of vision, therefore, the electronic web that encases the world becomes a battleground of perspectives. For the Americans, as we have noted, this complex ontology of progress and modernization is returned to the common theme of good prevailing over evil. For many commentators, in fact, the twin towers assaults had resolved and dissolved the relativism that had emerged in American (postmodern) life. According to this view, as it was propagated by Bush and his Wild West allusions, the world could now quite simply be characterized in terms of a cosmological polemic in which America was destined to prevail. America and its values had been assaulted for no other reason than their intrinsic correctness, their intrinsic decency. The amplitude of the events had distinguished perpetrators from the symbolic purity and 'innocence' of the Trade Center and its inhabitants. Undoubtedly, it is this symbolic divide which was critically deployed by US authorities and the media in order to mobilize public support for what was, as we have suggested, an ostensibly peculiar campaign – the location and elimination of Osama bin Laden. Of course, this enterprise is symbolically rendered as the pursuit of Satan, and authorities were astute enough to embed it in a more discursively persuasive project, the war on terror. Even so, the assault on Afghanistan and the inevitable maiming and killing of innocent (noncombatant) Afghans, including children, needed to be shaped as a convocation of the US citizenry against the gathering forces of evil. Thus, bin Laden, al-Qa'ida and the Taliban were imagined as religious fanatics, oppressors and terrorists. The flux of emotions experienced by the American and broader First World, non-Muslim citizenry created a powerful coalition of effects. Vengeance, jingoism and Orientalism mixed with a more moderate and liberal disdain for Taliban cultural practices in order to create a more or less galvanizing effect on American public 'opinion'. Along with the destruction of Buddhist world heritage relics and the prohibition of all modern practices, including communicational practices, the Taliban's oppressive denial of women's rights seemed to draw American liberals into a consensus which seemed to confirm the Bush polemic.

America's own culpability and responsibility for the Trade Center and Washington attacks were not, however, expunged by the state and a complicit media, as Chomsky fears. Rather, the flush of highly managed discourses which the US authorities and the media generated as they sought to fill the semiotic void created by 9/11 was neither stable nor sustainable. To this extent, and as we have suggested above, 'America' as a cultural conceit remained precarious: the crisis required the re-thinking, reviewing and reconfiguration of an America which was, to the shock of the President and much of the citizenry, 'so hated'. As with all crises, new ideas were invited – new thoughts, conceptions and choices. While drawing on a deep national heritage of self-righteousness and will-to-action, the US authorities nevertheless recognized that the cultural resources upon which they were drawing were both powerful and unstable. The significant financial and administrative effort devoted to the management of these resources betrays an underlying anxiety about the precariousness of culture, a recognition that history and cultural meanings may slip and transmogrify in the very moment of their invocation.

This is particularly the case with the concept of 'innocent victims', which, as we have noted, becomes continually vulcanized to the nobility and heroism of history and televisual narrative. The vehement attacks on commentators like Susan Sontag and Jean Baudrillard, who have sought alternative explanations for September 11, inevitably invoke the innocence of the victims. And in a very real sense, those people who were injured, maimed or bereaved by the 9/11 attacks did not deserve such inhumane and indiscriminate brutality. However, since bodies are semiotic tropes as well as biological entities, they are subject to alternative readings and the inscriptions of cultural politics. The bodies of the victims of terrorism are in this sense marked by the guilt of association: their signification is collapsed and renewed by a politics of resistance. In this sense, the attacks constitute 'return fire' for all the innocent deaths that have resulted from colonial and imperialist strategy. These are historical reprisals. The denizens of the twin towers were living on the blood of all of those who had fallen in the wake of American foreign policy, exploitation and global domination. Their comfort, lifestyles and security constitute a deep offence to those who have suffered for America's success.

This argument is not entirely consonant with Baudrillard's view that terrorism is a reaction to the excesses and singularity of modernity; however, the Islamic militants certainly see 'America' as the central cause for the suffering of many innocent people. Even the twin towers themselves, so heavily iconicized after the earlier bombings of 1993, were subject to counter-readings and counterclaims by the attackers. Promoted by US authorities as a defiant and enduring symbol of US global, capitalist primacy, the World Trade Center clearly represented something quite different to the militants – oppression, the deprivation of Palestine, exploitation, starvation in Iraq. These agonisms or language wars continued even as the

American government sought to reassert the authority and dignity of the buildings' meanings over the impiousness of its detractors: that is, even through the convocation of the American people and the American 'way of life'.

These language wars are deeply embedded in the processes of cultural and economic globalization. In particular, the export of American products, including cultural products and systems of semiotic order, expose American culture to alternative and agonistic interpretations and counterclaims. The twin towers, like dishwashers, computers or Hollywood movies, are de-territorialized as they are exported to alternative and external imaginaries. American culture, that is, becomes available, to the practices of adaptation, re-territorialization and re-inscription. Robert Fisk (1999) may claim, therefore, that Osama bin Laden has a relatively unsophisticated view of globalization and American cultural imperialism, but there can be no doubt that American cultural and territorial expansionism, part of the general programme of global capitalism and foreign policy, are implicated in the processes of global interaction. To this extent, the notion of 'United States' cannot be partitioned from the citizenry of the entire world. As a global presence, the United States is intricately bound to its products and policies, to the meanings it presents to the world community. At this level, there is no consensus; rather, there is an irradiating effect of language wars by which all of us claim and contribute to the formation of 'America', including the contribution of profound criticism and deconstruction. Put simply, there is no single 'America' or 'American effect'; there are multiple shapings of a broad and highly disputed discourse.

Perhaps this is precisely what the US President fails to recognize when he asks, 'Why do they hate us?' The multiple movement of globalization and the cultural relativism which many believe was ended by September 11 remain steadfastly unchanged. The symbolic resonance of the twin towers continues to evolve, even beyond the stark monuments of Ground Zero and the haunting space that the buildings once occupied in the centre of Manhattan. Baudrillard (2002a) suggests that it was in fact the parallelism of the buildings which made them so vulnerable to attack. That they were 'twins' emphasized the excessive stature of monopoly, global capitalism. The replication of the sign – a favoured theme in Baudrillard's earlier studies – indicates that they had already over-reached their believability. That is, 'If there were only one, monopoly would not have been so perfectly embodied. Only the doubling of the sign, truly puts an end to what it distinguishes' (Baudrillard, 2002a: 43). The meaning of the towers as the pinnacle of capitalism, Baudrillard explains, is bereft, even before the attacks and their destruction, a destruction that was predetermined by the excess of their claim.

We may suggest, further, that the replication of the towers anticipates the transformations of mechanical reproduction, as Benjamin describes it, to the perfection of simulation – the digital revolution. This replication principle is precisely that characteristic of representation, as we discussed it in Chapter 1. In this sense, Baudrillard's notion of 'excess', in fact, is an overcompensation for the problematics of meaning deficit whereby the compound of absence–presence is subsumed through the rapid reproduction of a supplement, a supplement which is never actually able to liberate its meanings from the unceasing volition of semiotic inadequacy. We suggested in Chapter 1 that volition, especially in news stories, is generated out of semiotic and financial deficits. The twin towers might represent this same volition, and the not-quite-real of a televisual world, as John Updike identifies it. The buildings' semiotic values are necessarily embedded in an unstable cultural and financial system, a global system by which the specific representations are not only not-quite-real because they are generated through the compound of absent–present, but because the disputes over their meaning necessarily irradiate across borders and modes of symbolic value and consciousness. They are not merely 'American' but global in the sense that they are formed in terms of a functioning system of financial, digital and semiotic exchange. The 'appearance' of trade has already been marked through the presence of a digital building-scape where the exchange is symbolic and virtual, a mere representation of 'product', credit or 'foreign exchange capital'. What might have been materially identifiable as 'trade' from the feudal to the mercantile periods, had already transformed itself as merely symbolic exchange; in a symbolic exchange culture what appears to be present (image, brand, stocks, credit) is merely a 'representation' of what is actually absent (value, product). The 'World Trade Center' and its twin towers are thus constituted as icons of this new age of simulacra and symbolic exchange. Baudrillard's notions of 'excess' and simulacra are concisely modulated in the towers:

> We must assume then that the collapse of the towers – itself a unique event in the history of modern cities – prefigures a kind of dramatic ending and, all in all, disappearance both of the form of architecture and of the world system

it embodies. Shaped in the pure computer image of banking and finance, (ac)countable and digital, they were in a sense its brain, and in striking there the terrorists have struck at the brain, at the nerve center of the system. (Baudrillard, 2002a: 44–5)

Modern buildings and even cities had been destroyed before – most notably by American military power in Dresden, Hiroshima and Nagasaki. But it was not merely that the assaults took place on 'American soil' that made this a unique event; rather, it was that the attacks, in Baudrillard's terms, *represented* a reactive and even self-reflexive assault on the American-dominated system of globalization, a system characterized by the economy of symbolic exchange.

FREEDOM

The iconography of the twin towers, then, is disputed within the broadening and ongoing context of language wars, and the meanings of 9/11. These clashes of meaning are entangled within the various gradients of cultural formation – community, religious, national and global. The cultural politics of these disputes, as we have consistently noted, cannot be reduced to a simple polemic, especially one which assumes the providential conquest of one over the other. Thus, bin Laden's justification for the attacks on America refers specifically to a deep hatred borne of an iniquitous imperialist history; this hatred is matched by an Islamophobia in the US which identifies the Orient with a seductive but insidious primitivism. Within these poles, critical discourses confront, shift and negotiate the meanings in terms of specific constituents and communities of interest (or indifference). These language wars are amplified through a televisual politics which is exercised through the media and its formational relationships within the electronic polis (Lewis & Best, 2002).

As we have noted, the notion of 'freedom' constitutes a central trope for the global polis. It is the moral and ideological virtue that George Bush most frequently invokes in order to distinguish Americans (and our 'friends' who also 'love freedom') from 'our enemies', who 'hate freedom' and 'hate America'. With the world's largest economy and undisputed military primacy, the US administration quite clearly feels justified in flagging the superiority of its political and moral systems. Freedom, along with democracy, assumes a cultural significance that overwhelms all contending ideals, virtues and ideas. In the constituency of its historical ethos, America is freedom. Its wealth, cultural productivity and military might are unquestionably superior to bin Laden's shadowy cultural fantasies represented in the cloaking of women, primitive dynastic political institutions, brutality, ignorance, inferior technology and calamitous social systems.

While the ideal of individual rights is enshrined in the American constitution, it is freedom of consumer choice which appears to be the central pillar of this discursive architecture. The (post)modern global capitalist economy has transposed the rights of writing democracy into a new form of individualism which is inscribed through the system of symbolic exchange. Little doubt, Bush's insistent invocation of the concept acknowledges the cultural significance of 'freedom', most especially as it is conveyed through the relentless deluge of consumer communication, branding and the formation of 'identity' which is directly linked to the symbolic inscription of product (Bourdieu 1984, Klein, 2002). It is not that writing freedom has been erased by consumer freedom, but rather there has been a transposition in the primary discourses which construct freedom and the status of the individual in modern societies. At this level, we may assume that freedom is captured within the dialogue of writing and broadcast cultures, and that the global electronic polis will necessarily dispute the force of these respective claims. This is particularly problematic since the concept of freedom, even in its Enlightenment incarnation, struggles to mediate the interests of individuals, communities and social elites. The ways in which individuals reconcile their freedom and self-determination against the freedom of all other members of a social group – and the social aggregate – remain largely unresolved throughout the period of modernity.

Jacques Derrida confirms in *Of Grammatology* (1974) that the notion of freedom cannot be disengaged from the contesting claims of social history. Derrida outlines how Jean-Jacques Rousseau's social ontology, which promotes freedom as the ultimate virtue, may be captured by both liberal and conservative interests. In seeking an origin of human nature and value, Rousseau unwittingly provides a political resource which may be mobilized for quite different ends. The problem, as Derrida explains it, is that language or more specifically 'writing' is fundamentally removed from its source: meaning is formed through the process of 'reading' which supplements the text with all that might be missing (see Chapter 1). For more recent political theorists, following Tom Paine and others, this cycle of representation and responsibility marks the essence of a successful modern democracy. Social order is assured as citizens will knowingly and willingly 'substitute' *absolute* self-determination, independence and 'freedom' for the greater security and freedom provided by the state. Rousseau initially idealizes this relationship by contending that the principle of majority rule necessarily concurs with the principle of self-interest and personal freedom; the decision of the majority can never be at odds with a deviating position since that position is necessarily neutralized by the greater good of community accord.

Ultimately, of course, Rousseau becomes disenchanted with this utilitarian paradigm, claiming that the practice of electoral representation removes the individual from the origin of his true nature and freedom. At this critical moment, in fact, the moment when freedom becomes attached to representation, the concept critically splits, forming one of the key contradictions of modernism. As it is forged through the armoury of institutional politics, 'freedom' comes to mean both the freedom of political expression through representation, and the freedom of choice. But even at the level of 'freedom of choice', the signifier splits again creating further political divisions, which, as we have noted, Martin Heidegger (1952) sees as a reductive exercise limiting freedom to a meagre freedom of product choice. For Heidegger this is the freedom which reduces politics to the level of consumer choice, a mode of Americanization which has neither dignity nor grace. This is precisely the criticism of neo-Marxists like Theodor Adorno and critical theorists such as Jürgen Habermas. For Adorno, consumer capitalism, dominated by the American culture industry, reduces freedom to a new form of social obedience: citizens as consumers move from conformity at work to a cultural conformity in which the melodramatic narrative or formulaic pop music determines the cognition of vast numbers of people. Habermas, equally suspicious of consumer culture, nevertheless recommends a form of communicative action which would restore the citizenry to a participatory public sphere and a freedom of expression that is no longer captured by the imperatives of representation.

George Bush's discourse of freedom assumes a particular validity for popular consumer culture as 'way of life'. While Bush doesn't specify which kind of freedom he is invoking, there is a continual ratification of a lifestyle and political system which privilege a certain type of choice as well as an assumed but extremely powerful mode of 'Americanization'. Within the walls of these discourses, 'oil' remains an unspecified agent of this consumer-freedom lifestyle, most particularly as it fuels the massive power of the American economy and its military machinery. Paradoxically, it is this oil-freedom which the Bush administration would seek to export and impose upon those in the Middle East who are its primary keepers.

Indeed, the 'freedom' of those whom the war machinery threatens, especially the Islamicists of the Middle East, is treated as a contradiction or perversity by the US. As Edward Said notes, it is as though the US authorities assume that the people of the non-west know or care nothing about freedom, since their understanding of the concept is historically and semiotically at odds with that of the west. In this sense, the approximation of freedom with consumer power is substituted by many Muslim societies, for example, for a freedom which is constructed around community and religious devotion. The freedom which George W. Bush espouses might appear merely as another form of oppressive decadence; the 'liberation' of Afghanistan and Iraq might appear as a new form of incarceration. For the radical Islamicists who have most violently opposed the imposition of this freedom, the American authorities have become deluded by their own unbridgeable narrowness.

SURVEILLANCE AND CONTROL

In many respects, the meaning of 9/11 and the war of terror is supplemented through other key language disputes, most notably the intersection between vision and freedom. Numerous critics have pointed out that one of the most prevalent meanings of 9/11 was the surrender of specific zones of freedom and rights for the greater security of the nation. As we have just noted, the dichotomy of collective and individual interests and modes of self-determination constitutes a key paradox for modernism and the modern state. Under the aegis of 'democracy', elected governments have sought persistently to reconcile the interests of the whole against the rights and freedoms of individuals and communities. This paradox has been intensified through the emergence of oracular and computer-based technologies which have vastly increased the capacity of governments to monitor and observe their citizens.

September 11 exposed gaps in the oracular system as it then existed. The failure of intelligence agencies to identify the risk and predict a cataclysm of this kind sent the authorities scuttling into various legislative paroxysms and public commissions. The pre-emptive strikes on Afghanistan and Iraq were the most spectacular responses to the 9/11 attacks and America's newly exposed vulnerability, but the US also led the democratic world into new modes of social surveillance and governmental management. If a handful of individuals could effectively hold the nation to ransom, then clearly some radical measures for controlling individual actions and thoughts needed to be devised. The Patriot legislations in the US, while aiming to enhance domestic security and limit terrorist penetration, have seriously impacted on the rights and privacy of individual citizens. Along with some astonishingly draconian measures affecting prisoners of war and any person suspected of a terrorist crime, these new surveillance measures constitute a significant challenge to the ideals of the legal protection of individual rights and access to law. In this context, the meaning of September 11 is forcefully linked to questions of civil and human rights, and the problematic confluence of individual and collective interests.

David Lyon has addressed the issue of surveillance and 9/11 very directly. Lyon (2003) argues that the development of transnational media networks has provided the technological facility necessary for an increasingly globalized surveillance system. At its seemingly more innocuous, we might identify this system with various kinds of synoptic and panoptic visions. A synoptic vision is typified by the satellite and cable television networks and the creation of a 'celebrity' system by which the many watch the few. As we have discussed, this networking has enabled the formation of new forms of political systems based around mediation. Representation, thereby, permits the delegation of authority to an exceptionally small minority who are at least visible to the majority whose interests they represent. Of course, and as we have also noted, this visibility proves uncomfortable to the powerful elites who, in turn, create elaborate machineries for managing their visible selves, most especially through the propagation of identity (celebrity image) and specific versions of the truth. While we have already noted this in terms of George Bush's propagated 'regular guy' image, a clear distortion of his actual genealogy, the practice of political identity creation is widespread. Media training and highly organized public relations profiles and systems enable politicians to selectively feed the synoptic vision.

The great danger of synoptica, of course, is that the information that is delivered to citizens, and upon which democracy is founded, may be compromised or positioned by those groups who have greatest control over the media systems. Thus, the synoptica of September 11 and the war on terror have generated an aesthetic of crisis and danger which can only be managed by the assertion of an uncompromising and unremitting authority. As Young and Jesser (1997) argue, during times of crisis, especially war, the citizenry are more likely to accept extreme measures of control, including the control of the synopticon itself. As we shall see in the following chapters, these extreme measures have manifested themselves through various military and informational actions, including the invasion of Afghanistan and Iraq. Measures such as the closure of the Baghdad bureau of the al-Jazeera Arabic news network (August 9, 2004) represent an extreme position on the control of information, and the processes by which the opinions of the citizenry are to be managed.

The panopticon, vision of the many by the few, is perhaps even more threatening for civil rights and the freedoms terrorists are supposedly assaulting. Borrowing from Foucault, Lyon describes the evolution of modern surveillance in terms of increasing state management and modes of 'governmentality' (Foucault, 1991). The state, Lyon argues, has generated and adapted a range of technologies and strategies of observation and checking to ensure that populations are acting, behaving and thinking in ways which maintain state legitimacy, authority and management principles. Beyond specific governments, the state seeks to negotiate individual freedoms against other individual and collective freedoms for the perpetuity of an orderly social and political system. Surveillance provides the ideal mechanism for the identification of crime and other 'excesses' of human action which may threaten this order.

Such measures, of course, may seem necessary where individualism is supported by a capitalist economic system which rewards adventurism, personal risk and self-interest, and which advantages specific individuals and groups over others. Differentials in rewards, pleasures and quality of life create a range of complex psychological and social problems which may manifest themselves in actions that threaten the security of individuals, privileged groups, the system and the social aggregate. An excess of individualism disrupts the orderliness of structured hierarchy; but an excess of order disrupts the potentiality of individual effort and the 'liberalism' of democratic processes. Democracy collapses where the individual is not able to express individuality. In order to prevent the unravelling of this nexus of opposite effects, states in the modern developed world have adapted surveillance as a principal mechanism for the control and coercion of its citizens. This has become particularly pertinent as modern societies have evolved through the processes of globalization, corporatization and marketization (Featherstone, 2002). These processes have created complex associative cellular social structures which frequently elude classification or delineations based around nation or other discursive borders. The citizen, that is, has become increasingly complex as s/he is formed through interactions with new modes of social agency and action, and new modes of information and media networks. With an increasingly cosmopolitan lifestyle, these interactions create the potential for cultural contiguities which usurp older meanings as they generate new conceptions, lifestyles and modes of social knowledge which inevitably threaten with fragmentation the perpetuity and security of the state (Jameson, 1991).

The state and its representative governments respond to this threat, of course, by a greater assertion of unity and control. The move to greater surveillance and restraint, therefore, is not merely a response to 'terrorism' and political violence. Yet terrorism has certainly become the rubric which justifies many of the recent legislative measures which extend social policing, creating conditions for greater controls on individual freedom and greater intrusion into the private lives of the citizenry. At its most basic level, this intrusion creates and determines an individual and a group's 'identity', creating new modes of prescription and obedience, new modes of inclusion and exclusion. Individuals are increasingly being required to identify themselves through various forms of documentation, including fingerprinting, identity cards and passports. A reasserted and aggressive form of border control has denied millions of refugees the rights of 'identification', including the sense of 'home'. Across the developed world, police and intelligence agencies have been granted increased powers of detention and powers to tap phones and access private email and web transactions. Digital communications, in fact, have created an ever-expanding resource for observation and information collection; private interests, beliefs and political actions are exposed to the panoptic view of suspicious intelligence services.

> One important aspect of this is that the flows of personal and group data percolate through systems that once were much less porous, much more discrete and watertight ... The use of searchable databases makes it possible to use commercial records previously unavailable to police and intelligence services and thus draws on all manner of apparently 'innocent' traces. (Lyon, 2003: 32)

Information derived from driver's licences, commercial transactions, banking, marketing, mobile phone billing, education records, email, television subscriptions and so on are all part of the individual's citizen 'observable' profile.

After 9/11, these sorts of data files were used to track the perpetrators. But they have also been used as the focus for extensions to security laws that were already causing concerns for civil libertarians and human rights activists. George Bush's rhetoric following the attacks, as we noted above, invoked a resurgent unity for the American people (and their friends); in practice this unity has enabled the imposition of radical new restrictions on civil and human rights. In Australia, the UK and the United States, the key (Anglophonic) partners in the 'Coalition of the Willing', a range of legislative measures designed to enhance the powers of security agencies were met with considerable opposition from civil rights advocates. Feeding on the profound anxieties of the public, the government and security officials in these countries devised a raft of legislative and managerial strategies which would enable greater synoptic vision of potential attackers, but which encroached considerably on the privacy and legal rights of ordinary citizens.

The authors of America's first Patriot legislation, for example, seem to have circumvented any wide-spread public objection through the adhesion of a nationalist discourse and by the very speed of the bill's enactment. Again, rushing to fill the discursive void created by 9/11, the US administration wrote the 342-page legislation, passed it with a 98–1 Senate majority, and signed it within seven weeks of the September 11 attacks. The acronym derived from 'Uniting and Strengthening America by Providing Appropriate Tools Required to Intercept and Obstruct Terrorism' was also adopted into a Patriot 2 legislation 'The Domestic Securities Enhancement Act' (2003) which extended the power to observe citizens and access data, as well as increase the range and reach of crimes that could be nominated and punishable as 'terrorism'. According to organizations such as the American Civil Liberties Union and the Village Voice, the new provisions would render organizations such as Greenpeace and Operation Rescue vulnerable to the 'terrorist' tag and hence penalties which would include the death sentence (American Civil Liberties Union, 2004). Moreover, the death penalty itself would be extended to include 15 new offences.

Security legislation in the UK and Australia, though somewhat less enthusiastic about the death penalty, has been similarly encouraged by the need for greater powers of surveillance and for restricting the legal rights of suspected terrorists. While there is an increasing level of public debate and disquiet over the more recent legislative programmes around terrorism and security in the First World, many Third World and non-democratic nations seem rather unrestrained in their use of terrorism issues as a justification for enhancing government control over their people. The 2004 Amnesty International Human Rights Report, while criticizing the US security measures, was even more concerned about a number of Third World regimes which use the rubric of terrorism to suppress legitimate protest and crack down on political or religious dissidents. Using the banner of 'controlling terrorism', these regimes are incarcerating and torturing minorities in places like Chechnya, the Democratic Republic of the Congo, Sudan, Nepal and Colombia. Muslim dissidents in China and Egypt have been labelled as Islamicists and terrorists, and have had their civil rights seriously impinged by hostile governments (Amnesty, 2004).

For Amnesty and other human and civil rights organizations, the 'freedom' that the US and other First World nations are trying to protect is in fact compromised by the restrictions they are placing on individuals' privacy and access to law. The discourse of 'freedom', of course, is challenged within the language wars we have been describing, and while it is certainly the case that the criminal perpetrators of September 11 should be brought to justice, using all appropriate strategies and technologies, it is also true that these measures must never be allowed to compromise the basis for that justice. Essentially, and as we indicated earlier, the contest of values which informs the discourse of freedom is embedded critically in our cultures and the meaning systems which support it. Indeed, the freedoms that are structured into the hierarchy of order we have outlined, are inevitably linked to their opposite effect. As governments seek to protect freedom, they restrict it; as these restrictions take effect, individuals and groups will seek out and exploit new expressive spaces in order to subvert restraint and enhance expressivity. We can take some solace in the inability of these restrictive structures to override the capacity of individuals, groups and communities to forestall the pervasive power of surveillance and governmentality, both through effort and through the underlying gaps of language and its supporting media systems.

These gaps are to some extent evident in the systemic deficiencies identified by the US Congressional Report on September 11 (2004). The failure of intelligence agencies to anticipate 9/11, and the failure of policing and military authorities to prevent it, are not merely symptoms of technological or strategic failure; nor indeed do they represent an intrinsic human fallibility. Rather, they represent the underlying gaps in text which will always and inevitably expose themselves through the dynamic of culture and the imperfections of systems, organization and communication. The Commission Report itself concedes as much, noting that 'nearly everyone' expects the terrorists to come again, even though 'the United States and its allies have killed or captured a majority of al Quaeda's leadership; toppled the Taliban, and severely damaged the organization' (US Government, 2004: 16). But the reason they will come again is not because of the material power of al-Qa'ida or other terrorist organizations so much as their discursive or 'ideological' force:

> The problem is al Quaeda represents an ideological movement, not a finite group of people. It initiates and inspires, even if it no longer directs. In this way it has transformed itself into a decentralized force. Bin Laden may be limited in his ability to organize major attacks from his hideout. Yet killing or capturing him, while very important, would not end terror. His message of inspiration to a new generation of terrorists would continue. (US Government, 2004: 16)

In other words, the governments of the First World cannot control everything – especially, they cannot control language or the things people will think.

While this is a particularly frightening prescience, it also indicates the source of hope. The gaps through which al-Qa'ida may move are also the passageways that are available for the freedoms of ordinary people. We need, that is, to recognize that at least some part of our freedom cannot be constituted or managed by governments, and in fact governments, like any other macro-institution, may actively constrain this dimension of liberation. The failure of the intelligence system is also a protection from its most complete excess – its capacity to marshal, manage and control us all. The gaps in the web of meaning, those spaces between the textual lines and discourses, are precisely the places in which alternative meanings may be generated. The digital network system, along with other global media networks, cannot be simply contained in the service of elite power. Hideous as bin Laden and his terrorist organizations may be, there is surely only a short step between the despotic brutality of the Taliban, and the despotic brutality of any ideological regime which detests diversity and alternative perspectives. It is at least gratifying, though terrible, that our intelligence systems are not perfect – as

9/11 and the debacle around Weapons of Mass Destruction indicate, the mechanisms of control have their limits. As we will discuss throughout this book, these limits create the possibility for alternative readings, and the capacity for citizens to engage in the expressivities of the September 11 crisis and its aftermath. The meaning of the crisis thereby remains open, even as the antagonists in the war of terror continue to assert their interests through the disputed terrains of the global media system.

CONCLUSIONS

1. The attacks on New York and Washington produced a significant rupture in the meaning of America. President Bush's discourses sought to fill this void with a convocation to patriotism and a divinely inspired retribution. 'Freedom' and 'democracy' became central discourses within this convocation. Much of this discourse, however, obscures the very significant American mission which seeks to exert greater control over the world's oil resources.
2. The major corporate media tended to support the patriotic discourse, contributing to an image of George W. Bush as a 'regular folksy guy' who was leading the nation against the forces of political and cosmological evil.
3. Critical voices were rare, especially in the months immediately following the 9/11 attacks. Critics like Tom Nairn, Noam Chomsky and Susan Sontag pointed to America's own inflated sense of (divine and political) inviolability as a contributing factor in a deficient foreign policy. These criticisms, however, were subsumed by the flush of patriotism.
4. Jean Baudrillard suggested that the deficiencies in specific foreign policy need to be understood within the broader context of 'the spirit of terrorism'. An American-dominated globalization inevitably produced a violent reaction. Within the progress of history, good and evil always advance together.
5. The Bush administration mounted the war on terror in order to mobilize the forces of good against evil. This war, like all other modern wars, required the consent of the public, as well as the media. This consent, however, remains problematic as it is ensnared in the language wars over the meaning of America.
6. Public opinion, in fact, is an unsatisfactory measure of 'consent' or the broader views of the electronic polis. Public opinion polling

often reduces the complexity of language wars to simple categories and calculations.

7. In fact, the meaning of America and the twin towers is available for various 'interpretations'. As a symbolic or cultural artefact, 'America' has been distributed across the globe. America clearly meant something hideous to the radical Islamicists who attacked the twin towers. The freedom espoused by George Bush means something very different to the many diverse peoples of the Middle East.

8. George Bush doesn't specify what he means by 'freedom', although the notion of 'freedom of consumer choice' is clearly a central part of the American-global mission. Even the civil freedoms, which may be attached to the ideals of democracy, are being compromised within the project of the war on terror. The civil freedoms of the people of Afghanistan and Iraq are threatened, even as the US-led forces seek to impose democratic liberation over the conquered territories. Similarly, the state is applying restrictions on civil freedoms within its own territories as a way of controlling the activities of terrorists.

9. The meaning of 9/11 is embedded in the meaning of America. The official discourses, which seek to impose a divinely guided America over the peoples of the world, are being challenged by alternative discourses within the broader sphere of language wars.

4
The Iraq Invasion:
Democracy in the Field of Battle

THE PURPOSES OF WAR

It is now abundantly clear that plans to invade Iraq were well advanced before September 11. In his book *Plan of Attack*, Bob Woodward (2004) has described the evolution of the Bush administration's foreign affairs and defence agenda. From the beginning of the Bush presidency, the possibility of an Iraq invasion was seriously discussed. As Woodward outlines, Vice-President Dick Cheney sought a briefing on Iraq from the outgoing Defense Secretary, Bill Cohen, days before the Bush inauguration (Woodward, 2004: 9). And on September 11 Donald Rumsfeld reportedly asked his Pentagon advisors to explore the feasibility of striking Saddam Hussein at the same time as US forces would attack Osama bin Laden and the Taliban (Woodward, 2004: 25). These claims and others like it were confirmed by the former treasury secretary Paul O'Neill, who believed that 9/11 was simply the catalyst for action (Mackay, 2004). According to the *Sunday Herald Online*'s journalist Neil Mackay, the Bush–Rumsfeld–Cheney team had been enthusiastic about a strike on Iraq from the beginning of the administration, as it would consolidate American control of the region, ensuring the on-going supply of Iraqi oil.

Of course Saddam Hussein had very little to do with 9/11 or Islamic terrorism generally. The US Commission report into 9/11 (US Government, 2004) states very clearly that Hussein had no connection with Osama bin Laden, al-Qa'ida or the Taliban. In accordance with their overall foreign affairs and defence strategy, however, the US administration deftly linked the Iraqi regime to the September 11 attacks through various rhetorical associations. These associations were deliberately aimed, it seems, at cajoling the US citizenry into supporting the pre-emptive attacks on Iraq and the removal of Hussein from power. There can be little doubt that the Bush administration would have had considerable difficulty persuading the public to support such an attack without the aegis of 9/11 and the powerful language of retribution. In the famous 2002 State of the Union address Bush attempted to absorb Iraq into the 'Axis of Evil' discourse, an ingenious allusion, compounding Third Reich horror with the ideological force of the current war on terror. With arachnid proficiency, the discourse of belligerent politics surrounded and entrapped Saddam and his regime into the web of terror.

As this discourse evolved, however, significant portions of the US public remained sceptical since Iraq, unlike Afghanistan, had no clear or direct connection with the 9/11 attacks. Academics, church leaders, military and intelligence strategists as well as leaders from across the world expressed grave doubts about a proposed attack on Iraq. Colin Powell, the Secretary of State in the first G.W. Bush administration, was perhaps the most irksome of these doubters. Powell, who sought constantly to work through the United Nations to resolve the Iraq issues, seems to have been regarded by the Bush–Cheney–Rumsfeld triad as a 'dovish' impediment to the strong action required to achieve the administration's Middle East objectives (Woodward, 2004). In particular, Powell seems to have had an entirely different view of Iraq's putative armoury of Weapons of Mass Destruction (WMDs). When Cheney announced to a Veterans of Foreign Wars convention that Iraq 'definitely' had WMDs, Powell was initially infuriated, though his responses soon turned to despair as his efforts at the United Nations collapsed and Bush's language became increasingly belligerent and determined. As in the UK and Australia, the discourse of WMDs became a central trope for the tyrannical and despotic power that Saddam exercised in the Middle East. This trope, along with the cloudy connotations of Islamic terrorism and the 9/11 attacks, assumed a particular discursive volition, one which neither Powell nor the millions of protestors who took to the streets across the globe could possibly deflect. Bush's rhetoric gathered the meanings of 9/11 and the WMDs into a concentrated trajectory of violence:

Eleven years ago, as a condition ending the Persian Gulf War, the Iraqi regime was required to destroy all its weapons of mass destruction ... The Iraqi regime has contravened all its obligations. It possesses and produces chemical and biological weapons. It is seeking nuclear weapons ... While there are many dangers in the world ... the threat from Iraq stands alone – because it gathers the most serious dangers of our age in one place. (Bush, 2002)

According to Bush, a regime that possesses such terrible weapons and which directs them against 'their own people' is surely the most evil of all regimes.

We are now all aware, of course, that the Iraq weapons programme had indeed been dismantled after the 1990–91 Gulf War and that, by and large, the Intelligence agencies in the United States, the United Kingdom and Australia seem to have assessed very poorly the actual conditions of Iraq's military power. It is now only a matter of speculation as to the respective governments' complicity in these assessments and to what degree the WMDs programmes may have constituted a mere ruse that justified war to the home citizenry. In either case, it is very clear that the pre-emptive invasion of Iraq was driven by a suite of purposes.

First, there was the perpetual question of oil. Numerous commentators, especially critics from the global peace alliance, have claimed that instability in the Middle East, especially around Saudi Arabia which is the world's largest producer and exporter of oil, perpetually threatens energy supplies to the developed world. The US has been a net importer of oil since 1973; its economic and military primacy is thus entirely dependent on oil supplies from the Arabic region. Saddam, once supported by the US against the threat of Iranian Islamicism, had become an unpredictable and increasingly rogue figure in the region, especially since the late 1980s. America's anxiety over oil supplies is undoubtedly a significant factor in its Middle East policy calculations. US relations with key oil supplier Saudi Arabia are central to these anxieties, most particularly because the ruling royal family, the House of Saud, is strongly influenced by Islamicist politics and is itself deeply divided over relations with the American state. According to numerous commentators, the House of Saud, which was established as a ruling monarchy in the new state (separated from South Yemen in 1963), has been a primary supporter and financier of various subversive or 'terrorist' groups, including al-Qa'ida; Osama bin Laden himself is the son of a wealthy Saudi with direct connections to the royal family. Paradoxically, however, the House, which numbers in the thousands, is also a key player in American foreign policy and global economic strategy. While the family invests heavily in American stocks and property, the most significant gesture of compliance to American interests occurred during the first Gulf War when the US installed command bases on Saudi territory. Bin Laden and other Islamicists, in fact, refer very specifically to the intrusion of the 'infidels' onto Saudi soil as a deep offence to the Saudi nation, the region and the Muslim faith. This peculiar and paradoxical interdependence of ideological foes has prompted a number of critics of American foreign policy in the Middle East to suggest that the US actually invaded the 'wrong country'.

Puzzling as the US–Saudi relationship may be (see Unger, 2004), it is clearly possible that the US administration feels comfortable dealing with the Islamic regime in Saudi Arabia, as it knows its enemy and has specific strategies in place that will exercise a certain measure of control. The same cannot be said of Saddam, who had continually defied American control. In this sense, there was a second purpose to the invasion which was, of course, to complete the task begun by George Bush senior – the task of punishing the Saddam regime for defying the hand that fed it. While clearly this purpose is linked to the issues of energy supplies, there is also a strong sense in which Saddam overstepped his delegated authority in the region, leading ultimately to the need for 'regime change'. This phrasing 'regime change' is linked directly to the third purpose we are highlighting, which relates to Saddam's brutal and tyrannical power. We know certainly that Saddam was a monstrous dictator who was prepared to use chemical weapons against the Kurds, most famously in Halabja on March 16–17, 1988. There is clearly a moral argument, one which was most potently and convincingly put by the British Prime Minister, Tony Blair, that Saddam was an entirely self-interested ruler who only represents an elite group of militarists and who suppressed the needs and interests of the vast majority of Iraqi people.

Saddam's power, of course, had been sponsored by imperial and postcolonial power. In many respects, responsibility for the removal of Saddam is directly linked to responsibility for his investiture. As a member of the minority Sunni Muslim community, Saddam was in a relatively precarious position, one negotiated by US military interests out of general concerns over rising Islamicism in the region. Setting Saddam against the Shi'a-based Islamicists in Iran – also an act of retribution – seriously distorted the cultural politics of the country that the British had established in 1932. In effect, the Shi'a majority in Iraq may have had far more in common with the Iranians than with their own Sunni-based regime. In either case, Saddam, we might reasonably conjecture, was impelled to assert a far more chauvinistic political authority inside Iraq than may have been necessary in a more homogeneous cultural constituency. This chauvinism, along with the essential characteristics of the man and his violent disposition, contributed no doubt to significant regional and global military posturing. The restoration of regional stability constituted the fourth purpose of the US-led invasion.

This was not merely an issue of WMDs but of conventional weaponry as well. In particular, Israel had felt threatened by Iraq's military potential, having been the brunt of missile attacks during the first Gulf War. However, the extent to which Iraq posed the sort of regional and hence global threat suggested by George W. Bush in the speech quoted above is extremely dubious. As many commentators have argued (see Chomsky, 2003a) and as the 2003 invasion demonstrated, Iraq's military capacity had been entirely devastated by the original Gulf War and the continuing UN sanctions. The decline in Iraqi oil revenues after 1991 and the sporadic but apparently effective rounds of weapons inspections seem to have limited markedly the regime's capacity to pose any sort of a threat to external states or to world security. Iraq's missile system had collapsed during and after the first Gulf War, and its military forces were in a state of general disarray. When the Coalition forces attacked in 2003, Iraq's defences rapidly capitulated, leaving nothing but a sporadic though viciously determined guerrilla resistance which continues through the period of occupation.

It is fairly evident that the Bush administration and the Pentagon were well aware of the weakness of the Iraqi defence system. The important thing for the propaganda machinery of the United States and its coalition of supplicant nations was that the invading forces were presented as heroic 'liberators'; this means that the informationists had to tread a very fine line between the impression of an easy or unheroic victory and a dangerous encounter which cost too many lives for too little return. An effective 'impression' of threat was necessary in order to mobilize the imaginaries and cultural politics of the home audience. Indeed, the discourse surrounding WMDs and the threat posed by Saddam's military was soaked in greater contentions and agonisms over America's global status generally and within the United Nations, in particular. The nomenclature of 'doves' defined the propensity for certain governments and officials to work through the collective responsibility and aegis of a United Nations governmentality; 'hawks' referred to those who were encouraging a pre-emptive attack on Iraq. The 'Coalition of the Willing', built around an Anglophonic First World order, represents an assertion of global governance that delineates the subordination of the Third World and the fatiguing cultural politics of 'Old Europe', as Vice-President Cheney and Secretary of Defense Rumsfeld were inclined to call it.

Thus, the fifth purpose of the invasion related directly to Saddam's continual breach of UN resolutions 678 and 687, and the assertion of US superpower pre-eminence. America was seeking to assert itself and its unique governmental authority over the world. Even as it came to neglect the auspices of the UN, America was announcing – or rather explicating – its rights and role as the world's only superpower. While Saddam was clearly using the resolutions as part of his own internal power-play, constructing them as part of the external threat of imperialist exploitation, they became increasingly significant to the legal debates around invasion. While many international lawyers supported the US administration's view that the resolutions themselves allowed for military action in the event of a breach, others were convinced that pre-emptive action was itself illegal in accordance with international law (Quinlan, 2004). In either case, the more recent Resolution 1441, in seeking to supplement the forcefulness of the earlier resolutions, seems to have been a somewhat desperate attempt by the UN to maintain its relevance and its authority within the context of America's clearly stated intention to 'go it alone' without reference to the international polity.

This belligerent and autonomous demeanour, the mood of 'with us or against us', radically shifted the veil of co-operative global governmentality through which the US had previously announced itself and its presence in the world. As numerous commentators have noted, it is as though the US suddenly realized it was the sole superpower (see Cohen, 2002, Kagan, 2002, Lewis, B., 2003) and it no longer had to be constrained by diplomatic pleasantries which merely compromised the substance and focus of its own interests. The invasion might, therefore, be characterized as the expression of American supremacy, and ideological force which distinguishes the US from the rest of the world. The compliant support of the UK and Australia sits within this framework, most specifically as it appends to the wider conditions of cultural politics and cultural expressivity. As we discussed in Chapter 2, these cultural agonisms contextualize the war on terror and the immediately obvious material purposes of the invasion. The invasion, effectively, was also a form of cultural expression, a charged and deeply violent iteration of the historical and cultural circumstances which led to, and support, America's cultural hegemony: this was the sixth purpose of the invasion.

The Coalition, dominated by the US, is really constituted around a form of Anglophonic elite. The clash of civilizations argument is certainly present throughout the purposes of invasion, especially as George W. Bush, Tony Blair and John Howard are all practising Christians, men whose value systems are informed by an unfaltering commitment to the cosmological reference of Christianity and notionally Christian values. When combined with an equally formidable affiliation to capitalist and liberal-democratic values, the Coalition leaders' Christian and cultural perspective might seem to lend weight to Huntington's clash of civilization argument. In fact, and as Tariq Ali (2002) has argued, the clash is more over what Ali calls distinct 'fundamentalisms' – a clash which is embedded in elite ideologies and modes of authority which would seek to promote themselves as pervasive and representative. The final purpose of the invasion then, extending the supremacy of the United States and its cultural perspective, can be understood in terms of the spread of ideologies and the transformation of Iraq into a modern state which participates fully in global capitalism under Anglophonic liberal humanist values.

FROM FREEDOM TO DEMOCRACY

As Slajov Žižek (2004) reminds us, there is ultimately a twisted and dream-like logic to these purposes, most particularly as they were so frequently articulated through the phantasm of Iraq's WMDs. The world publics became mesmerized by the narrative of the war, watching the British and American soldiers, clad in chemical protection masks and suits, marching into the desert, into the cradle of time. It was again as though the science fictions to which world audiences had become accustomed were being played out through the drill of another heroic certitude – an extemporized crusade in which good prevails over evil. There seems little question that if Saddam possessed the fabled weapons, now was his moment to use them: this was not a rehearsal.

Before the cynicism descended, however, it was with enormous relief that the chemical and biological weapons failed to materialize. The Coalition troops removed their protective clothing and marched, almost unhindered, into the capital, Baghdad. Yet as the dust of the conquest settled and weapons continued to evade detection, critical reviews were undertaken. The tragic sense of irony emerged out of these reviews, and even while the UK Prime Minister, Tony Blair, continued to hold out hope that the WMDs would be discovered, a dark shadow was being cast across the lives of those people who had been sacrificed for the campaign of violence. This shadow seemed all the more tragically rendered as many critics pointed out that the United States possesses undoubtedly the most deadly arsenal of destructive power ever known to humankind. In particular, the percussive and scatter bombs, which other Coalition partners had refused to use because of their imprecise and indiscriminate effects, had caused terrible harm to civilians and urban infrastructure in Iraq. Damage to water supplies and electricity, in particular, continues to wreak havoc on city populations and civilian health. A further dimension to this tragic irony, according to peace activists, relates to America's own forms of ethnic cleansing. Paralleling Saddam's treatment of the minority Kurds, America's treatment of its own indigenous, black and Hispanic populations has been constructed around a history of exclusion, criminalization and incarceration. Activists ask profound questions about the moral authority of a nation whose history is so steeped in blood and institutionalized persecution.

Thus, the image of the American Coalition as 'heroes' and 'liberators' has been questioned. Without the shield of the WMDs rhetoric, the march into Iraq has been more broadly vaunted as an emancipation from the tyranny of Saddam Hussein. No doubt that many Iraqis are happy to be rid of Saddam and his brutal military dictatorship, but they are asking very strong questions about the validity of the American invasion and its 'collateral' damage. According to Rampton and Stauber (2003), the image that was beamed around the world of Iraqis tearing down the statue of the hated tyrant may well have been a public relations stunt. Reuters, the BBC and the *Boston Globe* all reported that the crowd in Firdos Square that day was very small, and that American tanks had entirely ringed the area, admitting only a few Iraqis into the event. Long shots of the square were largely edited out of the final reports, as they showed only a few Iraqis joining the celebrations which the American troops had themselves orchestrated (Rampton & Stauber, 2003: 3). While Rampton and Stauber refer to these propaganda events as a 'clash of symbolizations', they are attached to a far more substantial cultural politics involving the critical discourse of freedom and liberation. As we noted in the previous chapter, this discourse is powerfully rendered by the Bush administration for the fight against terror and the 9/11 retribution.

In this light, the 'liberation' of Iraq, reaches to the more substantive dimensions of the ideology and meaning of America; this ideology would transform the liberation into a specific institutional politics. While the relics of its ancient history were being pillaged from museums and heritage sites across Baghdad, the toppling of the

Saddam statue announced the dawn of a 'new history'. According to the invaders, this new history would transform Iraq's social and political infrastructure into a modern, democratic state. As the WMD rhetoric fades, in fact, the discourse of democracy and transformation becomes the primary focus of the US propaganda machinery. The discourse of 'freedom' remains redolent within the war on terror, but its powerful and evocative abstraction – its theological and relentlessly Romantic intensity – is substantially fortified through its adhesion to the more pragmatic and politically precise discourse of democracy. As the 'graven image' of Saddam Hussein comes down, it is draped in an American flag, announcing not only the arrival of the conquering nation, but its raft of ideals, values and ideologies.

Indeed, while it is not possible to say with any certainty which of the purposes of the invasion is most important to the governments that directed them, it is nevertheless arguable that the discourse of democratic institutions and processes – the ideology and ideal of democracy – will prove the most resonant and far-reaching. That is, the expressivities of democracy, which include the more elusive, aesthetic and ontological dimensions of their cultural politics, will generate the most lasting effects for the invaders and the invaded. These expressivities are forged through the media representations of the invasion as well as the official and everyday public discourses with which the media interacts. As we discussed in Chapter 1, the media is far more than a conduit of these discourses, but actually contributes to their formation in various cultural modes and sites. Danilo Zolo has argued, in fact, that it is not possible in a contemporary cultural context to consider the issue of democracy without direct reference to its mediation:

The essential concern ... [is] the relationship between democratic institutions and the increasing complexity of post-industrial societies ... Our present theories of democracy fail to offer us conceptual instruments sufficiently complex to permit a realistic interpretation of that relationship ... Western political theory appears increasingly unable to cope with the massive transformation which 'the information revolution' is bringing about in the primary subsystems of industrialized society. These transformations seem certain to speed up the processes of functional specialization and consequently ... To bring about still further large-scale growth of social complexity. (Zolo, 1992: 54)

As we have also noted, this relationship between socio-cultural complexity, the media and democracy is manifest through the conflation of textual and political representation. The association between the media and democracy is entirely manifest in the context and conditions of the Iraq invasion.

In a later text, Zolo (1997) asks very directly whether it is possible to conceive of a world government, a question that has tempted a number of scholars interested in the effects and outcomes of globalization. Zolo argues that the first Gulf War represented for the first time in modern history the overwhelming pre-eminence and unassailable power of a single nation, the United States. The capacity of the US to assemble nearly half a million of its own troops, plus nearly 160,000 allied combatants from around the world, illustrated how dramatically the global political order has changed since the end of the Cold War. Unlike the conclusion of other major modern wars, when international forums such as the League of Nations or the United Nations were established to facilitate an enduring peace, the end of the Cold War left the US in an entirely unique position. Thus, the new 'cosmopolis' of international co-operation has been skewed in order to accommodate the unassailable primacy of the United States.

COALITIONS OF THE KILLING

As we have noted, a number of critics have argued that America's unwillingness to work through the United Nations over Iraq, along with its generally chauvinistic approach to pre-emptive invasion, is evidence of a new and more aggressive autonomy. This new autonomy confirms for these critics a belligerent self-interest which is also evident in America's refusal to sign the Kyoto Protocol and its continued evasiveness over the International Criminal Court. In fact, America's manipulation of its aid packages in order to silence criticism and generate support for its war crimes position (Traynor, 2003) illustrates for many critics a global political demeanour that is both imperial and autonomous. For these critics, the US barely tolerates the United Nations and other collaborative international organizations, indicating a deep antipathy toward global co-operation and democratic governance.

Despite its obvious concerns about the structure and representative formation of the United Nations, however, the US remains very focused on issues of global governance and the management of international affairs. The issue, especially for the current administration, is the degree to which internationalism mediates self-interest against co-operation, leadership against consensus, coercion against consultation. The shaping of national democracies, of course, deals with precisely these issues; the difficulty for international governance is the extreme disparities of power and the limited imperative for global unity. The 2003 invasion of Iraq demonstrated, above all other things, America's desire to express its power and self-interest within constituted hegemonic conditions. It is not that the US is not interested in world government: it is rather that it sees itself as the presiding authority for such governance. This is not a surrender of national sovereignty, as we might project in a form of pure globalism. It is rather a confirmation of the power of the state – especially the western developed liberal democratic state – to assert its technological, economic, military and moral–ideological supremacy. The ascent of the United States represents a move to a form of international totalitarianism.

The difficulty for America, however, is that totalitarianism of any kind profoundly transgresses significant dimensions of its own internal cultural politics, national identity and historical integrity. While critics like Noam Chomsky might suggest that the democratic coding of American culture is merely fallacious ideology, it is equally arguable that American democracy and the discourses of freedom are significant elements in the formation of 'America' and its cultural sensibilities. That is, the American mission is forged around a genuinely held belief in a divinely inscribed imperative to transplant its democratic ideals throughout the globe. As this book has argued, these discourses operate within a substantive composition of contention and language wars by which the signifier 'America' must be perpetually reconvened and re-established.

In this sense, the decision to by-pass the United Nations and act pre-emptively against Iraq did not entirely subvert the spirit of co-operation and collective 'responsibility' for the US. The alliance with the United Kingdom, in particular, but also Australia (Bush's 'Deputy Sheriff' in the Pacific region) provided a crucial rhetorical framework for eliciting the consent of the US citizenry. Clearly, the US has the military power to invade and conquer Iraq on its own, but the Coalition alliance imbued the military campaign with a moral and ideological density that approximated the notion of democratic duty. Rather than acting as a totalitarian state, the US was able to present itself as a 'coalition' of like-minded crusaders within the war on terror. The constant parade of democratic values seemed to be rendered more credible by the support of the UK and Australia, who were not the direct targets of September 11 and the belligerence of Islamic terrorism. The 'freedom' and 'democracy' that Bush vaunted before his citizens seemed all the more compelling in the triangle of Anglophonic states – as though America's supremacy were condoned and confirmed by those whom the US 'represented'.

It is thus possible to evince a version of democracy that is not subdued or compromised by the railings of Old Europe and the United Nations. In fact, the affiliation of the UK and Australia constituted a form of 'representationalism' which clearly suited the interests and ideals of the invasion project. Bush, Blair and Howard 'represented' their respective nations' citizenry – they were the polis incarnate, a collective of citizens who could parade themselves as a democratically constituted and representative body. This democratic pageant was conducted through the global media networks, creating a sense of collectivity that would help to mitigate the impression of American unilateralism and aggressive self-interest. The triumph of these democratic forces would translate, simply enough, into a triumph of democracy within the global media sphere.

DEMOCRACY IN THE AGE OF TERROR

Many commentators locate the period following the French Revolution as the etymological source of political terror. According to the Academie Française, a French dictionary published in 1796 claimed that the Jacobins used the term 'terrorism' to refer to themselves and their political strategies in a positive sense. The British philosopher and political theorist Edmund Burke referred specifically in 1795 to the French Revolution where 'thousands of those hell hounds called terrorist' were let loose on the people. Walter Laqueur (1987) argues that the 'Reign of Terror' marked a moment in the evolution of modern politics and the modern state when raw power dominated the rule of law. While a number of historians have identified significant changes to the ways in which the concept of 'terrorism' has been used since the eighteenth century, we can see nevertheless some continuities between the reign of terror and what Laqueur calls the current 'age of terror'. In particular, the violence of the French Revolution quickly shifted its target from the aristocracy to other citizens whose values or social allegiances may have transgressed the perceived interests of the self-constituting ruling party. In this violent gestation of modern democracy and the modern state, ordinary citizens were subjected to perpetual menace, including the removal of property and the threat of torture and death. Ideology and ethical systems were shuffled around as citizens sought to align themselves with any postulate or political group that could secure them against this brutality. This conjoinment of politics and violence actually percolated the dangers throughout the community; terror became a political instrument which combined persuasion with the underlying threat or actuality of violence.

Of course, there is nothing new about this deployment of threat and violence in political management, most especially in terms of rulers over subjects, warriors over workers, men over women, majorities over minorities. The emergence of the modern state and notions of citizenship, however, demonstrates how power can be broadly dispersed through an increasingly urbanized mass society. Foucault (1991) has identified this shift in modes of social management, suggesting that the modern state, which is created through broadly dispersed hierarchical systems of material exchange, has evolved highly precise strategies (technologies) of control which maintain order. Somewhat paradoxically, this evolving process of a widely dispersed system of 'governmentality' may, in fact, derive from the embryo of threatened disorder by which the citizens access and deliver power through terror. The French Revolution illustrated how the relationship between state and citizen is underscored by a mutual predisposition to violence: political thinkers such as Comte, the Mills, Carlyle and Matthew Arnold recognized that the potential for 'democracy' and 'representation' was necessarily and precariously balanced through the violent potential of this relationship. Social and political order must rest upon a fulcrum that balances authority and access, state and citizen, compulsion and critique. As we discussed in Chapter 1, 'writing democracy' has evolved as the principal strategy for maintaining this balance: for ensuring, that is, that the lexical form of order will reconcile the interests of the collective with those of the individual. In this sense, Hoffman's view that terror has moved from the state to the populace is dubious since, as has been argued here, all power in the modern state is effected through a process of exchange. The radical irruption of 'social order' by the secretive forces of terror is already inscribed in the notion of statehood: democracy becomes part of a fluid motion of orderly and disorderly engagements of power – itself a contingency of threat, persuasion and coercion.

Democracy, therefore, enshrines the rights and freedoms of the citizen within a political context of vulnerability: the citizen is vulnerable to the violence and persuasion of the state, as the state is vulnerable to the violence and freedoms of citizens (Lewis, J., 2003). It is precisely this mutual and contingent vulnerability which draws terror from its historical and discursive shadows as a military and political instrument. The discursive management of this contingency unravels (dissociates) as the raw effects of hierarchy expose themselves in a crisis of violence. Clearly, a democratic order which privileges hierarchies of obedience and control necessarily marginalizes specific perspectives, discourses and social formations. The notional 'majority' masks its absent other by excluding contrary views, especially radical views, from its discursive ambit. Political violence in Sri Lanka, Palestine, Northern Ireland, India, Atlanta and Fiji is associated with the limits of a democratic system by which the state and its 'majority' seek to impose their will over aggrieved social groups who feel their views are not being adequately 'represented'. At this point, the distinction between political and military strategy becomes functionally blurred.

In a televisual, globalizing world, characterized by broad flows of people, information, imagery, products and finance, the problems associated with the 'representation' of political interests are significantly intensified (Castells, 1997, Held, 1995, Zolo, 1997). As has been indicated in Chapter 1, the problems of representation become increasingly acute as the limits of writing democracy and its project of reconciliation are even more clearly exposed by the new broadcast and interactive communications media. This 'broadcast democracy' illuminates the failures of 'representationalism', most particularly through television imagery of elite power and elite interests; politicians, political institutions, plutocrats, police, the military and law are all exposed through the unceasing flow of narrative and informational televisual media. This synoptic view, as David Lyon calls it, contributes to an increasing awareness among the citizenry that representative (writing) democracy is failing to deliver on its promises of transparency, equality and access. For Danillo Zolo (1992, see also Held, 1995) representative democracy is a nineteenth-century solution to the threat of proletariat uprising; by providing the perception of equality and representation, the middle classes were able to enshrine in constitutional perpetuity their own class interests and privilege. Seeking to avoid the excesses of Revolutionary terror, the middle classes imagined and designed a political system which, while mediating differences and protecting property, would maintain the values of education, security and wealth within a hierarchical system that ensured obedience, order, law and the provision of low-cost labour.

The broadcast systems of representation, however, in demanding the televisual presence of politicians, institutions and the parliamentary system illuminates in the rawest way possible the incapacity of the state (and the citizenry) to escape its violent gestation. While condemning the WMD programmes of totalitarian states, we need to remind ourselves of the vast armoury of state-sanctioned weaponry and systems of coercion which persist as the fundamental and unerasable basis of modern statehood. While writing and writing democracy have been a primary 'civilizing' force for modernity, the contingency of violence remains as the principal definer of the relationship between the state and its citizenry – both within and outside its boundaries.

Such a claim, of course, might seem to contradict the general mission of a democratic system which is to resolve social difference by peaceful means. In the 'test of the public square', that is the capacity of individual citizens to openly criticize the government without fear of persecution, the democratic state is clearly well ahead of totalitarian regimes like the one presided over by Saddam Hussein. However, it is arguable that the advantage of democracy is forestalled when the criticizing individual speaks in a discursive vacuum – that is, when the speaker is not heard since the public square has already been transformed as a mediasphere and the criticism has already been neutralized within a relationship of legitimated and contingent violence. Contained within the armoury of the state is an ideal of obedience to a process of representation which by its own definition must exclude, suppress and control all individuals, groups and interests that would disrupt the sanctity of the borders and priorities that are assumed within its capitalist, hierarchical ideology.

This imperative of threat and exclusion, however, also functions outside the borders of a specific nation-state. Through the ongoing, but accelerating, processes of globalization, the modern state is evolving its liberal democratic ideology through a more open sphere of reference. At this level, the modern state is not being compromised by internationalization, as a number of critics are arguing. It is rather intensifying its 'presence' as a discursive force through the expansion of its ambit. While colonialism made this phase of globalization apparent, the current phase of economic internationalization – a process described as essentially imperialist by many critics – is certainly being led by the self-interest of many developed nation-states, especially, the US, Japan and European states.

The contingent state–citizen relationship is more acutely rendered through this current globalization phase, creating new spaces and boundaries for the imposition of its hierarchical systems, exercised as they are through the underlying force of violence. The banner of liberal democracy leads this violence into the international sphere, generating new zones of exclusion within an ideal of inclusion. Very obviously, the US and other First World states are imposing upon Third World countries and their economies governmental systems that are conducive to the First World's interests. More than this, however, the actual political institutions that are being imposed bear with them a hierarchical and exclusionary system which migrates the limits of democracy into a broader global sphere. Yes, democracy brings new opportunities and emancipatory values, but it also brings the economic, political and social programme of differentiation and the contingency of state–citizen violence. At this level, the internationalization of national hegemony will further marginalize the interests, rights, needs and political aspirations of specific social groups and discourses which do not necessarily subscribe to the dominant order. The globalization of economy and culture exposes the host of internationalization to the terror of political violence.

The deficiencies of democracy which are evident within nations become extra-territorialized as national hegemonies seek to maximize their constituent advantages within a globalizing hierarchy of interests. As it goes out into the world, liberal democracy assumes its primacy over all other ideologies and interests. As we are seeing in the conquered territories of Afghanistan and Iraq, the democratic systems that are being imposed are creating hegemonic alliances between elite groups and US interests to the general exclusion of many others within the boundaries of the new democratic states. The Islamicists, in particular, are not regarded as legitimate political aspirants, especially those who reject the idea of global capitalist integration. Moreover, while many of the dominant Shi'a community voted in the interim elections (January 2005), the Sunni Muslim communities, for a range of reasons, excluded themselves from a process which inevitably inscribed them as a 'minority' and subordinate group. Of course, this may be a better arrangement than the previous system of brutal coercion, but it is clearly associated with significant costs, including the radical transformation of culture and the obfuscation of violence through new modes of obedience.

In some respects, this ideological colonization parallels the historical template of all warfare: conquering nations seek to transplant their own institutions, values and ideologies into the conquered culture. The significant difference, as has been intimated, is the supreme power of the United States as a form of self-inscribing and more or less totalitarian mode of global governance. The paradox reveals itself through the ideal of representation, which continues to be locked within the borders of nation. Even as the system of democratic liberalism is imposed on the conquered nations, the super or *supra* power of the United States seems impenetrable for those who must live within the force of its cultural, economic and military ambit. At this level, we might all count ourselves to be citizens of the United States, but the ideal of democracy (representation) is not universal. While US policies have a powerful effect on most people's lives across the globe, relatively few members of the global polis are actually eligible to vote in US elections.

THE ELECTRONIC POLIS

We are returned, therefore, to a key question: how is it that the government and the citizenry have co-operated to create these new conditions of violence and insecurity? To emphasize the point, the evolution of a broadcast media reveals the critical limits of representational politics, as it reveals the general limits of a writing democracy. Nowhere is this more obvious than in the inability of the world-wide protest movements to make any impact on the resolve of US, UK and Australian governments to invade Iraq. The well-organized and orchestrated street protests, along with clear opposition to the planned invasion in public opinion polls (majorities in the UK and Australia), failed to move the Coalition leaders. Even in America, where the mood for 9/11 patriotic unity and vengeance remained potent, there was a very strong preference among the citizenry for a United Nations solution to the Iraq issue. However, while in Europe and Canada the protests may have exerted some influence on their own governments' thinking, the concerns were largely dismissed as irrelevant and unrepresentative by the US administration. In return, protestors themselves pointed to the despotic and unrepresentative nature of the US government which had barely received half of the votes in the Presidential elections at which only half the eligible voters cast a ballot. Protestors pointed specifically to the Florida college and the questionable punch-hole system which leaves no auditable paper trail. Protestors questioned, not without justification, how many US citizens the Bush administration actually represented.

Critics of this system of democracy would suggest, therefore, that the US President and administration not only 'represent' a mere 25 per cent of the US citizenry, they represent an even tinier proportion of the billions of global citizens whose lives are deeply impacted by US policy and cultural activities. In this sense, the 'majority' that the US administration represents is, in many respects, an arithmetic illusion. But what is perhaps more disturbing, at least in terms of the high principles of democracy, is the decision by around half the eligible voters in the US not to cast a ballot at all. While numerous scholars have investigated the possible reason for this low turnout, there are at least two explanations which are directly related to our interests here. First, disillusion with the electoral process and especially the honesty and integrity of politicians. This disillusion has many dimensions to it, but it is frequently argued that ethnic minorities, women and youth find only a limited connection between their personal and everyday lives and needs, and the megalith of democratic institutions. Governments, especially national governments, exist at a distance from the substantive interests and needs of these groups of citizens, especially as the personification of these institutions is shaped by a celebrity culture and celebrity politicians. These particular celebrities are practised in the arts of persuasion, evasion and role playing; their highly stylized media performances have contributed to the conditions of hyperreality and the compounding cynicism of many voters. The distance of politics is thus re-rendered as a contiguity that immerses the politician in the culture of televisualization: this mode of 'representationalism' is cast, thereby, as another narrative within the morass of images and broadcast illusion.

The second explanation for the disengagement of significant numbers of US voters from their electoral process relates more directly to the nature of the choice being offered. While western political systems have largely formed themselves around the central paradox of modernity – collective against individual interests – the historical shift toward a more free market and individualist economy has necessarily affected the polemic of democratic processes. As Anthony Giddens (1994), among many others, has noted, marketization and the ascendancy of a 'risk' society have contributed to the deconstruction of many of the key aspects of the welfare state as well as its ideological assumptions. The shift toward a more centrist political contest 'beyond left and right' has led to the collapse of many of the significant ideological and policy distinctions between the major political parties. While this has always been something of a feature of American politics, where a labour-based political party has never fully evolved, the convergence of perspectives is now a clear characteristic of British and Australian political life. Thus, in the US the choice is between a conservative, free-market party and a very conservative free-market party. The spectacular failure of Democratic President Bill Clinton to reform America's health system indicates how difficult it is for any modern western government to introduce new social support measures. The choice for the US electorate, therefore, appears to be between two prospective CEOs, not two distinctive ideologies.

While Giddens finds much to celebrate in this new political order since it emblemizes the possibilities for a new (postmodern) community and personal politics, we might also suggest that the collapse of ideological polemics marks the final victory of the bourgeoisie who created democracy as a form of political and material self-protection. The triumph of the market, that is, may be seen as the ultimate manifestation of the limits of writing democracy. Francis Fukuyama announces this new politics through the collapse of communism, arguing that the failure of the whole idea of state intervention introduces an 'end to history' where new political modes and freedoms are possible. More radical thinkers such as Ernesto Laclau (Laclau, 1991, Laclau & Mouffe, 1985), and Deleuze and Guattari (1987) welcome a new form of democracy that is centred on diversity, community and individual 'expressivity' within an unrestrained identity politics that provides a free flowing cognitive and creative space for self-exploration and expression.

It has been suggested above that the broadcast media, while denounced by some as a tool of the government and elite interests (Bourdieu, 1998, Herman & McChesney, 1999, Horkheimer & Adorno, 1972), may also provide a space for these new political expressivities. In this sense, the new media – broadcast and interactive – may well contribute to the formation of a broadcast or visceral democracy (Lewis, 1998, Lewis & Best, 2002), one that acknowledges the complexity of contemporary culture and the limits of institutional Enlightenment democracy. Critics of the broadcast media argue that mass mediation compromises the integrity of the traditional democratic ideal as it facilitates the spread of propaganda and reduces electoral and representative politics to a popularity contest (see Postman, 1987). As politics becomes immersed in the image-dominated mediasphere, a genuine policy debate is reduced to a parade of celebrity individualism. In either case, it is clear that writing and mass printing, which had traditionally 'mediated' the relationship between state and citizenry, are being supplemented by new modes of electronic mediation. As outlined in Chapter 1, this transformation of the media inevitably affects the nature of the state–citizen relationship: the broadcast media, that is, contributes to the formation of a new citizenry functioning through different modes of mediation and democracy. Within this new 'electronic polis' the political role of the media is itself radically altered. In particular, the role of a 'fourth estate', while maintaining some of its force in the thinking of specific informational zones, is subverted by the sheer mass and volition of generated imagery, narrative and information – the condition we are calling hyperreality.

As we have discussed, this new hyperreality, which combines a new orality (McLuhan, 1969) with a perpetually unfolding 'world as picture' (see Chapter 1), inevitably disrupts the purity of the fourth estate – the idea that the media should provide essential and objective information required for the effective functioning of the democratic political system. While referring specifically to radio, McLuhan's notion of a 'new orality', which facilitates communication across vast spatial and temporal zones, might seem to reinvigorate the immediacy of spoken language, restoring a greater potential for 'presence'. Heidegger's world-as-picture, along with antecedent theories of Walter Benjamin, Fredric Jameson and Jean Baudrillard, also claims a new status for the image which contends a new immediacy and the redundancy of time and space. This new imagistic immediacy might seem to create an intrinsic sense of the 'ever-present' human subject which is articulated in the ongoing and ineluctable conditions of a televisual culture (Lewis, 2002a). The new orality and the world-as-picture, that is, constitute a new media omnipresence which pervades all contemporary experience.

In effect, and this issue is intimated in the works of all these theorists though never quite explicated, this omnipresence is a feature of a more intense 'omni-absence'. The new orality, which is a permutation of mediated rather than interpersonal or communal voices, deftly intensifies the absent–present of writing. The expanding publication of broadcast media, along with the peculiar and somewhat paradoxical nature of the electronic artefact itself, seems to create an even more volatile context for the signifier; the electronic voice, as opposed to interpersonal orality or writing, subjects the signifier to a more rapid engagement with counterclaim, dispute, supplementarity and meaning deferral. The pervasive image and voice of the human subject and the less rarefied context of viewing (over reading words) create an impression of community that is at once immediate and 'real' but also profoundly deceptive. The immediacy of the imaged subject is not housed in a durable context of lived experience, but is duplicitously evanescent and intensely abstract, a seeming presence which is merely conditional, a life that has no depth-presence, no resonance beyond the memory of counter-memory.

As outlined in Chapter 1, meanings generated through the televisual media are in a state, not merely of deferral, but of perpetual deficit. A meaning debt is created by the professional media, along with a promissory note that the debt will be redeemed in the next bulletin, episode or instalment. The news media, in particular, works aggressively to overcome its deficit as it seeks to honour its social, semiotic, financial and historical responsibilities. As a component of writing democracy, the news media seems to take seriously its informational role as fourth estate; in general terms, it seeks to join the lived experience of the 'story' with the lived experience of the reader/viewer. In a broadcast context, however, the problem of deficit becomes critical, leading to a self-referencing whereby the media is its own lived experience and story. Meanings are generated through its own conditions and contexts, its own centralizing and institutional authority. The rabid and rapid engagement with the lived experience cannot overcome the effects of oscillation, and readers are left to wash about in a bewildering miasma of imprecise and ineffable facts.

Thus, the attacks on Afghanistan and Iraq are not solely determined by governments and the elite interests of oil corporations. These acts of political violence are shaped through complex discourses that necessarily implicate the citizen, the state and the media – as well as those who are deemed to be 'the enemy'. Governments may drive these policies and modes of governmentality, but the force of democracy draws together the aspirations and pleasures of an electronic polis into the web of decision-making and action. The attacks on Afghanistan and Iraq must therefore be treated as a broadly based responsibility – a mode of representation which implicates the agent and the viewer in every brutal act, every cry for mercy, every tear from every grieving eye.

BOMB THE WORLD

You can bomb the world to pieces
But you can't bomb it into peace.
'Bomb the world', Michael Franti

The condition of the hyperreal creates very specific problems for those who would seek to assert their ideals and discourses over others. As the media continually overextends itself, blurring the borders between perspective and narrative, it necessarily subverts its own truth claims. The hyperreal as not-quite-real demands the development of specific strategies of media management. The invocation of cultural narratives of freedom and democracy connects with specific kinds of historical knowings generated through a seemingly infinite corpus of mutually contingent texts (supplements). In this way, the war on terror, and its specific campaigns in Afghanistan and Iraq, are forged out of the expectation of a just violence, one which is ennobled through the televisual cultures of information and narrative. The first Gulf War, Baudrillard claims, was the first truly hyperreal war because it seems to have taken place through the sanitized effects of domestic television consumption. The electronic polis was engaged through the broad field of discursive effects, including the reconfirmation of the east–west divide.

The US administration and its supporters extended these strategies during the more recent invasion of Iraq. Not atypically, the government sought to control the representational breadth of discourses through various means of information management. In many respects, the powerful discourses of nation, culture and unity, most particularly as they were fortified by the post-9/11 rhetoric of freedom and democracy, seemed to quell even the possibility of alternative perspectives. The vitriolic criticism of Susan Sontag and others who raised questions about American foreign policy in the aftermath of 9/11 provides a clear prescience for a good deal of the social management that was to follow: a criticism of any aspect of US policy or government action was considered 'treasonable', an attack on all of America, its values and way of life. Thus, radio and television outlets refused to broadcast alternative perspectives on the Iraq invasion. Protest voices of musicians like Michael Franti and the Dixie Chicks were censored by various broadcasters in the United States. The Dixie Chicks, in fact, dramatically retreated from their musical dispute with the US government after receiving death threats which accused them of anti-Americanism. While many of these protest voices have found their way onto the Internet, there is no doubt that the patriotic fervour of the United States made it difficult for alternative perspectives to be produced and disseminated.

Rampton and Stauber (2003) have described the range of communications strategies which were designed to ensure the primacy of the government perspective. Within a globalizing market-based corporate economy, it is not surprising that the United States has adopted, among the more familiar PR strategies, a form of national branding that has been designed to promote the virtues and values of the US – especially the ideal of liberal democracy. In other words, and as Rampton and Stauber go on to argue, the new ideology of a corporatized and privatized democracy becomes both the tool and the object of the US communications strategy on the Middle East. In the aftermath of 9/11, preparing the way for direct military actions in Afghanistan, the US launched two advertising campaigns: the first featured the President's wife speaking in reassuring and maternal tones as she sought to lift the spirits of the American people and soothe their anxieties; the second was designed to remind Americans that they are part of a tolerant and virtuous society which is blameless but which must act to defend its greatness and high ideals. This second advertising campaign promoted US democratic pluralism – the idea that America is a tolerant and welcoming place which admits people from diverse backgrounds, ethnicities and nations into its national–cultural embrace. At around the same time, the US government established a number of instant communication offices in Washington, London and Islamabad (Pakistan). These PR offices facilitated regular contact between senior US officials and the Arabic media. The *Wall Street Journal* reported, in fact, that the US had exerted considerable pressure on Arabic TV and print news editors to release stories which were favourable or at least clarified the US perspective on events in the Middle East and South Asian regions.

This move toward a branding model is perhaps best illustrated by the appointment of advertising executive Charlotte Beers to the position of State Department Undersecretary for Public Diplomacy. In seeking to influence the opinions of Muslims and Muslim governments, Beers considered the possibility of using American celebrities, including sports stars, to generate a positive and more emotional impression of America and American culture. According to Beers, public diplomacy is 'a vital new arm in what will combat terrorism over time. All of a sudden we are in the position of redefining who America is, not only for ourselves under this kind of attack, but also for the outside world' (cited in Rampton & Stauber, 2003: 12). Beers and others who have been attracted from the private sector into the realm of 'public duty' are developing new strategies for neutralizing the antipathy of domestic and global citizens of the mediasphere. The branding of America might be the pre-emptive discursive strike against those over whom George Bush puzzles, those who 'hate us'.

While the deployment of propaganda processes is nothing new, the corporatization and branding model clearly acknowledges the transformation of democracy and the public sphere into a mediasphere, as we have been calling it. The Rendon Group, a major PR consulting firm employed by various administrations, now specializes in the corporate imaging of politicians and the support of US military campaigns. Having worked with the CIA to create anti-Saddam Hussein materials after the first Gulf War, Rendon has consulted for the US military in Argentina, Colombia, Haiti, Kosovo, Panama and Zimbabwe. Readers and viewers in various countries of the globe have been exposed to the perspective created by the Rendon Group and the US military. In fact, it was the Rendon Group that developed and financed the formation in 1992 of the Iraqi National Congress (INC), an assembly of key opponents of the Saddam regime. Under the leadership of Ahmed Chalabi and funded by covert CIA money (Jennings, 1998, cited in Rampton & Stauber, 2003: 43), the INC was able to forge strong links with the Project for the New American Century, a neoconservative thinktank chaired by William Kristol, a strong proponent of US military assertiveness in the Middle East (see Chapter 2). At the time of the war preparations in 2002, the White House began working with a new group, the Committee for the Liberation of Iraq, which was also closely linked with the New American Century people.

This stage-managing of the political transformation of Iraq is dramatically illustrated by the construction of specific stage sets. The first is the well-publicized stage set of US military command constructed in the small Middle Eastern country of Qatar. According to the *Army Times*, the military media centre, designed by Hollywood art director George Allison, is a high-tech stage set covering around 17,000 square feet. The set, while giving the impression of proximity, is constituted for journalists working at distance from the actual hostilities. Like the stage managing of the liberation of Private Jessica Lynch and the $45m military commission to the Institute for Creative Technologies, the Qatar media centre is charged with the task of creating an effective impression of the emancipation of Iraq. The second major media set was established on the US aircraft carrier, the *Abraham Lincoln*. On May 1, 2003 Bush was flown out to the carrier where, dressed in a naval flight suit, the President declared victory over Iraq. The image of Bush's declaration was played live on the media networks and replayed during the evening bulletins. The image of Bush in his flight suit, indicating a noble connection with the Iraq victory, became a centrepiece of the 2004 presidential election campaign. As a major public relations exercise, however, the bulletins omitted to tell their audiences that the *Abraham Lincoln* was actually situated only 39 miles off the San Diego coast and that Bush's pilot suit actually linked him to a barely reputable stint in the National Guard where he appears to have spent at least twelve months AWOL.

IN BED WITH AL-QA'IDA

This confluence of corporatized communications with the polemics of political positioning is clearly located within a hyperreal mediasphere which blurs the distinction between private and public interests. Through an electronic polis, public information penetrates the private domain within a broad field of competing signifiers, images, texts and media. Subjects receive the information within the private domestic setting, engage with it and create perspectives in terms of their own cultural resources. Thus, while Jürgen Habermas has called for a revitalization of the public sphere through an invigorated participative democracy and 'communicative action', this sphere is already being generated through the interaction of the hyperreal with the private–domestic.

In many respects, the strategy of 'embedding' allied journalists during the US-led invasion of Iraq represented an attempt by the US military to exploit this confluence of the public and private spheres by bringing the 'war' into the lived experiences of the domestic audience. As is typically the case, public support for the military campaign in Iraq increased once the troops were committed (Gallup Poll, 2003). However, in order to galvanize and maintain public consent, the US communications machinery sought to strengthen the sense of 'being with the troops'. While this strategy had been developed during the Vietnam–America War (Taylor, 1992, Carruthers, 2000), the strategy had turned against the US authorities as scenes of violence and bloody warfare had nightly invaded the domiciles of

American citizens. Sympathy and support for the home troops had been compromised by significant political questions which arose out of the vision of a close combat depicting Americans killing and being killed. The information managers realized that there needed to be a balance between propinquity, empathy and dramatic effect. The deaths of civilians and American troops were especially alienating and disturbing for home audiences; the propinquity needed, therefore, to maximize the sense of American courage and the justness of the war, and minimize the negative aspects of military engagement.

The practice of embedding journalists into the invading military forces represented a key strategy for managing sympathy and identification by home audiences with their troops without the exposure of excessive violence and loss of life. Embedding may be defined as a highly managed inclusion of accredited journalists in direct military action. Journalists are embedded as they are housed within specific military units under the direct control of military authority. The Pentagon guidelines on embedding (United States Department of Defense, 2003) include:

- no information on ongoing engagements will be released unless authorised by an on-scene commander, and information about previous engagement will be released only if discussed in general terms
- reports giving information on 'friendly force' troop movements and deployment are prohibited
- information on future operations is strictly prohibited
- journalists will be assigned to a specific unit
- no private transport
- no personal firearms
- all interviews with military personnel are to be 'on the record'

This management of death – or the story of death – is the focus of Jean Baudrillard's obviously ironical book *The Gulf War Did Not Take Place* (1995, see Chapter 1). The first Gulf War was largely deployed through aerial bombing and it was not difficult to parenthesize the significant numbers of Iraqi deaths (40–200,000) and camouflage the relatively few deaths of American and allied soldiers (around 200). The 2003 invasion campaign, which necessarily included ground assault, would inevitably produce greater numbers of American and Coalition deaths and allow considerably greater access for journalists to Iraqi casualties (around 100,000). As in the first Gulf War, the

US communications authorities devised a system of accreditation by which registered journalists would have access to information, protection and military personnel (as 'talent'), as well as a contiguous and intimate view of the invasion. Consequently, the vision and reporting were generated exclusively from the perspective of the American and Coalition troops. Using sophisticated digital imaging and satellite technology, reporters were able to present to the home audience a strong sense of immediacy, action and rapid success, the precondition of domestic public consent. Journalists would lose their accreditation if any of their stories 'compromised' American strategic interests.

The embedded and closely managed information releases were also designed to counter alternative news stories being generated by independent First World journalists and Arab-based networks, including al-Jazeera and al-Arabia. What was particularly troubling for the US communications authorities was the reporting and distribution of stories, especially through the Internet, of the slaughter of noncombatants, including women and children. The view from 'behind enemy lines' was to be minimized, if not censored altogether, since it represented the enemy as people and compromised the image of a highly sophisticated, targeted and liberational military conquest. Robert Fisk, one of the non-embedded journalists working from behind enemy lines, argues that American troops deliberately targeted independent journalists in order to eliminate these alternative perspectives. Fisk points specifically to the American attack on Reuters and al-Jazeera journalists, who were reporting from the Palestine Hotel, as evidence of information control in the Iraq invasion. The killing of these and numerous other journalists during the invasion indicates an insidious distrust by the Americans of a media they cannot directly control. Fisk asks: 'Is there an element of the American military which has come to hate the press and wants to take out journalists based in Baghdad ... working "behind enemy lines"?' (2003: 3).

Fisk's interrogation of the notion of 'enemy lines' points to a far broader problematization of geography in the war and its mediation. Clearly, the territory of Iraq is re-imagined through the reporting, as mainstream media networks recapture the territory for the informational and cultural gratification of the invaders' home culture. This is not the reporting at a 'distance' discussed by Phillip Taylor in the context of the 1991 Gulf War, and historicized by Paul Virilio in his book *The Vision Machine* (1994). Rather, it is an attempt by the private and military media networks to speak directly and 'immediately' to domestic audiences, giving them a sense of the presence and value of the US democratic mission. The war is conjured through the broadcast media as a presence, a reality and a lived community experience which compounds distance as simultaneously distant *and* contiguous. As we noted above, the media perpetuates itself and its vision in terms of a deficit of meaning. Each image, segment or instalment seems to confirm the story, and what is absent – death, bodies, scorched earth, contention, Weapons of Mass Destruction, Saddam himself. But this absence is irradiated through an insistent presence which generates its belief and verisimilitude through the gathering momentum of an emotional and dramatic narrative. This momentum is personified in the voice and body of the journalist who shouts from the back of an invading transport vehicle, assuring us that all is going according to plan and that the spearhead of this dawning democracy is not the abstract words of politicians and leaders at home, but the brave young men who represent all that is virtuous, healthy and good in the culture. These young men (and women), who may be as familiar and everyday as the boy-next-door, are prepared to risk all for the justness of the cause. By drawing the journalist and the soldier together and bringing them into the domestic living space of the home citizen, the distance and absence are folded into a moment of identification and forceful propinquity. The message is the medium; the soldier is the citizen; the citizen is the medium.

Of course, what appears to be present, is also absent. What is absent from the story of the invasion of Iraq is what is intrinsic to the information and imagery itself: that is, the actuality of the lived experience. The identification and the propinquity are always and inevitably ephemeral. Whatever the conjuration of the image–voice and the story, the imagining of the lived experience is always and inevitably a representation and a meaning deficit. This is not merely the financial deficit that impels the production of the story, but the deep demands of a meaning-rabid media which must create a story out of the bare bones of its own semiotic resources, its own 'lived experience'. In this way, the media feeds on its own proliferating and compulsive imagining, creating the story, as it creates itself, through an association or consonance of already existing supplements – images, ideas and texts which have already told the story of America's heroic democracy over and over again. These supplements, through fictional narratives, news bulletins or propaganda, create the preconditions for audience (public) belief or consensus which might constitute a self-actualizing semiotics that is grounded in what we conveniently epitomize as 'American culture'. This is not in an exact science of information control or simply the propagation of ideology, as many opponents of the war, following Althusser's paradigm, frequently proclaim. It is rather a complex interaction of signs and meanings over which governments and their information systems seek to impose an order that will somehow delimit the inevitability of semiotic stupefaction. The ideology or information structure that governments would impose, that is, inevitably encounters the whirring disorder of culture and a slippage that releases audiences' own expressive capacity.

Quite clearly, the US information authorities have entirely surrendered the notion of objectivity, replacing it with notions of 'values' and self-interest. The version of democracy to which they work is 'positioned', established through the perspective of what the Project for the New American Century might call 'the national interest': what's good for America is good for the world. It is precisely this alignment of political interest and communications strategy which is central to a broadcast democracy. Not surprisingly, the editors who manage information at home through the various national and global news networks are also critically positioned. As has been widely discussed, the editing process, particularly as it seeks to converge the interests of the private and public sphere of Coalition viewers, contributes significantly to the construction of meanings and the ways in which the representations are formed. Not surprisingly, the most watched TV coverage of the war in the US was the one with the fewest depictions of death, maiming and the complex politics of violence. The Fox network presented a war which closely aligned itself to the principles of nationalism, the invasion policy and a powerful, global democratic ideal, one which resolved conflict through the heroics of American enterprise and morality.

To this extent, the narrative of a pleasing but powerful nation is transposed from fictional to news texts by the Fox paradigm. And while there have been moves to interrogate the ethics and efficacy of its news model (see Greenwald, 2004), the Fox audience remains loyal to the illusion or ideals of a perfect state. The typical Fox war report is generated through three scales of interaction, each of which is designed to engage the audience through a narrative of information and entertainment. First, the embedded journalist tells his or her story, exclusively presented from the perspective of the invading American forces. The journalist often reports through real time, constructing a narrative of implacable American heroism and the force of liberation. This narrative interconnects with the cultural experience of the world as picture. Texts feed into one another and the embedded journalist, in a flak jacket and helmet, advances the story of American military might and right. The dichotomous national motif of victim–hero is the perpetually unfolding foreground of reports which are inevitably shot from the perspective of the American troops: the camera sees the world of hostility and violence literally over the shoulder of the obviously endangered American soldier.

At the second level, studio anchors – often a male and female – 'domesticate' the stories for homeland consumption. The anchors represent a critical framing for the extremes of adventure, bringing it into the realm of the familiar body; the TV host becomes an anchorage for fixing our understanding of the terrors of war and the excess of political violence. Now the story is moving from public experience into the familiar and private sphere, restoring the ideal of pleasure against the abominable and abnormal. The horrors of war and the distance of the military campaign become 'speakable' through what might be called the Ma and Pa Kettle effect – the translation of the unimaginable into the comforting values of home, parentalism and domestic familiarity.

A third framing is also frequently offered. This framing brings the 'expert systems' of advanced societies into domestic living rooms. In the case of the Fox network, and its imitators across the world, experts are drawn from the political or academic dominions of conservative thinkers. They provide a context and interpretation of events based on historical, cultural, strategic or political 'expertise'. While these experts will provide a bridge from the external to the internal modes of information and knowledge, they also confirm the ideological and cultural superiority of the invaders over the invaded. They are, in effect, a source of enlightenment and modernizing supremacy.

We might understand this process of informational and semiotic management through the following photograph, a cropped version of which was published by major newspapers across the world during the bombing raids on Baghdad and Basrah. The photograph was cropped in order to obscure the gruesome details of the child's injuries as well as the surrounding casualties. The uncropped version shown here was generally considered unpublishable.

What is silent or absent in the cropped version is the brute horror of the invasion and the political decisions that condone, and

Figure 4.1   A photograph which appeared in many newspapers, cropped in order to obscure the gruesome details of the child's injuries and surrounding casualties (courtesy of AP/Amr Nabil)

demonstrably perpetrate, the maiming and killing of children. This consent parallels the targeting by militants of children in Beslan (see Introduction), an atrocity that has been so savagely and so rightly condemned by the western world. What is also absent in the cropped version is a story of democracy which condones various kinds of murder and which continues to deny the rights, freedom and cultural integrity of the people of the non-developed world. The presence within the cropped photograph indicates the viability of the democratic mission that appears an almost innocuous or sublime act in which strange people and their strange customs may be embraced by the greater good. The image of an avuncular, exotic and gentle-looking man and the almost serene, angelic girl seem strangely to produce that presence which confirms the divine duty of the liberator. Beyond this content, the very framing of the photograph, the fact of mediation, gives legitimacy to the act of representation which is itself a form of social and cultural containment. The semiotic association, that is, parades its captives through a form of cultural appropriation (Said, 1993) which completely absents from view the implacable immensity of an industrialized media network whose singular motivation is the framing of the entire world.

While we may simply condemn the process of cropping in terms of political censorship, this would only partially explain the meaning of the cropped photo. In fact, and as has been argued throughout this book, the cropping itself constitutes a mode of representation whereby specific kinds of gaps and irruptions will necessarily occur. In particular, the fissure between the presence and absence of the photo expands infinitely as it enters the space of intertextuality. This intertextual flow constitutes a political space for meaning-making, the space in which alternative readings become possible. This is particularly the case in a hyperreal media culture where democracy is forged in relation to the everyday lived experience of televisualization and the destabilizing effects of signification. The media's ceaseless motion, its perpetual feeding of alternative texts and meaning potential effectively subverts the natural sensibility or *doxa*, as Barthes calls it, that might seek to construct ideology and purpose in the cropped photograph. The hyperreal swirls about an uncertain reading/viewing consciousness, creating its microcosms of doubt and futility. The shifting perspective of public opinion is the most obvious manifestation of a political consciousness that can no longer settle on a single truth. The innate violence of the state is never expunged by the propagated imagery of democratic projects;

the invasion and conquest of this foreign people will remain exactly that – even as the communications machinery sanitizes and organizes its hierarchies of meaning order. The child with the blood-smeared face is not left to her silence, but new voices, new modes of telling, intervene to speak her fate. The cropping obfuscates the image of death, but the silence is never lasting. The violence of the state is revealed in doubt, even at the moment of its imagined closure.

This silence, moreover, also encounters the resonance of history, including those discourses that would interrogate again the reasons for entering and attacking Iraq. Within this context, Roberts et al. (2004) have suggested that the mortality rates of the Iraqis, especially around the city of Fallujah, were estimated to be around 2.5 times higher during the invasion and occupation periods than before the invasion. In simple terms, this means that the regime change cost around 100,000 civilian lives, mostly women and children, which was about 92 per cent more than the Bush administration had estimated. The Basrah girl may seem a slight figure in the grand scale of global politics; but her mortality represents a calculated risk – collateral damage – for those powerful forces which seek to impose across the world their own particular version of progress and democracy. According to Roberts' survey of mortality rates, the risk of violent death was 58 times higher during the invasion and occupation periods than it had been in the last years of the Saddam government.

AL-JAZEERA AND THE ALTERNATIVE MEDIA

It is certainly true that the US communications strategies have contributed to a more general dislocation of the fourth estate ideal. Their direct involvement in media production and management, along with a powerful strategy of unsettling 'truth' through propagated perspective, leaves the 'public' in an uncertain reading position. As the public generates its own meanings around terrorism and the wars in Afghanistan and Iraq, it will certainly be drawing on a range of cultural and semiotic resources, including the ideals of freedom and democracy as they are being propagated by the Washington administration. But since these resources are themselves disjunctive and incomplete, and as the media continues to supplement their meanings through the unceasing volition of further instalments, publics in the mediasphere will themselves seek to overcome the deficit. The end result, as it has been argued here, is a broadcast democracy that ultimately collides with its representational and institutional forbear – writing democracy. As President Bush waves the flag of a democracy that is so inconsistent and incomplete, audience–electorates will seek supplements elsewhere. This may or may not lead readers to informed and alternative reportings of the invasion of Iraq, but it will certainly deepen the crisis for contemporary democratic culture – that is, the crisis of certainty.

In the midst of this crisis, the self-subverting impetus of the mainstream media is inscribed against the context of new readings and alternative perspectives of the war on Iraq. As noted earlier, the American authorities have a particular anxiety about the Arabic network al-Jazeera, which has been savagely attacked by the invading US troops, as well as by specific Arabic regimes. The relatively free and open reporting style of the network, a style which depicts the most graphic excesses of violence, constitutes a form of informational anarchy in the region. Funded by the Shah of Qatar and formed by a number of retrenched journalists who had been working for the BBC World Service, al-Jazeera from its inception established a policy of providing maximum detail. While frequently characterized by US information authorities and a number of US editors and journalists as a conduit for the promotion of al-Qa'ida propaganda, the network prides itself on its 'tell-all' independent status (el-Nawawy & Iskandar, 2002: 179).

Al-Jazeera's approach seriously challenges the highly managed information model supported by the US government and mainstream media corporations; however, this approach is based on a refurbished fourth estate paradigm which seeks to return responsibility for decision-making and the agency of warfare back to those citizens who, by ignorance or active assent, are necessarily engaged in the conflict. Al-Jazeera conflates the ideal of information with the volition and cultural ubiquity of televisualization. In its view, the people of all nations are accountable for the actions of their governments and military, at least inasmuch as they must know as much as possible about these actions. Within the global mediasphere, al-Jazeera is seeking, that is, to refurbish the fourth estate principle, allowing publics to make informed decisions about policy, political violence and government.

During the invasion, of course, both the US and Iraqi officials were somewhat confused about the role and status of the al-Jazeera network since, at various stages of the war, the reporting provided for the predominantly Arab audiences both sympathetic and critical reports on the respective sides and their legitimacy. Essentially, however, the US denounced the network and its open information philosophy, citing in particular the airing of the bin Laden post-9/11 video as evidence of al-Jazeera's naïve approach to al-Qa'ida propaganda. This 'scoop', as el-Nawawy and Iskandar (2002) call it, personalized the perpetrator of the US terror attack, providing a vehicle for the dissemination of his ideas, ideology and recruitment drive. As Alan Cullison (2004) points out in his analysis of the al-Qa'ida computer discs seized during the Afghanistan invasion, bin Laden's major objective in attacking the US was publicity, recruitment and funding. The air time provided by al-Jazeera, the US officials claimed, served the interests of terrorism as it compromised the fight for freedom. Nothing, of course, is said about the 'oxygen', as Margaret Thatcher calls terrorist publicity, provided by the US networks which have illustrated globally that the al-Qa'ida publicity strategy has actually succeeded.

An even more significant resource for alternative information about global political violence, of course, is located through the Internet. A whole body of academic and public discourse emerged during the 1990s which promoted the Internet as a new public sphere for the expression of a new participative and emancipatory democracy (Ess, 1994, Lewis 1998, Lewis & Best, 2002, Negroponte, 1995, Poster, 1995). This idealism has inevitably unravelled somewhat, as the interests of private corporations, government authority and the mainstream media have invaded the Internet, creating new spaces for more culturally ubiquitous forms of mediation and expressive hegemony. Significantly, though, these spaces and representational systems, while seeking to reproduce the hierarchies of information that characterize broadcast media systems, are finding it far more difficult to constrain the effectiveness of alternative textualities. This is due in large part to the flexibility and convergent character of the Net; the same communications infrastructure is available at relatively low cost for broadcast, narrowcast and interactive telephony, including email.

The facility of the Internet, thereby, provides significant opportunities for the production and dissemination of alternative texts. As an intrinsically global matrix, one which is shaped by flows and vectors rather than nodal distributions, the Internet permits a broad interface for writers (producers) and readers. Quite clearly the Internet has been crucial for the organization and co-ordination of worldwide protests against the Iraq invasion and for the dissemination of alternative perspectives, information and news reporting. In particular, independent journalists have been able to present their perspectives through the web system, bypassing the structures and strictures of the American communications authority. Through web logs (blogs) and organized alternative e-journals such as *Znet* and the *Guardian Online*, alternative perspectives and information have been produced and globally distributed. The uncropped photograph of the Basrah girl discussed above was globally distributed through the Net, thereby making its way into alternative newspapers and educational institutions.

For many people in the west, the Internet has provided direct access to al-Jazeera and other Arabic news sources. It has become a central forum for debate among numerous Muslim communities which are being directly affected by the current phase of global political violence. As Karim Karim (2000a) points out, the Internet has become a critical communications tool for these communities, belying the idea that the Middle East and the Muslim faith are somehow intransigently opposed to modernization processes and modern technology. Muslims across the world who are being vilified by the cultural divide arguments, especially as they were being constructed in the United States, are able to discuss important aspects of policy, as well as theological issues pertaining to terrorism and counter-terrorism. The Net, in these terms, is a critical part of the more encouraging dimensions of globalization.

On the other side, the Internet is also part of the more pernicious dimensions of global communications. In the war of terror the Internet is a widely used facility for the dissemination of propaganda, hatred and incitements to violence. As we have noted in our discussion of the war of vision (Chapter 3), the oracular technologies that have integrated themselves throughout the digital telecommunications system have enabled new forms of surveillance and social management which clearly impinge on citizens' rights. In their pursuit of publicity and recruits, militant Islamic organizations use the Internet to disseminate their values and horror. The kidnapping and horrific execution of foreign workers in Iraq constitute perhaps the most spectacular example of this strategy. The Internet thus becomes a facility for the propagation of language wars that are shaped through political violence and a relentless trajectory of terror. Perhaps this shouldn't surprise us since the Internet was originally conceived as a communications weapon, a military facility clearly imbued with the violent potential of the democratic state. Its appropriation by the proponents of knowledge, humanism and 'gift culture' replicates the contentions and contentiousness of the wider political and cultural spheres.

Even so, the Internet does not itself inflict direct physical violence; it is merely a facility for engaging in the inevitability of language war. And indeed if we might, in a utopian sense, restrict conflict to language, where various perspectives on any issue may be expressed and processed, if not actually reconciled, then the Internet might be an ideal forum for a 'democratic' mediasphere. But of course the crisis of violence emanating from the Middle East is far more evolved than this participative ideal would like. The democracy that is being brought into Iraq – and Afghanistan for that matter – has been forged out of a deep history of exploitation, retribution and violence. The communications system that supports and directs this democracy is based, paradoxically, on strategies and principles of the destabilization of trust and certainty. With very little left to believe, it is hardly surprising that the Iraqi people seek no greater certainty than to be left to their own devices and destiny. While the US authorities seek to manipulate the information system and the mediasphere, they are by the very project of destabilization condemning them to volatility and disorder. It is difficult to believe that such an unstable system of mediated democracy could achieve anything like the success propagated by the US administration and its military.

CONCLUSIONS

1. The principal purpose of the invasion of Iraq was to secure American supplies of oil and hence US global primacy.
2. This purpose was supplemented by others, including the installation of American values in Iraq and other parts of the Middle East. In particular, the imposition of economic capitalism and 'democracy' will have the most far-reaching and lasting effects in the region. These values, while regarded by the invaders as worthwhile in themselves, will provide the basis for the security and management of oil resources.
3. It is almost certain that the invading authorities were aware that Iraq's WMD programme had been dismantled following the 1990–91 Gulf War. The discourse of WMD threat was appended to the war on terror in order to galvanize public support for the invasion.
4. The Bush administration deploys the discourses of freedom and democracy as a justification for its extra-territorial or imperialist

ambitions. While dismissing the United Nations co-operative model, the US appears to be seeking to establish a form of world government over which it alone presides.

5. Democracy is invoked as the 'natural' mode of nation-state governance by the US administration. However, democracy, which is designed to resolve difference through peaceful means, actually obfuscates its own intrinsic violence. In particular, the relationship between the state and citizen has been forged out of a contingency of violence. Through the processes of representation, writing culture has merely deferred or parenthesized this contingency of violence for the protection of middle-class and capitalist interests.

6. In a broadcast democracy the limits of representation have become even more acute and volatile.

7. The Anglophonic governments within the Coalition of the Willing have sought to exert control over the mediasphere and broadcast representation. In particular, they have sought to convince the polis that democracy is not violent and the invasion of Iraq is justified.

8. Various strategies have been employed by these governments and their military. These include the embedding of journalists, the negation of alternative perspectives, the creation of stage sets and the camouflage of death.

9. Alternative perspectives inevitably emerge, both from the confusion of deception and through the active engagement of global citizens. Al-Jazeera and Internet 'bloggers' have produced and globally distributed significant opposing perspectives in the language wars of the Iraq invasion.

5
Globalizing Jihad:
The Bali Bombings at the End of Paradise

OCTOBER 12 AND GLOBAL JIHAD

On October 12, 2002, separate bombs exploded in Paddy's Bar and the Sari Club, two popular nightclubs in Bali's tourist district. The bombs killed around 200 people, mostly young tourists from Australia, the UK and the US. To the rejoicing of the perpetrators, the bombs ignited the nightclubs' propylene gas bottles and cane-grass walls, creating a massive fire, which quickly engulfed the walls and lightweight timber framing. Before many people could escape, the roofs collapsed, crushing some and inflicting terrible burns on others. Many of those who perished had suffered extensive, third-degree burns or scorched lungs, which made it impossible to breathe. This was neither an isolated nor a spontaneous assault; the members of Jamaah Islamiyah who carried out the attacks had been planning it for many months. Like the twin towers, in fact, the nightclubs were deliberately targeted both for their publicity and symbolic value: militant Islam and jihad were engaging very directly in a battle against the excesses of western globalization, moral degradation, and the 'soul' and territory of Indonesia.

Our focus is drawn to the terrorist activities in Bali for a range of reasons. First, Indonesia is the most populous Muslim nation in the world and marks the outward spread of radical and revolutionary Islam. The influence of organizations like al-Qa'ida on the ideologies and strategies of South-East Asian Islamic groups is evident in many of the attacks in the region. Second, these groups, such as Jamaah Islamiyah and Laskar Jihad, are in many ways reacting to the local conditions and broader processes of globalization and modernization, which have been discussed in previous chapters. The tourism industry in Bali, in particular, evinces those aspects of globalization which are transforming the cultural territories of the world. Bali, in fact, is somewhat unique as an 'eastern' tourist destination, as it is a Hindu cultural enclave inside a predominantly Muslim nation. Moreover, its popularity with western tourists and its relative geographical proximity to Australia have contributed to increasing levels of cultural exchange, hybridization and contiguity, which challenge the conventional imaginary of an east–west divide. Radical Islam constitutes a reaction and a mode of direct opposition to the global 'mediascape', which propagates these spaces for the pleasure of the First World imaginary.

Third, Bali and Indonesia represent a clear case study in the language wars of civil society and democratization. The bombings were, as much as anything else, a manifestation of the discursive contentions which are issuing from the country's transformation to a modern, civil society. Out of the viciousness of the New Order regime, this transformation is bringing the discourses of modernization into direct conflict with traditions and a pre-modern imaginary that seeks to uphold community values and belief systems. As in the Middle East, Bosnia, Afghanistan and Chechnya, these clashes and contiguities are bringing the society into deep crisis. The rise of Islamicism, therefore, is as much associated with the context of these specific local and national transformations, as with the broader global ambit.

Indeed, the collapse in 1965–66 of President Sukarno's fragile civil state of Indonesia ushered in the repressive military New Order regime of General Suharto. Around a million people were killed during military purges which removed all semblance of communist or civil opposition, as well as Sukarno's nascent vision of an equitable, pluralist, modern society. With seemingly intractable poverty levels of around 16 per cent, massive international debt, and a protracted history of colonial exploitation, Indonesia has been highly susceptible to social and political instability; this instability has been further exacerbated by the conflation of an extraordinary cultural diversity (17,000 islands, 300 ethnic groups, 250 languages) and the pre-eminence of the Muslim-Javanese. Suharto's primary governmental strategy during his presidency (1966–98) was to crush all opposition, repress freedom of speech, limit political assembly and labour rights, and maintain power through the support of a plutocracy of the military elite. As *Time* magazine reported after Suharto's forced resignation in 1998, the President's family had amassed around fifteen billion US dollars during a career that facilitated the unrestrained plunder of the Indonesian economy, its workers and people. Thus, Suharto's internal security agencies, which pervasively surveilled and eliminated all modes of social and political contention, were supported by an equally complex system of economic patronage, nepotism, commission and corruption. As numerous commentators have noted, Indonesia's efforts to modernize were continually frustrated by this system and the rigid social structures that were designed to protect the interests of the military elite.

For all its significant deficiencies, however, the Suharto government found favour with US authorities, since it was both anti-communist and secular. The latter quality, in particular, has become increasingly important since the collapse of international communism and the rise of Islamic radicalism. As the most populous Muslim state in the world, Indonesia carries significant potential for radical Islam and the international jihadists. Suharto's strict enforcement of the nationalist pluralism enshrined in Pancasila, the Indonesian constitution, seems effectively to have contained the potential of Islamic radicalism to disrupt the ideal of national unity, security and order. On the other hand, Suharto's repressive regime may have actually contributed to the simmering of discontent, which seems inevitable in a country with such high poverty levels and a government which habitually steals from its people.

Even so, and despite an appalling record of human rights abuses, economic mismanagement and corruption, Suharto maintained a substantial level of international sponsorship and support – at least until the severe weaknesses of the economy and the modernization programme were exposed by the Asian monetary crisis in the mid 1990s. Like President Marcos in the Philippines, Suharto ultimately capitulated to old age and the powerful intersection of opposition forces – students, liberal politicians and activists, Islamicists and a middle class whose wealth had been dramatically diminished by the monetary crisis. The US, Australia and a range of international financial and donor organizations supported the opposition groups' call for a change in direction and the restoration of democratic processes. The first free election, held in 1999, marked a significant move toward the formation of a modern state and civil society. However, the Wahid and Megawati presidencies struggled to institute a programme of effective social and economic reform which might ameliorate the continuing crises and insecurities that have beset the nation.

In many respects, the Bali bombings were a symptom of these problems. The international jihad, however, has appended itself to these broader issues, implicating the east–west divide in the processes of democratization, modernization and globalization. The aim of this chapter is to situate the bombings within the general context of global terror, most particularly as the Islamic jihad confronts the national aspirations of civil society and the cultural economy of global tourism. The chapter also focuses on the severe social and economic impact of the bombings and the processes by which the Balinese and Indonesian communities are seeking to reconcile themselves and recover from the tragedy. In particular, we will interrogate the strategy of a tourism-led recovery which seeks very directly to restore Bali's status as a safe destination for western tourists seeking an authentic experience of the exotic east.

JAMAAH ISLAMIYAH

It is generally thought that al-Qa'ida is a more or less amorphous organization which is neither cohesively structured nor governed. Most commentators now agree that it is built around ideologies or perspectives which are shared through various global 'cells'. Alan Cullison (2004) has argued that even around the eve of 9/11 the primary cell, which was being housed in Taliban Afghanistan under the leadership of Osama bin Laden, was still rent by critical debates about strategy and principles. Bin Laden, it appears, was very enthusiastic about the idea of attacking 'distant' enemies, while others in the group wanted to attack and overthrow Arabic regimes that repressed Muslim people and denied the legal primacy of Islam. According to Cullison, bin Laden won the day, as he believed the organization needed a significant publicity boost in order to attract more funding and recruits. With the viability and effectiveness of the organization under pressure, the 'big job' as it was eventually called would provide an impetus for the organization's global jihad. The death of women and children was also, apparently, a significant matter of contention, though in the end it was felt that the greater good of God would prevail over the misfortune of inglorious casualties.

Muslim scholars and theologians across the globe have strongly rejected the radical Islamicist interpretation of jihad. The notion of a 'struggle for the good of God' has been broadly adapted by Sayyid Qutb and later Islamicists to mean a war of faith by which the entire world would be conquered by 'Islam' (see Chapter 2). In more recent times, this notion of a holy war was particularly inspiring for many of the Muslim warriors fighting against the Russians in Afghanistan. Bin Laden and many other key members of al-Qa'ida and the Taliban shared their ideological and theological views during the campaign and ultimate victory.

A number of the foundation members of the South-East Asian Islamic group Jamaah Islamiyah (JI) were also engaged in the Afghanistan campaign; clearly, their views on jihad were strongly influenced by al-Qa'ida and the horrors of this warfare. While initially focusing on Christian groups and other non-Muslims in the region, JI made its most spectacular contribution to the global jihad with the bombings on the Indonesian island of Bali. However, as the International Crisis Group report of December 2002 indicates, JI had been active across the region since around 1999. Led by Indonesian nationals and organized loosely around more or less autonomous cells, JI has been linked to a series of deadly attacks in Malaysia, the Philippines and Indonesia. In the Christmas Eve attacks of 2000, for example, JI bombed churches and attacked priests across eleven Indonesian cities in six separate provinces. These attacks indicated a reasonably high level of organization and co-ordination across a wide area of the country.

The ICG report confirms much of the recent intelligence information on JI, most particularly the belief that Islamic high schools and boarding schools (*pesantren*) are the central platforms for the promotion of radical Islamic ideology and the training of young JI operatives. The report names Abdullah Sungkar and Abu Bakar Ba'asyir (Bashir) as the co-founders of Pondok Ngruki, a *pesantren* in Central Java which appears to be a primary hub for Jamaah strategists. These strategists are mostly Indonesian nationals who fought in Afghanistan against the Russians, but who now reside primarily in Malaysia. Beneath this loosely organized leadership, a second tier of trusted foot soldiers is responsible for managing operations, delivering money and co-opting local operatives. This last group is usually comprised of young men from the local *pesantren*; they are the ones at most risk of arrest, injury and death in the operations. As with other Islamic militant groups, the suicide bombers are largely drawn from this low skill, lowly educated group of single young men.

While there are broad speculations about the primary motivation of Jamaah Islamiyah, it is clear from evidence presented at various Jamaah trials that the operatives' motives combine political, social and religious interests. A deep faith in Muslim values and the strict interpretation of holy law is combined with a strong sense of social justice which includes the repudiation of all non-Islamic political power (Abuza, 2003). The operatives have adopted the ideology of anti-Americanism which is frequently articulated as anti-Christendom and pro-Islamicism. The massacres of Muslims by Christians in

Maluku, North Maluku and Poso seem to have been used as a primary motivation for many of the earlier attacks on Christians in Indonesia. The recruitment and training of general operatives seem also to have been associated with discussions and videos on the Maluku and Poso killings. However, the trials of Amrozi and other Bali bombing perpetrators indicated a distinct shift in JI towards a strategy which more clearly accords with the motives of Osama bin Laden and the al-Qa'ida network. While not surrendering the strategy of killing Indonesian Christians, the organization appears to have embraced the notion of jihad against America and its allies – especially the UK and Australia. Just as al-Qa'ida turned from Arabic to international targets, JI has turned from Indonesian Christians to the 'excesses' of international tourism.

Amrozi states specifically that he developed a deep hatred for Australians and Americans while working as a construction labourer in Malaysia (Anggraeni, 2003: 129–31). Having studied at one of Bakar Ba'asyir's *pesantrens* in Indonesia, Amrozi appears to have embedded this hatred into his own religiosity and a desire to subvert the wrongs he observed in social life. As an Indonesian villager who was forced to work for pitifully low wages constructing buildings that are part of the megalith of economic and cultural globalization, Amrozi's biography appears to personify the transformation of JI itself. While bin Laden experienced an awakening to American global hegemony during the US occupation of Saudi Arabia in the first Gulf War, Amrozi must have seen the unrestrained growth and building boom in Malaysia as a sign of profound global inequity.

In fact, we can observe very clearly that the engagement of Jamaah Islamiyah into the global jihad becomes an almost epiphanal event, as the key tacticians come to acknowledge the significance of globalization. The 'success' of the 9/11 attacks, perhaps, convinced the Bali bombers that bin Laden's distant enemies strategy was an effective publicity, retributive and recruitment tool. Just as bin Laden had encouraged an attack on America as a mechanism for promoting the cause of radical Islam, the Bali strategists seem to have believed that a direct assault on tourists would dramatically advance the cause of global jihad. As we have noted, Jean Baudrillard claims that it is the forces of globalization which are necessarily inciting their own opposition. Tourism as a central conduit of globalization is clearly implicated in the bombings and their percussive economic and cultural effects.

PARADISE DEFILED

A number of anthropologists interested in discourse and social con-
structionism have defined the history of Bali in terms of an 'imagined
community' (Anderson, 1991, Hamilton, 1990) and 'created paradise'
(Vickers, 1990, also Lewis, 1995, Connor & Vickers, 2003). Adrian
Vickers argues, in particular, that with the emergence of European
tourism in the late nineteenth and early twentieth centuries, Bali was
promoted as a spiritual and sensual idyll, a site in which the 'authentic
Orient' could be genuinely experienced. The Dutch colonists, for
example, retreated from the equatorial climate and squalid urbanism
of Jakarta to the beautiful beaches, temperate mountain villages
and Hindu ambience of Bali. From the early 1930s the island of
Bali became a favoured destination for Dutch and other western
writers and artists. Its rather unique version of ancient Vedic culture,
hybridized through local animism and long periods of isolation,
was also very attractive to anthropologists like Margaret Mead and
Clifford Geertz. Indonesian President Sukarno, whose mother was
Balinese, saw the island as a unique window into the original culture
of the archipelago; similarly entranced by the island, India's President
Nehru described it as the 'morning of the world'.

During the 1960s and 1970s, with the emergence of relatively
cheap international air travel and mass tourism, the island became
popular with young travellers who were seeking some alternative
spirituality and non-western aesthetic (Hamilton, 1990). Following
the generation of painters like Walter Spies and Donald Friend,
young artists came to Ubud to work and share in the crafts and
insights of their Balinese mentors. Popular Hollywood films such as
Road to Bali (Walker, 1952) and *Honeymoon in Bali* (Griffith, 1939)
contributed to the sense of mystique, providing a basis for the works
of a new generation of film-makers including John Darling and Albie
Falzon. Darling's films extended the anthropological vision of Mead
and Geertz, presenting the island people as a genuinely beautiful
and creatively distinct social and cultural group. Falzon's 1972 surf
movie, *Morning of the Earth* (see Lewis, 2002c), presented a particularly
idealized image of the island and its promise of surfing perfection.

Both the Dutch and Sukarno governments were well aware of
the cultural and economic value of this constructed paradise.
But the Suharto regime developed a far more aggressive strategy
of development and marketing for the promotion of Bali as an
international tourist destination. From the 1990s, tourism-based

development on the island accelerated enormously as the Suharto family and its allies sought to profit from the island's integration into the global tourist economy. At the time of the bombings, tourism was Indonesia's second highest export earner after oil; by far the greatest majority of tourism income was generated out of Bali. It is fairly accurate to suggest that, along with oil and international aid, the Indonesian economy had become substantially dependent on Balinese tourism.

For the Balinese themselves, of course, this rapid 'modernization' was ambiguous, bringing opportunities for employment and financial advancement but also significant cultural, social and environmental disruption. By the turn of the millennium, Bali was receiving an average of 140,000 international tourists a month, along with increasing numbers of local tourists. As a United Nations Development Program report (2003) indicates, tourism had contributed significantly to a substantial reduction in poverty rates on the island – around 4 per cent as compared with a 16 per cent Indonesian average (UNDP, 2003: i). Even so, the high level of local and international investment, especially around Ubud, Sanur, Kuta and Denpasar, has significantly impacted on the cultural and physical integrity of the 'tourism triangle', creating high levels of social dislocation, internal migration, inter-ethnic tension and increased levels of crime (Pastika, cited in Lewis, B. & Lewis, J., 2004). The social and physical environment of Kuta, in particular, has been transformed into a global cosmopolis in which the ideology of hedonism and recreational pleasure predominates. The identity of the Balinese has become enmeshed in the services they perform and the clients they serve. While the traditional *adat* (religious rituals and practices) remains a powerful force in Balinese culture it is being severely strained by tourism development and global integration (Lewis, B. & Lewis, J., 2004, UNDP, 2003). The Balinese themselves, while maintaining strong social and community links with their villages and *adat* practices, are being swept into a cultural and economic matrix over which they appear to have little direct control.

While a number of commentators have suggested that the Balinese retain a deep integrity which protects them from the excesses of development (Darling, 2002), there is also a very strong suggestion that the Balinese have been subsumed by a development which perpetually grounds itself in economic discourse (see Harris, 2001). Indeed, as local activist Viebeke Lengkong argues, the Balinese have assumed the role of 'houseboy' or 'sweeper' in the new economy (cited in Lewis, B. & Lewis, J., 2004). In a tourism industry that is dominated by international and Jakartan–Chinese investors, the ranks of senior and middle management have been largely filled by non-Balinese.

This view is confirmed, at least in part, by Gordon MacRae (2003), who believes that the Balinese participation in global capitalism through tourism supplements an intrinsic cultural predisposition to silence, obedience and 'apoliticism'. In particular, the Balinese themselves, especially in the post-bombing period, have actively promoted a notion of social and political 'harmony', which in many respects constitutes another variation of the 'created paradise' discourse. At a cosmological level, this harmony is articulated in terms of the Hindu concept of *rwa bhineda* or the 'two in one' principle (see Connor and Vickers, 2003). According to this principle, good and evil are locked in a perpetual battle, and it is the task of mortals to limit the damage that might issue from the excesses of evil doing. The *adat* is largely constructed around the maintenance of this balance – this conflictual harmony. In accommodating the extraordinary transformations of their social and cultural environments, especially over the past two decades, the Balinese have adapted the *rwa* principle, integrating it into the everyday demands of economy and survival. The projection of a harmonious island, as the brochures remind us, is critical to the imagining of Bali as an international tourist destination.

Bali's transition to a civil society, most particularly in the post-bombing environment, seems captured, in fact, by this discourse of harmony and the imperatives of a tourism-led recovery. According to MacRae, the combination of a deep cultural reverence for the Hindu rituals of the *adat* and the active production of a commodified social harmony disinclines the Balinese to civic and political debate. While Vickers (2003) argues that this imagining distorts the underlying realities of a complex and often belligerent Bali, MacRae claims that the constituted harmony itself is contributing to the formation of a new political reality. At the level of civic action, this politics consolidates older social hierarchies, intertwining them with newer forms of discrimination and inequality; the traditional 'silence', by which the Balinese supposedly revere order and harmony, is thus translated into the context of a truncated and passive civic process. In much the same way as the European class system is reworked by modernism into a form of what Gramsci calls hegemony (multiple 'negotiated' hierarchical systems of domination), the Hindu caste system provides a basis for new modes of compliance and hierarchy in a modernizing Bali.

Thus, the *adat* is being mobilized by economic elites and by the Balinese themselves in order to support a hierarchical social infrastructure. Even in a post-Suharto context, the combination of the *adat* and the economic imperatives of tourism contributes to a civic community in which authority is delegated upward and problems are subsumed within a culture that values and rewards silence and compliance (Reuter, 2003). According to this perspective, the confluence of tradition and the tourist economic imperatives of globalization tends to defer significant issues of inequality, poverty, the environment and social management. While we will discuss a number of these issues later in the chapter, it is worth noting that the key political forums on the island, including the traditional village councils or *banjars* and the nine district governments, seem disinclined to address these critical issues in any direct or forceful way. This is particularly problematic since most of these issues are deeply embedded in tourism and tourism development, which many believe to be the economic life-source of the island (Lewis, B. & Lewis, J., 2004).

The bombings themselves have been explained by many Balinese in terms of cosmological imbalance, requiring the reassertion of the *adat* and the release of the *rwa bhineda* from the cloying effects of modernization. Referred to euphemistically as 'the tragedy', the bombings have generated a new set of appeasement rituals within the *adat*. For MacRae, however, this discourse of harmony is generating a profound apoliticism which exposes the Balinese to the most negative and exploitative effects of globalization and modernization. Global tourism has deprived the Balinese of their own capacity for self-determination. The *adat* further weakens the force and potential of social reform, as it encourages an acquiescent theologism which consistently draws the Balinese away from political action toward the appeasement of the gods.

CLASH OF IMAGININGS: GLOBAL AND NATIONAL CONTEXT

As we have indicated above, Bali has become a significant feature for the global tourist itinerary. By and large, this has taken place through a reshaping of the western imaginary. Postcolonial and Orientalist theory (see Said, 1978, 1993) has suggested that this cultural shaping is largely an exercise of imperialist and political appropriation: the west defines itself in terms of an eastern 'otherness' which it then absorbs into its own mode of cultural superiority. It is this sense of superiority which provides the ethical basis for exploitation and appropriation. Historically, Said notes, Orientalism has produced various forms of imagining, including 'the mystical East', a play-space for sexual, intellectual and poetic adventurism, and 'the primitive East', a place of irrational resistance, heathenism and brutality. This latter space, in particular, provides justification for the imposition of the civilizing effects of empire, administration and economic integration.

Paradoxically, this Orientalist theory, as we have noted in Chapter 2 (see also Lewis, 1995), tends to reconfirm the cultural ontologies it is aiming to deconstruct. In seeking to counter the neoconservative essentialism of arguments like Samuel Huntington's 'clash of civilizations', a good deal of postcolonial and Orientalist analysis generates a resistant identity for the subjugated Asian. Despite Said's intention, his work tends to surround his oppressed subjects with a discourse of resistance which is formed by the essentialization of the western oppressors. Moreover, the ontology of an east–west divide, which is an important aspect of western neoconservative responses to 9/11 and the war of terror, is also adapted into the more strident discourse of the jihadists generally, and the Jamaah Islamiyah, in particular.

Homi Bhabha (see Chapter 2) suggests that the exchange of power between an 'eastern' and 'western' subject is a far more complex process than the more polemical modes of postcolonial theory and resistance seem to acknowledge. In essence, Bhabha argues that there is a far greater level of interactivity and interdependence in subject exchanges than the self–other thesis appreciates. This is not to say that power is not a feature of these exchanges; it is to suggest rather that the exchange of power is multiply-forming (Lewis, 2002a). At the level of globalization, this argument would confirm the processes of hybridization and adaptation, whereby the categories of dominant and subordinate nations and subjects are disrupted by a cultural exchange which alters the *episteme* of both parties. As has been argued throughout this book, the concept of language wars provides a useful tool for understanding the complexity of these exchanges.

Thus, the integration of Bali into the global tourist economy and culture is being forged through these ambiguities and language wars. In many respects, the thesis here resembles the notion of the *rwa bhineda* as we have outlined it above, and Jean Baudrillard's

Manichean account of globalization – both of which acknowledge the complex progression of positive and negative effects and the improbability of absolute resolution. There is a broad exchange and inter-flow of cultural imaginings sourced through Europe, America, Japan, Java and Australia. As a more or less isolated Hindu enclave within the most populous Muslim nation on earth, Bali has a history of violence and resistance which belies the propagated images of 'harmony' and 'paradise'. However, the successful conjuration of these images has infiltrated the cultural imaginings of many First World tourists, providing a resource for a rethinking of their own nation, culture and subjectivity. The contest between history and a contemporary imaginary leads inevitably to the language wars we have been discussing.

For western tourists, Australians in particular, Bali is part of a cultural geography, a 'thirdspace' as Henri Lefebvre calls it, which operates through at least two distinguishable cultural flows. First, Bali exists as an imaginary land-bridge connecting Australians to the region and the rest of the world. Bali constitutes for many Australians the first interface of global contact which is not merely or exclusively generated by international popular culture: the journey to the extraneous territory of Bali represents a 'reaching out' into the world, as opposed to being 'reached for' through domestic television, movie or music texts sourced primarily from America. For Britons and Americans, Bali – and indeed Australia – also constitutes another land-bridge to an alien South, a space which is vastly removed from the industrialized First World order of the North. Bali is a zone of confluence, a cosmopolis which brings together people from around the world within a 'convivial' Asian context.

This reaching out to Asia or 'the South' also constitutes its own countermove. That is, the reaching out is counterbalanced by an equally forceful movement toward self-interrogation or 'interiority'. The otherness of space provides a cultural resource for self-reflection and the exploration/expression of personal and collective identity. Westerners' imaginative and bodily engagement with the cultural geography of Bali facilitates new forms of self-expression. At this second level, the journey to Bali is inevitably an expression of an overlapping imaginary where the self and the other are sustained by communion, contingency and new modes of cultural contiguity. In Bhabha's schema, the movement into Bali stimulates 'change' and the shifting of identity. The interactions of the cosmopolis provide the cultural resources for reconfiguration and the exploration of new modes of self. This is not merely an experience for the visitor, but is also and inevitably part of the globalizing experiences of the host.

In this sense, Bali is genuinely global and cosmopolitan. The significant presence of Australians, in particular, provides a disarmingly comfortable interface between the Hindu Balinese and the Muslim Javanese who have migrated to the island for work. The beaches, bars, restaurants and nightclubs are themselves hybridities, bringing together culinary and recreational practices that are both familiar and exotic. This familiarity allows the First World visitor to engage in various forms of exotic excess; even their currency and spending power are extravagantly extended by the conditions of a Third World economy. The low-wages and low-cost regime of Bali enables even the most humble First Worlders to enjoy a luxury they could never afford at home. But as much as the Balinese have adjusted and accommodated the reconfiguration of their economy, social practices, culture and territory, the visitors too have modified their subjectivities in order to embrace the conditions and sensibilities of the alien space. This, after all, is the reason they have come to Bali – for the exchange of ideas, customs, clothing and ways of thinking about themselves and their familiar world.

As has already been suggested, however, the cultural contiguities associated with tourism and globalization are also implicated in the formation and sustenance of significant social and political tensions. In many respects, these tensions challenge MacRae's claim that the Balinese are essentially apolitical, since all aspects of their lives have been affected by politics and the multiply flowing exchanges of power. Clearly, the definition of 'politics' applied in this book is far more inclusive than MacRae's, which tends to restrict politics to the conscious act of civic participation and contention; within the framework we are applying, 'apoliticism' is barely possible since power affects all dimensions of social engagement and even silence or capitulation constitutes a political action. As noted at the beginning of this chapter, in fact, the modernization and democratization of Indonesia generally have created a context of substantial social and political instability. Within this context, Bali's specific cultural, economic and environmental conditions have clearly contributed to an intersection of tensions which have manifested themselves through the crisis of the Bali, Marriott Hotel and Australian Embassy bombings. This 'crisis of contiguity' (Lewis, J. & Lewis, B., 2004b) is deeply embedded in the ongoing transitions of globalization.

Thus, the post-Suharto policies of de-militarization and decentralization have created significant opportunities for social and political activism. As part of the transition to civil society, these policies have been designed to reduce the pervasiveness and power of the military, distribute civic authority more broadly through the provinces and districts of Indonesia, and construct a form of 'policing' and social management which would facilitate greater public autonomy and community participation. While the new political space may constitute a forward move for the values of participative democracy, it nevertheless provides opportunities for radicalism, including the violent radicalism of Islamic groups like Jamaah Islamiyah, Islamic Defenders Front and Laskar Jihad. Both the International Crisis Group (2003) and the Australian government (Sherlock, 2002) reports on the Bali bombings suggest very directly that President Megawati's inept management of this space and related security issues – specifically her failure to act against Islamic militants – was a major contributing factor in the Bali attacks. But in broader terms, there is little doubt that the disengagement of the military from direct policing and social management activities in Bali has also permitted the expression of new tensions and forms of social disharmony which are both directly and indirectly related to the bombings (Lewis, B. & Lewis, J., 2004). In particular, a new form of Hindu chauvinism has arisen in Bali, one which both reacts to the rising aggression of Indonesian (and global) Islamicism and appends itself to the very strong sense of cultural and religious isolation on the island. This sense of cultural isolation tends to blame 'outsiders', especially the *orang java* (nominally Javanese), for all political, criminal and social disharmony. Community revenge attacks on outsiders suspected of committing a crime appear to be increasing; with little more than circumstantial evidence, communities have imposed summary executions, including death by stoning, on many Javanese who have been accused of minor theft or various forms of 'loitering with intent'.

The ICG report on the Bali bombings identifies the rise of private security organizations in Bali as a major contributor to inter-ethnic tension and insecurity. As the military was withdrawn from social policing, village-based groups like the *pecalang* asserted a new and sometimes quite menacing authority over communities. As the traditional 'spiritual' protectors of the village, the *pecalang* have evolved into a private security agency, supplementing and in some cases replacing the authority of the police in civil management.

According to a number of commentators, however, the new *pecalang* has been drawn into the vortex of civil authority without substantial organizational planning, training or clearly defined goals. Many of the men who are performing the policing roles in the *pecalang* have no obvious managerial aptitude and are often 'conscripted' out of a context of unemployment or underemployment, as well as a more politically motivated dislike for outsiders.

Beginning with the spontaneous protection of Megawati and the PDI-P congress in 1998, this transformation of the *pecalang* from spiritual to civil management became most evident in April 1999 when the village guards, dressed in traditional garments, attacked the migrant workers and street sellers along the Kuta-Legian beach strip. The burning of the vendor stalls (*kaki lima*) focused international attention on Bali, leading to a significant downturn in tourism for the following year. The economic impact led, in turn, to a more subdued and administrative model for the *pecalang* to follow. New laws formalized the power of the *pecalang* who, following the Bali bombings in October 2002, assumed responsibility for managing and deporting innumerable non-Balinese. In the months that followed the bombings, the *pecalang* also engaged in identity checking and various forms of licensing and tax collection. Members of the Islamic community, migrant workers and other putative 'aliens' were the focus of significant social abuse, exclusion and discrimination, all of which was justified by the authority of the *adat* and the constituted notion of 'Bali harmony': '*Pecalang* are now seen not only as a village security body but also as a pro-active deterrent to increased migration and the eventual marginalisation of the indigenous Balinese' (International Crisis Group, 2003: 7). Rapid population growth, associated with employment opportunities and violence in East Timor and Maluku, placed enormous pressure on the social and community infrastructures of the Balinese capital, Denpasar, and the tourist precinct of Kuta-Legian. Various regulations required non-Balinese to carry official identity cards and pay much higher residency fees and work permit fees than were charged to local Balinese. The prohibitive costs resulting from these efforts to reduce overcrowding in Denpasar forced many migrants to leave the island or simply become invisible residents by going 'underground' and perpetually evading the authorities (Lewis, B. & Lewis, J., 2004).

The bombings of October 2002 served to deepen these tensions. As the *pecalang* and other locally constituted civil gangs became more overtly chauvinistic, the migrants fell further into the background.

Around 30,000 Balinese lost their jobs as an immediate economic effect of the bombings, and a mood of desperation fell across the island. One private security group, the Forum Peduli Denpasar, engaged in a vigorous exercise of surveillance and control:

> After the Kuta bombs, ÏPD also screened returning migrants and newcomers to determine whether they had jobs, valid travel documents and sufficient funds to support themselves during their stay in Bali and whether they could show proof, in the form of a letter from a Balinese friend or employer at the village level, that they were legal residents and workers. These efforts had an immediate impact. The number of residents seeking identity cards rose by 800 per cent, and between 12 October and early December 2002, over 8,000 non-Balinese migrants were sent home to Java. (International Crisis Group, 2003: 10)

It is impossible to say how many non-Balinese were dislocated as a result of the bombing, as many of the migrants and drifters remained *personae non gratae*. What is clear, however, is that the long-standing tensions between the Balinese and non-Balinese Indonesians remain simmering beneath the surface of a constituted Bali harmony. The expulsion of ICH Indonesian head, Sidney Jones, and the repudiation of the ICG report on the emergent system of private security and surveillance in Bali, exposed considerable anxiety within the Indonesian hierarchy about the economy, social cohesion and any form of criticism that might affect the tourism-led recovery in Bali. The propagated image of security and harmony in Bali, while understandable, may distract the Balinese from the substantial issues and problems the community is facing – most particularly in terms of the resurgent processes of modernization and globalization.

THE CRISIS OF CONTIGUITY

As we have noted, MacRae and others claim that the Balinese commitment to the *adat* and to the propagated tourist-based discourse of harmony creates a mode of silence which deflects serious political engagement. Our own empirical work in Bali (Lewis, B. & Lewis, J., 2004) illustrates that the move to a civil society model in Bali is at best uneven, reflecting the problematics of an adapted European democratic discourse, as much as the specificities of Balinese and Indonesian political conditions. But we would also claim that the *adat* is itself a highly political discourse, especially as it intersects with the language of global tourism. This is not apoliticism, but a serious form of cultural politics which ultimately espouses the values of cultural integrity and especially the ideology of Vedic Balinese community and lifestyle. As much as this integrity is threatened by the contiguity of Balinese and western subjectivities and the effects of modernization, it is also threatened by deep anxieties over the overwhelming presence of Muslim cultures and peoples, and the force of Javanese-dominated political and military order. The expressivity of Bali–Hindu rituals and values is both a mode of self-assertion and identity-building, and a manifestation of profound social and cultural insecurity. The Bali harmony discourse and the *adat* may be regarded as part of the language of resistance, especially as Bali confronts the overwhelming force of globalization – including the globalization of political violence and terror which international tourists (indirectly) and Jamaah Islamiyah (directly) have brought into their midst.

The politics of the *adat*, in particular, are central to the tensions surrounding the bombing and to the mechanisms by which the Balinese are seeking to overcome the crisis. In many respects, the *adat* represents the crisis of cultural contiguity – and the broad issues of transformation, language wars and power – which has been a central feature of Balinese history. In this sense the *adat* has functioned as a cultural shield, a mode of resistance against the external threat posed by centuries of Javanese–Muslim propinquity, regional wars, Dutch colonialism and more recent effects of modernization–globalization. The very famous *puputan* of 1906, where the Balinese nobility and priests led nearly 4,000 islanders to their certain deaths in a final gesture of resistance to Dutch colonial conquest, invokes the powerful cultural politics of the *adat*. The absorption of Bali into the colony and ultimately the nation of Indonesia has never entirely expunged the deep ontology of Balinese difference, most especially as it is invoked by the Balinese themselves.

To this extent, there is a subtle but unmistakable dissonance between the Balinese *adat*, and the overarching authority of the Javanese-dominated government. When, during the 1999 presidential elections, the head of the United Development Party, A. M. Saefuddin, denounced Megawati Soekarnoputri's candidature because she was both 'a woman' and 'a Hindu', the serious limits of Indonesian pluralism were exposed. While Megawati's actual religious status remains ambiguous, the Balinese expressed the primacy of their loyalty to the *adat* over civil politics by staging a protest against Saefuddin, which brought together supporters of the different political parties in a show of solidarity; this solidarity, however, could not disguise the force of ethnic difference upon which it was based. Thus, even as it is enshrined in the constitution, Pancasila, and was at times brutally enforced by the Suharto government, Indonesian pluralism has never been able to expunge the ongoing ethnic and religious tensions that have manifested themselves throughout the postcolonial period. As Prayudi has noted in his study of the reporting of ethnic tensions during the New Order period, Suharto's strict controls on the media, which were designed to give the impression of social order and harmony, never fully obscured the violence that was perpetually simmering in ethnically mixed areas of Indonesia (Prayudi, 2004).

The *adat*, therefore, becomes a central feature of the Balinese mode of ethnic and cultural self-assertion and resistance against the dominating force of Javanese hegemony. Yet, as we have noted several times in this book, the ontology of self-ascribed difference may move politically from a mode of resistance to a mode of domination. Especially where the difference is grounded in some greater cosmological force, the move to a fixed signifier – identity, culture, community – appears to generate new and 'grounded' modes of exclusionism, segregation and threat toward outsiders. This appears to be what is happening in Bali where the sense of cultural isolation within a Muslim-dominated national structure is translated into a new hegemony against minorities who enter the isolation precinct. The Hindu–Balinese move, that is, from being a minority in the national corpus to become a majority within their own regional and sovereign imaginary. As we have noted, the *adat*, in fact, rallies the Balinese against Muslim (and Christian) transmigrants, who are frequently regarded by the civil government, the *pecalang* and community members as a critical threat to economy, law and security (Lewis, B. & Lewis, J., 2004).

General Made Pastika, the Balinese Chief of Police and head of the Bali bombing investigation team, argues that the bombings were underscored by a criminal intensity that is being generated by the worst excesses of globalization and modernization. The social disharmony that produces killers like Amrozi, the General claims, is spiritually derived. For Pastika, the bombings are a manifestation of a disharmony created by compromises to religious devotion: a greater level of religious observance would restore the *rwa bhineda* to balance. The presence of Javanese prostitutes and the transgression of traditional *adat* values, especially in rural villages, are considered to be compromising the moral integrity of the Balinese.

Pastika's view is shared by many Balinese, who believe that the island's rapid development has disrupted the integrity of the *adat*. The cleansing ceremonies that were arranged through *banjar* (community council) leaders and priests after the bombings were designed to restore harmony. Thus, the discourse of harmony, which is frequently attached to the *adat* and which has been central to the marketing strategy of the post-bombing tourism recovery, is critically woven into the fabric of community and cultural politics. From the highest level of national government through to the beach sellers in Kuta, the integrity of the *adat* and its cosmologically referenced harmony has been the principal focus of restoration and recovery. Yet, even as the *adat* is espoused by senior representatives of the emergent civil society, Pastika included, the underlying paradox of the *adat* as a mode of resistance and domination is never quite explicated, most particularly as it confronts the forcefield of Indonesian pluralism and the Pancasila. As Pastika and others promote the *adat* as the central and unifying ideology of Balinese society, there is an implied sense of cultural and religious primacy, one which risks, and at times actively promotes, the exclusion and marginalization of all other ethnic and cultural groups. The *adat*, in effect, constitutes a resistance–domination oscillation for the Hindu-Balinese. The ethnic violence which was broadly predicted after the bombings didn't eventuate in any substantial sense because the oscillation drew back to a propagated harmony and pluralism which would underpin the tourism-led economic recovery upon which the Balinese lifestyle has become so dependent. Another serious economic or social crisis, we believe, could see these tensions erupt into bloody violence (Lewis, J. & Lewis, B., 2004b).

A number of other community members have seen the *adat* as a serious impediment to the modernization and transformation of the Balinese people themselves. Viebeke, who was instrumental in negotiating the return of the Kuta beach to community governance, believes that the *adat* occupies excessive importance, and consumes excessive time, in the Balinese community. Women and men demonstrate their unreliability as modern workers as they are frequently required to participate in *adat* ceremonies and other devotions. Along with the daily libations, these frequent disruptions compromise the work rhythms required to run a successful business. The low level of business ownership and managerial participation by the Balinese, as we have indicated above, may also be associated with the *adat* commitments. In this sense, the *adat* constitutes a limit to Balinese participation in the economic and governmental bases of liberal democracy.

Viebeke claims, further, that the exclusion of talented women from the *banjar* and other significant decision-making civic institutions, while satisfying the demands of the *adat*'s patriarchal order, excludes valuable intellectual resources from effective governance. Even as the *banjar* becomes conscripted into the broadening ambit of civil participation, the *adat* traditions seem to be resisting the political evolutions which accompanied European modernization. A number of commentators have suggested that the seemingly endemic poverty of Bali's eastern and outer district, and the very serious environmental problems associated with rapid tourism development, are at least in part due to the compliant tenor of the *adat* and the amount of time and moral energy it occupies in the lives of ordinary Balinese.

Of course, and as we have noted, modernization, development and globalization do not, of themselves, produce social equality and civil participation, even though these things are inscribed in the ideals of liberal democracy. Indeed, the ambiguity of the *adat* is further evinced in its invocations against the excesses of capitalist materialism and the hierarchies that are constituted through hyperbolic individualism. For Pastika, Viebeke and other community leaders, the spectacular inadequacies of western cultures emerge from this excessive individualism and a material greed which leads westerners into all manner of unattractive and dissolute behaviours. To this extent, the *adat* also has parallels in the ideology of radical Islamicism. Even so, the *adat* encourages a spiritual reflection which seeks to negate the harm created by materialist hedonism and an excessive focus on the sensate pleasures of the body. Like Islamicism, the *adat* demands absolute reverence and fidelity to meticulous religious practices and rituals which protect the spirit from obsessive secularism.

On the other side of this paradox, however, the *adat* and the Vedic mythology have been essential features of Bali's modernization and cultural transformations. While western film-makers, writers and scholars have sought to represent the Balinese culture as a spiritually refined contrast to western materialism, Bali's art, dance, temples, rituals and music have all been commodified for mass tourist consumerism. As we have noted, the dichotomy that generated the east–west difference has been modulated by global cultural contiguities, creating new hybrid spaces which clearly compromise the propagated discursive boundaries of the divide. As Stuart Hall has so aptly described it, significant Difference becomes consumable difference in the 'global postmodern'. The bombings themselves exposed the level of this disruption, as the militants identified the Balinese themselves with the unpalatable practices of western materialist hedonism and the western imaginary. For the bombers, Bali had become a mistress to western decadence and to the violence of its international hegemony. Even the Balinese, upon whose homeland the JI attacks were perpetrated, came to recognize that their culture and lifestyle had become integrated with, if not tainted by, western tourism, ideas, values, practices and culture. Bali had become a feature in the western global mediascape, the western global imaginary.

The bombings, thereby, exposed the degree to which this contiguity had been effected. Nearly 190 Australians, 60 Britons and 20 Americans were killed; Balinese, Japanese, Javanese, Brazilians and Germans were also among the dead. As with the twin towers, this was a cosmopolis of death. The cleansing rituals that had been sponsored by government, tourism interests and the local *banjar* sought to restore the *adat* to its pure form and the *rwa bhineda* to balance: the ultimate aim of the rituals was to appease the evil that seemed to be hatching out across the tourist precinct. But while this cosmological work was being dutifully undertaken, there seemed to be no relief from the complexities and ambiguities of the modernization and globalization processes themselves. The immediate focus of the recovery was the restoration of this trajectory; even the cleansing rituals were sponsored by private businesses and interests. In fact, the *adat* and the Bali harmony discourse became the central platform for a US $4m tourism campaign. Businessmen like Kadek and Gede Wiranatha, who were making considerable fortunes out of the tourism industry, were very quick to finance tourism recovery projects, including those that used the *adat* as a central feature of cleansing rituals, international media releases and market promotion. As the owner of one of the nightclubs attacked in 2002 and a primary shareholder in the new, Bali-based international airline, Air Paradise, Kadek Wiranatha was committed to the rapid restoration of tourism. In this context, rather than being a restraint on commodification, materialism and modernization, the *adat* was used in the cultural politics of capitalist expansionism and the revivification of hierarchical social order.

THE BOMBINGS: MEDIA AND POLITICAL DISCOURSES

There is a frightening synergy in the timing of the Bali bombings. Occurring on 10/12, a little over a year after 9/11, the attacks on Paddy's Bar and the Sari Club came between the American-led invasions of Afghanistan and Iraq. At the time of the bombings, the US and its principal Coalition allies, the UK and Australia, were engaged in the advanced stages of a propaganda campaign that was designed to convince their respective citizens of the legitimacy of a pre-emptive strike on Iraq. While peace protestors, who were marshalling their own forces against the proposed invasion, regarded the bombings as retribution for Afghanistan and the proposed invasion of Iraq, the leaders of the Coalition nations saw them as another manifestation of brutal and mindless terrorism. For Australian protestors, in particular, the high number of their nationals killed in the bombings represented the profound threat posed by their government's unswerving fidelity to US security policy. According to protestors, as Australia appended itself more fully to America's aggressive posturing on Iraq, it also exposed itself to the hostilities that were primarily targeted at the superpower. During the ensuing weeks, these claims were amplified as the US deviated further from United Nations processes and the issues surrounding the Bali bombings became more fully illuminated.

In Britain, the Prime Minister, Tony Blair, while politically more moderate than George Bush or the Australian Prime Minister, John Howard, nevertheless appeared equally evangelical in his support for the US approach to Iraq. The leadership of this formative 'Coalition of the Willing', as Bush called the group of nations prepared to attack Iraq, was unanimous in its rejection of the protestors' claims. The attacks in Bali were a manifestation of the spreading web of terror. Neither Australia nor the UK was more vulnerable for its support of the US war on terror; everyone was at risk and everyone 'who loved freedom' was duty-bound to fight in the war against the insidious evil of global jihad. Commenting on the deaths of British citizens in the bombings, Blair warned that 'the world must rid itself of terrorist evil'. In a voice which was echoed through many of the grieving nations, Blair emphasized the 'innocence' of the victims, and the inhumanity of the 'terrorists', 'who are not interested in the destruction and devastation they wreak upon whole communities and families who have lost their loved ones' (*BBC News Online*, 2002).

US Secretary of State Colin Powell included the attacks on Bali in his broad repudiation of those nations that fail to take arms in the war on terror. In this sense, Indonesia was considered entirely culpable for not dealing adequately with terrorist organizations like Jamaah Islamiyah:

> This has been a very sobering experience for the Indonesia leadership when they see this kind of tragedy. So we now can see that you are not exempt from this, you cannot pretend it doesn't exist in your country. It exists everywhere where conditions are right and where this kind of terrorist organization can thrive. And that's why we have to go after them wherever they are. (*Washington Post*, October 16, 2002)

As we have frequently noted, the discourse of ubiquitous evil enshrines the specific details of policy and history within a cosmological jurisdiction. America is not simply fighting humans and exercising specific policy options: it is involved in a spiritual battle on behalf of God. This rhetoric may actually obscure the very specific and pragmatic content of Powell's warning. It also hides from view the considerable pressure the US and global financial agencies, like the International Monetary Fund (IMF) and the World Bank, are able to exert on the Indonesian economy. In a sense, too, Powell's rhetoric points back to the pre-9/11 plans to invade Iraq, plans that were hatched out through the broad context of the war on terror and the manifestations of the Bali bombings. For the US, in fact, we can see that the intricate matrix of foreign policy and modes of US global governance are precisely woven into Powell's account of the bombings and the somewhat understated rebuke of the Indonesian government.

Appending itself to the economic and military force of the United States, Australia's official response was also constructed as a repudiation of those who were not prepared to confront the terrorists. Echoing the mantra of national victim–hero, a discourse so effectively used by George Bush after 9/11, Howard invoked an ontology of terror against which all Australians must be united – thus, 'the war against terrorism must go on with unrelenting vigour and with an unconditional commitment ... People should get out of their minds that it can't happen here. It can and it has happened on our doorstep' (quoted in Dodson, 2002: 4). For Howard and others in the national government, vulnerability pre-exists action because the assailants are perversely antagonistic to the nation's value system and, as such, Australians are vulnerable across all geographic and cultural boundaries. The 'doorstep' motif has a particular cultural resonance for Australians who, unlike the US or UK, are bordered by a densely populated Muslim country; Australia's own history of decolonization, immigration and foreign relations is marked by a profound invasion anxiety. The doorstep reference, thereby, resonated through the psyche of national language wars which link the bombing to Australia's own profound sense of being culturally isolated within the Asia-Pacific region. Piers Akerman, a former editor of one of Australia's major newspapers, expands on the Prime Minister's views, arguing that the bombings invoke a deep sense of history. Reflecting on the first anniversary of the bombings, Akerman (2003) comments:

> Next Sunday, we will mark the first anniversary of the Bali bombing, Australia's shock introduction to the nightmare world of Islamic terrorism ... The scars are still fresh. There's no doubt we are a vastly changed nation. Although Bali can't be ranked with Gallipoli on a scale of national disasters, nor the losses compared with the wholesale slaughter of World War 1, the raw immediacy of the coverage ensured that images of survivors stumbling from the burning ruins of the Sari Club have been seared into the national psyche.

Akerman's comments represent a view that has been broadly expressed through media and political commentary. Just as the 9/11 attacks invoked a deep sense of the American cultural imaginary, reflections on the Bali bombings and the nearly 180 Australian casualties seemed to synthesize historical anxiety with the revivified discourse of nation and its place within the latest incarnation of the east–west divide.

Akerman's invocation of Gallipoli points directly, and somewhat ironically, to the substantial language wars which lie behind this divide; Turkey, a Muslim nation, was defending its territory on the Gallipoli coast against the invading British and Australian Imperial forces during the First World War. While the British and Australian forces were savagely defeated, the campaign has infused itself as a propitious moment in Australian cultural history. This strange and pointless colonial adventure, by which Australia confirmed its fidelity to British military and economic hegemony, has been shaped into a formidable motif for the popular imagining of nation and national identity. While the disaster exposes for many Australians the tragic deficiencies of an imperial system, over time 'Gallipoli' has assumed an even greater epiphanic power in the celebration of Australia as an independent, free and heroic nation. The paradox of constituting a national ideology around a fatuous and humiliating military failure has been frequently noted; as with the Eureka disaster (ennobled as 'rebellion'), Gallipoli allows Australians to imagine a heroic imperial parturition, one which seems to valorize the status of the political victim. The invocation of Gallipoli during the Bali bombing commemorations resonates with a similar ideological motive, a desire to transform the hideousness of the event into a discursive unity, a triumph of national valour. For the official discourses of the state, the Gallipoli–Bali association galvanizes the popular imagining against a common enemy: the disparate sensibilities, practices, ethics and ideas that constitute a social assembly are drawn together through an overarching political postulate, one which affirms the ultimate authority and validity of the nation-state itself.

The poetic elegance of this unity, however, serves only to parenthesize its component parts – its absences. The very invocation of Gallipoli as a discourse which announces, as it obscures, the coercive authority of the state, necessarily dislocates the internal language wars which compose it. Thus, the seeming presence of unity in the Gallipoli discourse immediately unravels as it seeks to identify itself *as* the 'nation': that is, as an inviolable and absolute semiosis. The slightest glance at the internal composition of the signifier 'Gallipoli' reveals that it is composed of agonistic elements which may be read in a variety of ways. Indeed, while Peter Weir's film *Gallipoli* might seem to synthesize the beach landing through a romantic–resistant valorization of Australian 'identity', the composite elements nevertheless continue to exist beyond the borders of a propagated textual (and national) unity. There remains, for example, a series of distinct tensions around the ethical and ideological validity of empire, nation, class, gender, ethnicity. The nation (and the empire), after all, has sent young men into an alien war and a battle that has nothing at its core but slaughter. As Fredric Jameson (1981) noted some time ago, these agonisms and textual elements pre-exist their withdrawal into the absolute and constituted synthesis of 'interpretation' or analysis (the secondary text). That is, the multiply layered and infinitely complex elements that made up the original experiences of Gallipoli are reduced and synthesized in order to create Weir's film text; the film itself is then reduced as it is interpreted by viewers and critics. This flow to synthesis, however, is subverted by the pre-existence of the elements which constitute it. The synthesized version of Gallipoli which might heroize Australia and its culture must confront alternative discursive elements – for example, the military elite in all the warring nations which sacrifice the lives of common class soldiers in order to protect their own class interests; Australia's military aggression, racism and Orientalism which has taken its soldiers to fight on foreign territory; an imperialism which validates its territorial claims through brutality and coercion; a patriarchy which affirms power in masculine violence and militarism; death and maiming which have become the shared borders of individuals without regard to nation, ethnicity, class status or gender; and a banality which exists as a neutral underpinning to the grand projects of ideology.

These alternative linguistic tropes, however, are themselves engaged in a battle for primacy. Weir's film – indeed all representations of Gallipoli – must struggle internally and externally against the agonistic potential of alternative meaning and semiotic dispersal. Hegemonic social groups, of course, seek to 'enlist' Gallipoli in the assertion of their own particular interests and ideological order. For a range of reasons, Gallipoli appears to be particularly susceptible to this sort of discursive conscription, combining as it does the possibility of heroic ascent, with a resistant (postcolonial) victim consciousness, a pathos which rails against an externally imposed, iniquitous authority. This conflux of opposite potential seems to facilitate the broader convergence of state interest and popular imagining, a necessary precondition for the maintenance of an essentially hierarchical social system. And while this symbolic order is not as implacable as Althusser has claimed, it nevertheless draws together its contingent agonisms into a 'presence' that allows for the subjugation of potential disorder. Paul Virilio (2002) has suggested, in fact, that this subjugation has been actively pursued by a military class whose historical project has been the domination of the remainder of humanity. While Virilio's claim may seem excessively totalistic, we can say with some certainty that the state itself represents the latest incarnation of social violence and coercion – militarism is the 'constant' of a hierarchical order which establishes itself in the cartography of nation and empire. Concepts like national 'identity', 'consciousness' or 'psyche' (Anderson, 1991) are part of the grand signification of modernization.

In Australia this process of becoming modern is necessarily implicated in the formation and expression of militarism. Having been established for principally military and strategic reasons, the colonies of Australia participated in a number of extra-territorial campaigns well before Federation (1901) and Gallipoli (1915). Under the imperial banner, colonial troops fought against Zulus, Sudanese, Boers, Chinese Boxers, Indians and Maoris. Since Federation, the

Australian military has fought against a range of Muslims and 'Orientals' in Japan, Korea, Vietnam, Kosovo, Afghanistan and Iraq (twice). While its sovereign territory has only been threatened once (during the Second World War) since British settlement, Australia has continued to centre its security policies on a perceived threat, most frequently associated with Asia and Islam – China, North Korea and Indonesia. Not surprisingly, this militarism has both propagated, and responded to, a somewhat diffuse sense of national anxiety, appending itself to the perceived greatness of 'natural' allies, the United Kingdom and the United States. This 'Great and Powerful Friends' foreign policy model has expressed itself culturally and psychologically as a sense of presence within the perpetual imagining and re-imagining of an east–west divide.

Gallipoli, as it's forged into contemporary discourses, seems constantly to reinvigorate this otherwise precarious 'presence'. On the first commemoration of the Bali bombings, the Premier of Victoria, Steve Bracks, made explicit, for example, the link between Gallipoli and the national psyche. Terrorism becomes the new unnamed enemy of the state and the values which Gallipoli represents: 'Not only did it bring terrorism to our doorstep, it has led to the indelible mark on our national psyche ... Like Gallipoli, it's my hope that the lasting legacy of Bali will be a peaceful and unifying one' (quoted in Dubecki, 2003). Within a resurgent east–west divide, Bracks' reading of history clearly situates the perpetrators of the bombing with the adversary in the Gallipoli context. This radical inscription on the national psyche is as much a 'loss of innocence' (*The Economist*, 2002) as a realization that 'As Australians, we are faced with the reality of having the world's largest Islamic nation on our doorstep ... [with] a highly volatile system of government' (Akerman, 2003: 2). Whereas the Turks are safely situated in another hemisphere, the contiguity of Indonesian Islamists poses a more immediate and inescapable threat: it is the mere fact that these are 'Muslims' in our near north which constitutes a significant danger to Australia's national security. This 'threat' is also identified by the Zionist Federation of Australia, which published the following poem not long after the bombing:

> You hurt us bombing Bali, but we can take the pain,
> But if you think you'll beat us, then you can think a-bloody-gain,
> We battled at Gallipoli and we fought the bloody hun
> Of all the arseholes we've had to face, you're just another one.
> (Holland, 2002)

The menace of terrorism 'at our doorstep', therefore, is generalized in terms of a national consciousness that battles against external enmity. Gallipoli symbolizes a unity of purpose in which the state and popular imaginings are drawn together as 'national psyche' within a seemingly ineluctable context of the east–west divide. The Bali bombings are another iteration by which nation can express itself against the agonistic counterflows of diffuse interests and individual perspectives and values.

It is perhaps for these reasons, more than any other, that the US has been so enthusiastic about Australia's participation in the war on terror. As an international minnow, Australia seems to represent for the Bush administration that part of its world 'democratic' governance that voluntarily delegates its power upward for the greater good of the majority. Australia's interface with its Asia-Pacific region, in a sense, encapsulates the margins for the United States. While the UK represents the historical integrity of the state itself, Australia confirms for the United States the legitimacy of its own hegemony and global domination. Combined, the United Kingdom and Australia have ennobled the American cause, lending moral and ideological legitimacy to the war on terror. The deep ambiguities of history are thus washed up into the vectors of power, leading Australians into a war that has no clear boundaries nor justification – other than the maintenance of the Great and Powerful Friends philosophy. Not surprisingly, the invocation of Gallipoli and an imagined heroic nationalism enables the Australian government to construct this compromise of its sovereignty as a gesture of social and moral virtue – one in which the victims of heinous action become the heroes of national self-assertion.

THE BLIND PUPPETEER: ATROCITY AND CIVIL SOCIETY IN INDONESIA

There is now very clear evidence that intelligence organizations in the US, the UK and Australia have served their nations very poorly over the recent past. Commissions of inquiry in each of these nations have criticized the intelligence agencies for failing to prevent atrocities like 9/11 and the Bali bombings. In these mature civil societies, intelligence has an ambiguous role, performing security functions which putatively require constraints on the rights of citizens, most particularly in terms of privacy, surveillance, organizational transparency and public information. In essence, these organizations betray the very essence of democratic values and rights, creating for themselves a unique context of secrecy for clandestine operations and data gathering. In a country like Indonesia, where civil society is barely re-emerging from a context of military totalitarianism, these sorts of ambiguities become critically intensified within a complex socio-political system (Anderson, 1990) that remains coded through patronism, nepotism and corruption. While the *reformasi* or reform programme is seeking to rehabilitate the political and civil organization of Indonesian society, it is meeting formidable opposition from those who had been so favoured by Suharto's totalitarian military infrastructure.

The International Crisis Group team led by Sidney Jones in Indonesia has been extremely critical of the *reformasi* presidents, Wahid and Megawati. According to Jones, the Wahid and Megawati governments' failure to confront the endemic corruption and power of the military–intelligence agencies contributed significantly to ongoing instability in Indonesia. Farish Noor (2004) has suggested that the expulsion of Sidney Jones from Indonesia in June 2004 was clearly related to these criticisms, especially as Indonesia seeks to re-establish itself as a 'model' Muslim state supporting the US war on terror. For Noor, however, these efforts at appeasing the US authorities obscure the entrenched problems of managing a volatile state in which, as Jones discovered, the military and political elites continue to thwart the efforts of democratic and civil authority. The appointment of former Suharto general A. M. Hendropriyono as head of the new counter-insurgency intelligence service is indicative, Noor claims, of the deep malaise in the *reformasi* modes of governance. Hendropriyono was well known in Indonesia as a senior member of Suharto's counter-insurgency unit, a group that was responsible for much of the suppression and human rights abuses that maintained the brutal authority of the New Order regime.

Like former general Wiranto, who is accused of directing many of the massacre killings in East Timor and who emerged as a presidential candidate in 2004, Hendropriyono is part of a re-emergent military class which refuses to relinquish its privilege and power. Indeed, as various political elites jostle for control of Indonesia, dangerous allegiances are being forged between sectors of the military, specific politicians and Islamic militants. In particular, the head of the militant group Laskar Jihad, Jaafer Omar Thalib, claims to have strong links with the Jakarta political elite. This claim is supported by Stephen Sherlock in the Australian Department of Foreign Affairs, who has identified strong connections between Laskar and Hamza Haz, who was Indonesian Vice-President until the 2004 change of government. According to Sherlock:

> The Vice-President is a leader of the United Development Party (PPP), an Islamic-oriented party which was one of three parties which were allowed to exist under the Suharto regime. Hamza has openly associated himself with some of the more extreme Islamic organizations in Indonesia, the most notorious example of which was his visit in May 2002 to an imprisoned leader of Laskar Jihad, a group which gained prominence for its violent campaigns against Christians in eastern parts of the country. (2002: 3)

The complicated allegiances and support agreements which facilitated Megawati's ascent to the presidency, almost certainly facilitated the engagement of dubious external political forces in the official hierarchy; they seem also to have limited the capacity of the President to pursue effective policy and decision-making. The strength of Islamicism in the Jakarta government and its complex associations with the military have contributed to the context of the Bali bombings and other atrocities. Laskar Jihad and its campaigns of 'moral cleansing', which involved violent attacks on bars and hotels, have largely gone unpunished.

Concerns over Megawati's ability to manage these acute security issues were broadly expressed by the US and Australian governments. During the 2004 presidential election campaign, these governments endorsed Megawati's primary rival and ultimate victor, Susilo Bambang Yudhoyono, another former general from the Suharto era, but one who appears more moderate and less tainted than Wiranto. Not surprisingly, many Indonesians themselves have publicly and electorally expressed their disappointment with Megawati's presidency. While some of this concern is related directly to Indonesia's continued economic problems since the monetary crisis of 1997, much of it also centres on anxieties over security, especially the activities of Islamic militants. Ongoing instability has been generated by violence in West Papua (Irianjaya), Ambon, Bali, Jakarta and Aceh, even after the Tsunami disaster. The attack on the Australian Embassy, targeted after the fortification of and increased security alerts around the US Embassy, was certainly linked to the Coalition attacks on Afghanistan and Iraq. Public and international demands for a stronger government response to political violence and Islamic or secessionist militancy have gladdened the military elite.

This satisfaction, according to commentators like Sidney Jones, may be more than serendipity. Farish Noor, for example, suggests that

> Groups like Laskar Jihad, Fron Pembela Islam and Majlis Mujahideem Indonesia also played a role in creating havoc in troubled regions like the Moluccas, which in turn served as the pretext for further military intervention there, as well as in other places like Timor and Aceh. (2004: 3)

The idea that the military and secret intelligence services actually promote violence in these troubled regions is neither new nor unique. In particular, attacks on Christians, including the Catholics of East Timor, have a dubious history. The pattern of violent assault, neglect and then military intervention and appeasement has been repeated frequently throughout the Indonesian archipelago. The ICG Report on Asia (May 17, 2004) notes, for example, that the resurgence of violence in Ambon has been exacerbated by the poor response of government:

> The response of the Indonesian government at both local and national levels has been poor, from the short-sightedness of police to the unhelpful portrayal of the violence in some quarters as Christian independence supporters against Muslim defenders of national unity ... But as the *Jakarta Post* editorialised on 6 May, events in Ambon may be part of a larger political game. The question ... is whether anyone benefits by making trouble there. (International Crisis Group, 2004: 1)

As in the complex politics of American democracy, a propagated east–west divide may serve the interests of particular power groups, not only the Jihadists but those groups, like the military, who have the 'capacity' to neutralize them. The processes of decentralization and a move to civil society, according to numerous critics of the Indonesian government, have left the way open to a chaos that suits the interests and aspirations of a resurgent military elite. Even the Bali bombings investigations under the direction of a committed policeman, Made Pastika, is clouded in doubt. It is certainly suggested that Pastika displeased his commanders in West Papua when he protested against the excessive brutality and corruption of the province's military management; his move to Bali as Chief of Police has generally been seen as a demotion. The Bali bombings, however, thrust Pastika into international prominence and his commitment to ethical standards and civil policing was sorely tested. While Dewi Anggraeni (2003) saw the investigation as a triumph, Robert Finnegan, editor of the *Jakarta Post*, had his doubts. For Finnegan, the Balinese and the international investigation teams were dismally inept in the management of the crime scene, forensic evidence and the investigations more broadly. The rapid identification and elicited confessions of the principal perpetrators, Amrozi and Samudra, constituted a significant mystery for Finnegan:

> If indeed there is one thing that has been glaringly apparent throughout this investigation, it is perhaps that nothing close to the truth has been told as of today. It is also apparent that something is very, very wrong not only with the procedural aspects of this case, but also with the suppression and outright destruction of evidence. The international investigators bear a heavy responsibility for this and should be held accountable. (2003: 6–7)

The contamination of the Bali crime scene is well known. In fact, the cases against the bombers were largely based on Amrozi and Samudra's confessions and identification of fellow perpetrators. Finnegan alerts us to the convoluted processes of law which tried and convicted the criminals; the convictions ultimately collapsed under constitutional challenge.

For conspiracy theorists, it may be tempting to suggest that the investigation and trial processes were largely staged in order to lessen external pressure. Amrozi's extraordinary daily press conferences generated from the context of incarceration may thus be seen as part of a language war through which the Indonesian public are being courted. The sympathy that some Indonesians feel for the bombers indicates the very deep disharmonies that are affecting Indonesian society. Even the inability of the Indonesian legal system to manage the notional spiritual head of Jamaah Islamiyah, Abu Bakar Ba'asyir, indicates an impotence that derives as much from the nascent character of civil management, as it does from a profound anxiety over what it is that Ba'asyir actually represents. The Ba'asyir problem, along with the successful constitutional challenge by the Bali bombers and the accosting of another key JI figure, Hambali, by US authorities, is indicative of the significant challenges facing civil democracy in Indonesia. In overturning the retrospectivity of the terrorist legislation, the constitutional court confirmed many of the doubts about the Megawati government and its ability to deal with security issues. It remains to be seen whether the new President, Susilo Bambang Yudhoyono, will be able to mediate the formidable power of the military with the demands of civil governance. The successful management of these competing interests will determine whether Yudhoyono can stem the rising force of Jihadist Islamicism in Indonesia, most particularly within a context of chauvinistic US interventionism. The tsunami disaster in Aceh made explicit, among many other things, the close tagging of US and Australian foreign aid to specific political and social programmes which draw Indonesia more tightly into the web of global capitalism and the security interests of the US war on terror.

DEVELOPMENT AND RECOVERY IN BALI

Against the background of Indonesia's continuing economic crisis and Islamic agitation, Bali continues to seek pathways to recovery. As we noted at the beginning of this chapter, the severe downturn in tourist arrivals created problems not only for the Balinese, but for the broader Indonesian economy as well. The dramatic decline in tourist numbers that followed the bombings led to reductions in employment and family incomes in Bali, as well as declines in foreign investment and foreign currency reserves for Indonesia more broadly. In the grip of substantial international debt and under the strict policy control of international financial organizations like the World Bank and the IMF, the nation as a whole is struggling to deal effectively with continuing contraction of the economy, endemic poverty levels of around 16 per cent and severe social inequality. While other nations in the region have forced their way out of the 1997 monetary crisis, Indonesia seems condemned to ongoing economic difficulties. These difficulties are clearly exacerbated by the contraction and current instability of Bali's tourism industry.

Not surprisingly, the Indonesian government has courted various donor and development agencies in order to elicit support for a tourism-led recovery in Bali. The United Nations Development Program report to which we referred earlier in this chapter is largely focused on a tourism-led recovery. While acknowledging the importance of social and cultural issues in Bali, especially around inequality and ethnic–community tensions, the UNDP centres its interest on the economy of Bali and the mechanisms required for restoring tourism. Donor and development organizations such as USAID, the World Bank, Dutch Trust and AusAID have also developed a range of social and infrastructure programmes, mostly focused on the restoration of tourism. The World Bank, for example, has provided funds for the upgrade of drainage around the main tourist area of Kuta-Legian, the site of the bombings. Australian funds have been directed into emergency response facilities which are now of First World standard.

Thus, while the national government is directing funds into 're-securing' Bali (US $4m), significant funds are also being allocated directly into tourism promotion, events and conference promotion (US $1–2m). These funds, managed by the Ministry of Culture and Tourism and a tourism development planning committee, have contributed to a range of activities, including the establishment of a media centre which will distribute tourism promotion information to Indonesian embassies across the globe; the establishment of a national tourism marketing campaign; the co-ordination of events such as an internationally profiled music concert, sports, surfing and other recreational activities; and the recruitment of international consultants such as Gavin Anderson (Australia) and Marketing Garden (Japan). Promotional activities overseas have included advertisements on CNN and exhibitions in key international tourism fairs.

A key element of these promotions, as we noted earlier, is the discourse of Bali harmony. While still at odds with diplomatic travel warnings, the Bali harmony discourse insists that Bali has recovered and that the issues and problems that led to the bombings have all been resolved. Our empirical research (Lewis, B. & Lewis, J., 2004), however, suggests that, while the Balinese themselves clearly understand the economic and social value of the discourse and are prepared to use it with good grace when dealing with tourists, there is also a very persistent anxiety in the community. This anxiety is centred on an awareness that the recovery is brittle and that their island and nation are anything but harmonious. While inevitably faithful to the discourse of economic development, even the UNDP acknowledges that Bali's social and community issues must be addressed in order to create a genuinely sustainable recovery:

> Despite the significance of these impacts from the crisis in tourism, it is vital that government, industry and donors do not lose sight of the long-term agenda of tourism and sustainable development in Bali ... [T]he growth of tourism in Bali and Lombok has been spontaneous and has occurred outside of a well-regulated planning framework. The process has often involved opposition from local people who felt that their interests were not given sufficient importance in the decision-making process ... The challenge is for government to develop processes and approaches which provide

opportunities for local people to have a say in future development and
influencing government policies and priority programs. (UNDP, 2003: 59)

While the report recommends the diversification of the Balinese
economy, it offers no alternative to the inevitability of Bali's global
integration. The harmony of Bali remains a vacuous mantra against
the overbearing certainty of this fundamental surrender to a globalism
which is embedded in political violence and seemingly irresolvable
language wars.

Thus, while Bali has been conscripted by globalization into the war
of terror, its notional saviour and protector, the United Nations, is
also critically embedded in the aegis of global capital and commerce.
According to the UN report, there is no alternative to the economic
development programme of global tourism for Bali and Indonesia. It is
perhaps a little ironical that the war on terror, by which George Bush
so seriously compromised the credibility and effectiveness of the UN
forum, has so thoroughly ensnared the international organization.
Its role in a conquered Iraq has been extremely problematic. The
bombing of its headquarters in Baghdad, like the report on Bali's
recovery, critically positions the UN as a servant of international
capitalism and the globalization that is dominated by US interests.
Perhaps Bush and his other Coalition leaders are correct when they
claim that there is no free space in this conflict, that no country or
people can distance themselves from its effects. The UN has shuffled
its feet and been humiliated by American xenophobia and aggression
in Iraq. Like the International Red Cross, also attacked in Baghdad,
and Médecins Sans Frontières, attacked in Afghanistan, the UN's
self-ascribed independence is merely another discourse that can be
assaulted or conscripted by ideological antagonists. This is precisely
the point US Secretary of State Colin Powell made when he claimed
that the donor and aid agencies were part of the US front line against
terror. Thus, the radical Islamicists and nationalists in the Middle
East seem uninspired by the discourse of democratic humanism and
collaboration by which the UN presents itself to the world. The UN
failed to prevent the attacks on Iraq, as it failed to prevent Saddam's
attacks on the Kurds. It failed in Rwanda, Ethiopia and the Sudan. It
failed to prevent the hideous carnage that followed its own sponsored
referendum in East Timor.

Not surprisingly, there are those in Bali who feel rather deserted by,
or sceptical about, the UNDP work on the island. While the UN would
profess its independence, there is certainly a strong sense among

many Balinese that the agenda of development has been largely wrested from their control; the UNDP merely continues a tradition of external forces defining for the Balinese the best way of dealing with their inescapable integration into the global economy. In some ways, of course, the UNDP model denies the fidelity of the Balinese to their *rwa bhineda* or 'two in one' principle, according to which evil will always progress with good. While the UNDP assumes a progress to an ideal economic condition, the *rwa bhineda* assumes that threat and danger will always accompany pleasure – and vice versa. The lesson of the Bali bombings in this sense is not that tourism must be restored with better hotels, clientele and drainage; the lesson of the bombings for most Balinese is that the excesses of an unrestrained and externally imposed development have unbalanced social, commercial, environmental and cosmological conditions. While the discourse of civil society may express these things differently, there can be little doubt that the majority of Balinese are exhausted and fearful for themselves and their future.

Recovery is not, therefore, the resolution of good triumphing over evil. It is the reconciliation of contending elements – development, environment, tradition, progress, pleasure, struggle. While the UNDP report extols the protective power of the Balinese cultural and community fabric, within the weave there is something terrible and tragic. For all its undoubted value to a modernizing society, the transition to civil society must necessarily mediate the conflux of life and death, good and evil, pleasure and pain. While tourist numbers are returning to the pre-bombing levels, there is no sense that the Balinese themselves are ready to be swept again into the vortex of a frenetic global mediascape nor its reactive context of global Islamic Jihad. Despite the claims of governments, marketers and tourist brochures, the Balinese are clearly aware of the dangers of globalization and the western imaginary which has ensnared them in the web of terror and political violence.

CONCLUSIONS

1. The Suharto New Order regime (1965–98) was characterized by nepotism, repression, corruption and economic mismanagement. The fall of the regime, along with the severity of the Asian monetary crisis (1997), left Indonesia impoverished, dependent on international aid, and with a vastly underdeveloped civic, social and economic infrastructure.

2. Against this background and with the rise of international Islamicism, a number of dissident groups became increasingly active and violent in the post-Suharto period. One of these groups, Jamaah Islamiyah, had been influenced by al-Qa'ida's principles and personnel. Following the 9/11 attacks, JI changed the focus of its violence from Indonesian Christians to international targets.

3. The nightclubs were targeted because of Bali's perceived cultural affinity with America and Australia. The nightclubs were seen as Satanic manifestations of western materialism, decadent hedonism and self-interested individualism. Bali was seen as corrupting itself for the sake of international tourism and America's global hegemony.

4. In fact, Bali has been constructed as an available paradise by the western global imaginary. An ascendant discourse of harmony obscures many of the island's historical and contemporary tensions.

5. The traditional Hindu practices, beliefs and rituals – the *adat* – are critical to the cultural politics which emerge out of Bali's transformation as a 'created paradise' within the global tourist cartography. These cultural politics are pivotal to the bombings and to Indonesia's transition to a modern, civil state.

6. The *adat* is embedded within the community and ethnic politics of Bali. In the post-Suharto period, community security agencies like the *pecalang*, invoke the *adat* as a mechanism for social control, migration management and policing. The *pecalang* and other community forces have been active in the promotion of civil order and the harmony discourse. Transmigrants, in particular, have suffered considerable social oppression in the wake of the Bali bombings.

7. The bombings have provoked a complex response from nations like Australia. As was the case in the US following the attacks on New York and Washington, the Bali bombings incited a strong nationalist response in Australia. Bali has been a psychological and symbolic land bridge for Australians to their 'Asian' neighbourhood. The bombings provoked the familiar hero–victim reaction, though Australia turned even more aggressively toward its great and powerful friends (the UK and the US) for solace and security. Australia's participation in the Iraq invasion was substantiated by the bombings.

8. This response intensified Australia's paradoxical relationship with its region, and with Bali in particular. Australia's response to the

Indonesian tsunami disaster is further evidence of this paradoxical and confusing relationship.

9. While Indonesia seeks to maintain and enhance its relations with the US and Australia, it is struggling to deal with the transition to democratic civil society. The bombings and their aftermath are symptoms of Indonesia's struggle. In particular, the successful constitutional challenge by the Bali bombers, public sympathy for Abu Bakar Ba'asyir and Islamic anti-Americanism, America's own expropriation of Hambali, and intrigue over interaction between radical Islamicists and leading military and government officials are all manifestations of the precariousness of Indonesian civil society.

6

The Occupation of Iraq:
Rule of Law and the New Public Sphere

RESOLUTION

It has been suggested throughout this book that a new political sphere has formed around broadcast media. In particular, I have suggested that the public and private dimensions of political life have merged somewhat, creating new forms of political expressivity, subjectivity and modes of social knowledge. Enlightenment-based writing democracy, with its ideals of representation and responsibility, has not been expunged by a new televisual context; rather, writing democracy has been absorbed through new modes of representationalism and a hyperreal consciousness which is perpetually being shaped and reshaped by the proliferation of images, information and electronic texts. In this context, political and public debate is constituted in terms of the not-quite-real of the mediasphere. As much as anything else, the events of 9/11 were so intensely shocking because they exposed the underbelly of a culture that is barely coming to terms with its own radical and intrinsic transformations. September 11 revealed, in fact, how far these changes had gone, and how deeply they had cut into the social and political system that dominates the globe. Much of the discourse, prescience and policy programming that has issued from the events has sought to recover the semiotic fissures. The US government and its Coalition partners embarked on a project of fighting violence with violence so that the history of language wars could finally and absolutely be resolved through the triumph of 'the chosen' – good over evil, democracy over tyranny, freedom over anarchy, law over chaos, west over east.

Thus, the cultural fissures that 9/11 exposed were quickly sealed by a frantic and aggressive reassertion of Enlightenment or quasi-Enlightenment ideals and discourses. In particular, the Bush administration embarked on a rapidly engineered policy of retribution and violence in which 'freedom' and 'rule of law' would be imposed on those states and peoples who threatened American supremacy; the media would be simply marshalled in the service of the state, its conquests and its discourses of global order. The electronic polis would be captured within the project of American self-interest which, according to neoconservative philosophy, was tantamount to the interests of global security and prosperity. Thus, the citizenry could be enlisted into the project through a strategic management of the new public sphere, the mediasphere. The ideals of writing democracy – humanism, freedom, law – would be asserted through the mobilization of broadcast culture's expansive but dangerous expressive potential.

In this context, the invasion of Iraq was something of an anticlimax. As brutal and as appalling as it was, the war was swiftly won (March 9–May 1) by the overwhelmingly superior firepower of the United States and its primary military ally, the United Kingdom. Quite clearly, the first Gulf War, ongoing sanctions and the continued weapons inspections had entirely decimated the Iraqi's capacity to defend their country. Indeed, despite the insistence of the Coalition governments and their express reasons for going to war, a series of inquiries have confirmed that the much-vaunted weapons of mass destruction were largely dismantled after the first Gulf War. While the invasion was quickly completed, the calamities of this phase of the war on terror have become more apparent during the occupation. Since Bush's declaration of the cessation of hostilities (May 1, 2003), there have been many more Coalition casualties than during the invasion itself. Donor agencies are in retreat, and attacks against international reconstruction companies and their personnel have become acute. Moreover, and as Robert Fisk (2004a) has so powerfully reported, militant resistance, especially by Islamicists and Sunni nationalist supporters of the former dictator, is making travel anywhere outside Baghdad extremely perilous, if not impossible. Governments within the Coalition core are under increasing pressure from their domestic publics, even in the aftermath of the general elections of 2005.

The current chapter will interrogate the conditions of the conquest and occupation of Iraq, most particularly in terms of the Coalition's primary objectives. The chapter is especially interested in the ways in which the media and culture have been implicated in the occupation, and how the discourses of democracy and freedom have been marshalled through Iraq's new 'rule of law'. This rule of law, as the alternative to Saddam's rule of tyranny, is sponsored by the democratic states that are occupying Iraq by force; our investigations, therefore, necessarily involve the intersection of global interests and discursive practices within the formative public sphere.

THE FIRST CASUALTY: DAVID KELLY AND TRIAL BY ORDEAL

One of the most significant issues for the occupation forces is, of course, their own credibility. The invasion was justified on the grounds that Iraq possessed weapons of mass destruction and that Saddam Hussein was a tyrant. In order to make the world a better and safer place, the US, the UK and Australia embarked on a 'just war'. A genuinely just war can only be conducted by a nation that has a particular moral authority, graced we might assume by the auspices of democracy and civilization (Keane, 2004). In many respects, the United Kingdom, more so even than Australia, provided for George Bush a moral legitimacy for the pre-emptive strike against Iraq. As the founder of the modern parliamentary system and global industrial capitalism, the UK might seem to have less obviously selfish motives for military intervention in the Middle East than the US. Under the ideological banner of Labour politics and a social justice agenda, the Prime Minister, Tony Blair, presented his arguments for a pre-emptive strike within a context of very strong objections from his own party and the citizenry generally. At the centre of Blair's rhetoric were the WMDs and a powerful conviction about the moral degeneracy of Islamic militants – and of Saddam himself.

Not surprisingly, the British government and Tony Blair, in particular, have struggled to maintain their moral authority during the course of the invasion and the period of occupation. The problems associated with the WMDs and the occupation itself were accentuated by the 'suicide' death of a chemical and biological weapons expert, David Kelly. Kelly appears to have committed suicide because of the immense professional, political and media pressure exerted over the WMDs issue. As a casualty of the war, Kelly personifies many of the critical issues associated with the cultural politics of 'truth' and the media representation of the invasion, issues which ultimately prompted the Hutton Inquiry and a fundamental crisis for public broadcasting in the United Kingdom. This crisis, in fact, reflects many of the issues we have been discussing around the transformation of the public sphere and the discourse of liberal democracy.

During September 2002, about a year after 9/11, the British Prime Minister, Tony Blair, was becoming increasingly committed to the US invasion plans. In order to convince both a reluctant Labour Party and the public, Blair announced on September 3 the imminent publication of a dossier on Saddam Hussein's weapons of mass destruction programme, which would prove beyond doubt that Iraq posed a 'real and unique threat to the security of the region and to the rest of the world'. Compiled by intelligence services, the dossier first appeared in draft form on September 5, but Alistair Campbell, Blair's director of communications and strategy, suggested that 'the dossier needs a substantial rewrite ... as per T.B.'s discussion'. Around September 10–11 an intelligence claim that Saddam could launch chemical or biological weapons with only 45 minutes notice first appeared in the dossier. When the final version was published on September 24, it also included a section from a PhD thesis dated twelve years earlier. On the day of the dossier's publication the London *Evening Standard* led with the headline '45 Minutes to Attack'. Many of the other newspapers and broadcast bulletins focused on similar details, establishing a context which clearly exacerbated public anxiety over terrorism and Iraq's weapons capacity. In October the Bali bombings occurred and in November the UN issued an ultimatum to the Saddam regime, insisting they comply with all resolutions and admit a new weapons team into Iraq. While the Iraq government acceded to these demands, it was too late and the Coalition bombing raids began on March 20, 2003.

As a scientist and public servant working for the Ministry of Defence, David Kelly became ensnared in a very difficult ethical dilemma, a dilemma which beset many members of the Coalition intelligence communities at the time. Kelly believed that the likelihood of Saddam holding chemical or biological weapons was little more than 30 per cent and that the dossier had significantly overstated the threat. Kelly, it seems, offered his views on Saddam's weapons programme and the inspections that were then taking place in occupied Iraq to Andrew Gilligan, the defence correspondent for the BBC's *Today* programme. Gilligan used the meeting with David Kelly for a series of reports which argued that the government, knowing that the 45 minute claim was 'dubious', had made the dossiers 'sexier' in order to persuade the party and the citizenry of the need to go to war. It was Gilligan's reports which precipitated a deeply divisive row between the government and the publicly funded national broadcaster. Blair was clearly infuriated by the BBC's apparent delight at the failure of the inspections to find WMDs and the government's obvious embarrassment at this outcome.

With what appears to be a disproportionate sensitivity to the dossier criticism, Alistair Campbell attacked the BBC, Gilligan and his 'unnamed' source. In evidence to the House of Commons Select Committee investigating the dossier and intelligence processes and in a formal complaint to the BBC board of governors, Campbell severely criticized the professional and ethical standards of the BBC. The critical moment for David Kelly himself, however, was his eventual naming in the press. In what may well have been a leak from the Blair government, Kelly was exposed to intense professional, media and political scrutiny. On July 16 Kelly himself appeared before the House of Commons committee and the next day he committed suicide. In the deepening crisis the Blair government announced that Lord Hutton would chair a new and independent judicial inquiry into the events surrounding Kelly's death. While conceding that Kelly was put under significant political pressure, especially by the Secretary of Defence, Geoff Hoon, the Hutton report ultimately exonerated the government, while vilifying Andrew Gilligan, and the managerial and reporting standards of the BBC.

Tony Blair and his government, of course, have felt entirely vindicated by the Hutton report, though the public seemed far less convinced. Not only did the polls show a steady decline in support for the UK's participation in the Iraq invasion and occupation, but they have also demonstrated a significant decline in support for Blair himself. Indeed, just prior to the release of the Hutton report, one poll showed that the majority of the public trusted the BBC more than they trusted Blair. According to Jackie Ashley, writing in the *Guardian*, the media and public commentary have not been convinced by the Hutton findings,

> For it feels as if Labour in general, and the Prime Minister in particular, has suffered a radical loss of authority. One minister asks: if Blair has been cleared of everything by Hutton and is still portrayed as a liar, and a fraud, what does he do next? (2004: 2)

Much of the discussion around the Kelly affair centres, in fact, on key questions of veracity, political integrity and accuracy of reporting. The ideals of democracy require an educated and informed public that is capable of making sound judgements based on quality, objective information. While a free public education system is the cornerstone of this electoral ideal, journalism has also been charged with the responsibility of the fourth estate – the mechanism by which the interests of the public are 'mediated' against the excesses of government (see Chapter 1). It has been suggested throughout this book, however, that this mode of Enlightenment–writing democracy is being supplemented by alternative political expressivities, most particularly as they are being formed through the broadcast and new digital communications systems. One reading of the David Kelly story would suggest that the scientist has been entrapped by the collision of altering webs of political consciousness and the processes by which the media now convenes its realities. As has been suggested in our discussion of the Iraq invasion (Chapter 4), the global networked corporate media, in particular, is driven by relentless semiotic and financial deficits. The 'excess' or proliferation of information, images and texts is actually a reaction to these deficits; the corporatized media especially seek to overcome deficit by engaging in excessive production. One dimension of the Kelly story is his conscription into the disputed semiotic territories of writing and broadcast democracy: while the ideal of truth and the fourth estate persist in the former, the latter is dominated by the irradiating effects of persuasion, perspective, image and the over-generation of information and entertainment. In this sense, Kelly is not merely a pawn in the politics of the Iraq invasion; he is actually a casualty of a war over truth and its basis in democratic 'rule of law'.

In this context, the resignation of senior BBC executives, while parading itself as a confirmation of professional standards and objective reporting, is actually a side effect of this clash of political consciousness. The not-quite-real of hyperreality creates a story out of the media itself. Andrew Gilligan, the journalist who challenged the probity of the government's WMD dossier, is not sacrificed to the high standards of journalism he breached, but to the politics of media war. As a participant in the new public sphere of the media, Gilligan embellished his story and his reputation by challenging the government's own questionable veracity. Within the boundaries of the persuasion game, Gilligan and the public broadcasters are not supposed to expose the mirrors of their own hyperreality. In some respects, this is precisely what Mary Riddell has in mind when she suggests that the resignation of the BBC executives is an overreaction, a hyperbole that bears little resemblance to the realities of the situation. Arguing against John Lloyd's view that the media wields vast power over politicians and the judiciary, Riddell claims that the Kelly affair reflects, more than anything else, the limits of the media and its capacity to challenge endemic institutional power:

Pause here for a moment. Gilligan was wrong. The BBC was stupid not to nail his mistake and say sorry. But the issues thrown up by the Iraq war, most of them scrupulously unaddressed by Lord Hutton, were an indictment of politicians, not their chroniclers. When a judge handpicked by a prime minister obliges that prime minister with a silly benign report, the media are entitled to ask some questions. (2004: 1)

But these questions, Riddell insists, are not to be framed as exceptional. They are part of a public discourse that seeks to engage with issues in ways that resist hegemonic or intellectual authority. Arguing against a censorial overreaction to the Hutton criticisms of the BBC, Riddell concludes:

Newspapers are not best produced by those with a taste for censorship, 'good news' stories and Downing Street canapes. Nor is a vision of a civic journalism half as beguiling as it might sound. The dream may be of a media respectful of politicians, mindful of their democratic duties and shorn of fatty stuff about Beckham's tattoos and Jemma's marriage. The result would be newspapers of such turgid blandness that nobody would ever buy them … Certainly we need a new kind of politics. But a neutered media and GOSES obedience at the BBC would further wound democracy, not heal it. (2004: 1)

Riddell's version of democracy here is a vibrant and even slightly chaotic mediasphere in which many views are heard and questions asked in ways that engage the public. Engagement is generated largely through the flow of popular as well as serious media texts. Riddell, while not explicating the point in any detail, dismisses the elite view of the media which would elevate organizations like the BBC and the broadsheet newspaper companies over those popular media groups that are interested in everyday community matters and pleasures. In other words, Riddell supports a mode of journalism which acknowledges the legitimacy of the body and a politics which is both personal as well as social. David Kelly's death, in these terms, personifies this intersection of democratic discourses. The body and its personal effects – biology, emotions, relationships – are conscripted into a mediasphere of colliding and interconnecting intensities: truth, social utility, ethics and ideology capture the body in their own kaleidoscope of mysterious political logic.

Whether it was Tony Blair or someone else in government who authorized the release of David Kelly's name to the press is perhaps unknowable. What is clear is that Kelly's body becomes transformed as identity through the processes of representation. The new democracy of the mediasphere functions at this level. In speaking to the media, Kelly was exercising a choice. Confronted with an irresolvable ethical dilemma, the scientist decided to take the risk of direct engagement with the 'mediated' public. Kelly's choice, which would lead ultimately to his death, was to play actively in the game of mediated politics. Thus, while some commentators are prepared to suggest that David Kelly was actually and literally murdered by a paranoid state apparatus (see Rarey, 2003), at least metaphorically this is certainly the case. David Kelly's body was absorbed into the vortex of a political mediasphere to which he was ultimately made a sacrifice.

This is not merely a trial by media, but a trial within a highly politicized mediasphere which implicates producers, governments, the public–audience within the context of an extremely complex and often contradictory culture. In many respects, Kelly's experience hearkens back to the pre-modern trial by ordeal in which individuals were dragged from their private lives into a public forum, then brutalized as a form of legal examination (see Ashley, 2004). If a lord or religious authority were not able to adjudicate an accused person's guilt or innocence, the suspected criminal would be required to hold a hot iron or be immersed in a river. In the latter case, if the accused person floated, they were guilty; if they sank to the bottom of the river they were innocent. In some cases of course, the ordeal constituted its own punishment as victims who sank to the bottom of the river, proving their innocence, were hauled back to the surface already dead. David Kelly's career and professional ethics were put on trial in a similar way. Surveilled and enlisted by a media which is constantly propelled by its own intrinsic fallibilities, Kelly immediately placed himself within the mediasphere. Perhaps unwittingly, Kelly's participation in the cultural politics of the mediated public domain exposed him to a semiotic realm that has already sacrificed truth to the whirring uncertainty and frenetic supplementarity of an ungrounded and highly illusory broadcast democracy. The rule of law which seems to be present is actually already subsumed within the orbit of the law of persuasion, the mediated law which tries the participant through the ordeal of mediated exposure. Like Kafka's Joseph K., David Kelly is led to his slaughter by a rabid media and a mode of government that is now, more than anything else, a product of the mediasphere. Kelly is denied 'natural justice'; his ordeal is constituted within a precarious cultural politics which reaches into

Whitehall, the Middle East and Washington. Like that of the medieval witches, Kelly's guilt is assumed in the accusation and the ideology of globalized violence. His execution is convened by the fear of his accusers; his innocence is an attribute of his death.

THE NEW IRAQ

While many commentators characterize the trajectory of the Enlightenment and modernism in terms of truth and certitude, in fact, the basis of that certitude is doubt. 'Doubt all', Descartes recommends, since it is only through doubt that truth can emerge. In many respects, the centralization of doubt as a philosophical conceit is not an inversion of the Enlightenment trajectory, but an acknowledgement of its alternative force. Poststructural and postmodern theory, which seeks to valorize doubt and the imprecise nature of language and meaning, is simply focusing on that dimension of modernism which doubts its own certitude: poststructuralism, that is, seeks to draw doubt from the shadows of its hierarchical otherness. In many respects, too, the rise of the hyperreal mediasphere broadens the field of doubt and 'undecidability' for a public which must confront daily a cast of players – politicians and public figures – whose primary purpose is constructed around discourses of perspective and persuasion. These rarefied beings are themselves contingencies of the mediasphere and of those media professionals who might seek to unravel the script or the political performer in order to maintain the momentum of the hyperreal, earn their salary, sustain the organization, advance the idea – and *resolve* the doubt.

Yet doubt, especially in a time of crisis, seems almost irreducible. As discussed in our analysis of the invasion of Iraq, the tight management of information seems only to confirm public uncertainty. During the period of occupation, public uncertainties have been intensified as the three key Coalition governments have conceded that the putative reason for invading Iraq, Saddam's WMDs, has proved apocryphal. Of course, the respective governments have tried to assuage public anger over the deception, shifting their discourse to other dimensions of Saddam's great evil and directing fault to the quality of information provided by their intelligence services. Each government has appointed commissions of inquiry all of which have concluded, inevitably, that the governments didn't lie about the WMDs and that Saddam's slippery diplomacy was the key to the failings of western intelligence services.

Clearly, the US government had been convinced by the CIA's report of October 2002, around the same time as the UK dossier on WMDs was released. In addition to the story of Iraq's import of uranium from Africa (later found to be false), the information provided by the respective intelligence agencies prompted the US and British governments to commit to war. According to the US Deputy Commander in the Iraq war, General Abizaid:

> Intelligence was the most accurate I've seen on the tactical level, probably the best I've seen on the operational level and perplexingly incomplete on the strategic level with regards to weapons of mass destruction. It is perplexing to me that we have not found weapons of mass destruction when the evidence was so persuasive that it would exist ... I can offer no reasonable explanation. (cited in Joint Standing Committee, 2004: ch 4)

In order to resolve this 'perplexity' against the 'persuasive evidence', President Bush commissioned a Review of Intelligence Capabilities of the United States Regarding Weapons of Mass Destruction (2004). While the review's findings were predictably benign, Bush had already moved his discourse beyond the WMD issue, arguing that Saddam's demonic regime needed to be removed in order to liberate the people of Iraq and bring democracy to the Middle East. In the UK the Privy Council Review of Intelligence Services and Weapons of Mass Destruction (2004), chaired by notable establishment figure Lord Butler of Brockwell, produced a benign account of intelligence failings which entirely exonerated the Blair government. In Australia the government-dominated Parliamentary Joint Standing Committee on Foreign Affairs, Trade and Defence reported that, since 'intelligence is not an exact science' nor is it 'evidence', many perspectives are possible. While hindsight might have enabled a more accurate reading of the WMD situation and provided a more effective basis for intelligence assessments, the government acted on the best information available at the time: 'The parts of the jigsaw are never completely there, and the information is often suggestive rather than definitive' (Joint Standing Committee on Foreign Affairs, Trade and Defence, 2004: ch 4).

Of course, these august commissions have been attacked by opposition parties, critics of the Iraq war and various media commentaries. Within this context, the noble ambition of democracy has been invoked in order to explain the increasingly prolific and distressing media images of subversion and confusion that have been laying siege to Iraq's reconstruction and 'liberation'. For supporters of the invasion, the ongoing killings and warfare in Iraq are seen as part of the agonies of a difficult birth. To this extent, the investiture of the first elected government of post-Saddam Iraq, a coalition of religious Shi'ite parties (50 per cent of votes) and Kurds (25 per cent), was seen as the first expression of a modern, secular and democratic state. The basis of this state, as the Project for the New American Century claims, is a constitution containing 'the strongest guarantees of individual, minority and women's rights and liberties to be found anywhere in the Arab world' (Kagan & Kristol, 2004a: 9). According to Kagan and Kristol, the success of the invasion and occupation is manifest not only in these immense advances in freedom and liberty, but also in the social conditions of the country:

> There are hopeful signs that Iraqis of differing ethnic, religious and political persuasions can work together. This is a far cry from the predictions made before the war by many, both here and in Europe, that a liberated Iraq would unleash a bloodbath. The perpetually sour American media focus on tensions between Sheites and Kurds that delayed the signing [of the interim constitution] by three whole days. But the difficult negotiations leading up to the signing and the continuing debates over the terms of the final constitution, have in fact demonstrated something remarkable in Iraq: a willingness on the part of the diverse ethnic and religious groups to disagree – peacefully – and then to compromise. (Kagan & Kristol, 2004a: 9)

The self-exclusion of the Sunni Muslim community from the 2005 elections might seem to disrupt Kagan and Kristol's optimism, though for neoconservative supporters of the Bush strategy in the Middle East, democracy and rule of law are the ultimate, rather than immediate, effects of invasion. In the 'test of the public square' Iraq has made enormous steps forward; a fully participative public sphere, the Project for the New American Century proclaims, will come in stages. In many respects, Kagan and Kristol's utilitarian perspective recalls former White House advisor Richard Perle's belief that a justification for the American-led invasion need only measure the number of civilian casualties inflicted by the Coalition forces against the number of deaths inflicted by Saddam (see Chapter 4). While overlooking the estimated 800,000 deaths inflicted by a decade of UN sanctions on Iraq, as well as the estimated 100,000 invasion deaths (Roberts et al., 2004), Perle argues that the invasion and occupation are entirely justified (see Kagan & Kristol, 2004a).

The capture of Saddam Hussein, the establishment of the interim government, restoration of electricity and oil production to pre-invasion levels, and a vibrant reconstruction programme might all seem to suggest that things are going well in Iraq. However, and as we intimated at the beginning of this chapter, the now decreasingly 'embedded' media appears to be rediscovering an interest in alternative perspectives, at least at the margins. The patriotic fervour which captured the United States after 9/11 and which seems to have limited the critical capacity of some sections of the news media seems to be subsiding somewhat – especially within a legislative context which is compromising press freedom. The *New York Times* and the *Washington Post*, for example, have 'apologized' to their readers for surrendering some of their own critical edge in reporting the war on terror. And it appears that journalism and media scholars in the US have become increasingly vocal over the severe restrictions on freedom of speech being imposed for the sake of 'security'. Most famously, the incapacity of media outlets to depict American coffins returning from Iraq and the limits on reporting or publishing specific parts of the Patriot 2 bill have outraged a number of US media and freedom of speech advocates (see, for example, American Civil Liberties Union, 2004).

Publishing through the Internet and the London-based *Independent*, Robert Fisk tells a very different story of the occupation of Iraq to the one proposed by the New American Century writers. Fisk notes, for example, that on the departure of Paul Bremer, the Coalition-appointed administrator of Iraq, and the accession of the Allawi interim administration, new laws governing the use of motor vehicle horns were enacted. At the same time, three US soldiers were torn apart by a roadside bombing (one of 60 attacks on US forces over that weekend), US military strategists were devising plans for quelling the resistance led by Shi'ite cleric Moqtada Sadr, UK forces were involved in skirmishes in Basrah, and Islamicist militants were threatening to behead a Turkish citizen who had been working for a transport company in the new liberated Iraq. The 'handover' to the Allawi interim administration served merely to deepen Fisk's trepidation and despair:

> Most of the American CPA men [interim administration] who have cleared out of Baghdad are doing what we always suspected they would do when they had finished trying to put a US ideological brand name on 'new' Iraq; they have headed off to Washington to work for the Bush election campaign. But those left behind in the 'international zone' – those we have to pretend

are no longer an occupation authority – make no secret of their despair. The ideology is gone. The ambitions are gone. 'We've no aims left,' one of them said last week. 'We're living from one day to the next. All we're trying to do now – our only goal – is to keep the lid on until January 2005' [when the first Iraqi elections were to be held]. (Fisk, 2004a: 1)

This bleak image of the new 'sovereign' Iraqi administration needs to be understood within the context of America's continuing military presence and the billions of dollars that are being generated out of reconstruction contracts for which the American and Coalition countries have priority. The interim Prime Minister, Iyad Allawi, is himself a former CIA and MI6 operative, someone who was once a member of the Bathist party and close to Saddam. Having failed to win a majority in the 2005 elections, it remains clear to Allawi and everyone else that the newly elected Iraqi government will continue to rely on the 146,000 American troops who are still based around Baghdad.

Fisk himself believes that concentration of US power around Baghdad actually limits the perspective of foreign journalists. While the capital itself is reasonably secure, most other parts of the nation are extremely dangerous for journalists and other visitors. One of the most dangerous uprisings took place in the holy city of Najah, where radical cleric Moqtada Sadr sought to resist the force of American military control. According to Fisk, sedition of this kind is neither sporadic nor isolated, reflecting the critical limits of government in Iraq. Despite the massive US–UK assault on Fallujah, the Muqawama resistance controls hundreds of square kilometres outside Baghdad; persistent and dangerous uprisings continue to be reported in Fallujah and Ramadi in the west, Fao in the south and Kirkuk in the north. Sunnis continue to resist the elected majority Shi'ite government, while radical Islamicists battle the 'infidel invaders' on all fronts. Baghdad, like Kabul in Afghanistan, remains entirely isolated within a dangerous context of political unrest and violence.

Fisk maintains, in fact, that discussion of the situation by politicians and public commentators in the US and UK is largely based on limited information and hence limited understanding. The discourse of freedom that is attached to the occupation of Iraq largely falsifies the extreme volatility of the situation and the new government's precarious hold over power:

As in Afghanistan, so in Iraq, US air strikes are becoming 'uncoverable,' as the growing insurgencies across the two countries make more and more highways too dangerous for foreign correspondents. Senior US journalists claim that Washington is happy with this situation; bombing wedding parties and claiming the victims were terrorists – as has happened three times in a year – doesn't make good headlines. Reporters can't be blamed for not travelling – but they ought to make it clear that a Baghdad dateline gives no authenticity to their work ... Here is the central crisis of information in Iraq just now. (Fisk, 2004a: 1)

As Fisk himself concedes, it is simply too dangerous to travel outside Baghdad without the permission and management of the Muqawama resistance. Even under the protection of the Muqawama, it is necessary for journalists to disguise their nationality. Many journalists remain inside their hotels, while others move about Baghdad only with the protection of armed 'security advisers'. Like the employees of foreign reconstruction companies, the journalists are ever vigilant against those broad range of political activists who might abduct and execute them in their own 'trial by ordeal' conducted through the global mediasphere.

PRIVATIZATION AND OCCUPATION

The revival of Saddam's 1984 anti-strike and anti-labour laws are distinct evidence of the influence of neoconservative American market ideology in the newly liberated state of Iraq. Naomi Klein (2003) corroborates this view, pointing to Paul Bremer's legacy of privatization and tax-break incentives which are creating the conditions for a substantive sell-off of Iraq's social and commercial infrastructure to American interests. Klein makes the case that Iraq constitutes a form of social and economic 'experiment' for the neoconservative interests in the US administration. On September 19, 2003, only a few months after George Bush declared an end to hostilities, the CPA's chief administrator, Paul Bremer, instituted the now infamous Order 39, a move which *The Economist* declared a 'capitalist dream'. According to the Order, around 200 state-owned enterprises in Iraq would be privatized, making them available for foreign ownership; banks, mines and factories can now be 100 per cent foreign owned and 100 per cent of profit can be repatriated to the foreign country.

The occupation of Iraq, therefore, is not merely a military or diplomatic imperative, but is clearly linked to powerful economic interests. Given the chaotic state of the Iraqi economy and the effects of protracted UN sanctions, it is unlikely that Iraq's own private companies or financial institutions could successfully outbid foreign, especially American, corporate interests in the privatization fire-sale. Moreover, while the Order 39 rules may apply to any form of foreign ownership, it is very clear that foreign companies already working in Iraq – mostly American-based – will be advantaged in the bidding process. Since the beginning of the invasion, the US administration has made it very clear that its own corporations and national economic agencies will have priority in all reconstruction contract negotiations, adding further options for the total annexation of Iraq's corporate economy. The risks involved in participating in the occupied economy are thus offset by the prospects of lucrative reconstruction contracts which would outlive the current dangers of occupation and terrorist assaults. To this extent, the withdrawal of occupying forces from Iraq would have little effect on the country's integration into the global capitalist system, and its transformation into a US satellite economy. For Naomi Klein, this radically broadens the definition of 'occupation':

> The 'troops out' debate overlooks an important fact. If every last soldier pulled out of the Gulf tomorrow and a sovereign government came to power, Iraq would still be occupied by laws written in the interest of another country; by foreign corporations controlling its essential services; by 70% unemployment sparked by public service layoffs. (Klein, 2003: 1)

With perhaps a third of Iraq's major enterprises already owned by international corporations and with the sell-off of basic public infrastructure – including water – this unemployment rate is unlikely to be reduced in the near or medium future. Bremer claims, of course, that Order 39 was an attempt to 'deconstruct' the power of Saddam's Bathist party and its control over the public infrastructure. However, there is little evidence to suggest that Bathist influence reached beyond the senior management levels or that middle and lower-level public employees contributed to the heinous conditions of Saddam's regime. Bremer's approach is undoubtedly modelled on the neoconservative disdain for public enterprise and notions of social responsibility.

It is precisely this modelling which underpins much of the Bush administration's approach to the war on terror and globalization generally. Simon Cooper (2004) has suggested that the privatization of the US military, most particularly through its security and computer-based weapons and surveillance operations, is a manifestation of US economic ideology. Thus,

> while the US army has downsized its personnel by over forty per cent in the past decade, many of these have transferred their labour and expertise to private firms. Indeed, private corporations are the second biggest contributor to the coalition of the willing, well ahead of the United Kingdom, Australia and others. (Cooper, 2004: 111)

Cooper goes on to argue a familiar neo-Marxist case that the war on terror and the Iraq invasion are themselves manifestations of a liberalist ideology which demands the perpetual volition of economic growth: war provides a major stimulus to productive activity, resource exploitation and materials demand.

We would not need to look far into modern history to find that these arguments are by no means universally applicable since many economies have been devastated by major military conflict. Even the UK, nominally a victor in the Second World War, suffered serious economic damage – including severe debt – as a result of armed conflict. However, the United States may seem to constitute a unique case, since its economic and military superiority are such that war may provide a Keynesian stimulus that is not compromised by excessive infrastructure damage or unmanageable debt. In a country where public spending is a very low percentage of GDP compared with other (especially European) First World economies, government spending on military activities may provide a catalyst within a stagnating economy. We can certainly see in Figure 6.1 that the US economy was in relative decline, virtually from the moment of Bush's inauguration as US president.

While authors like Simon Cooper see the war on terror and a promulgated sense of security threat and crisis as a reaction to the general economic decline of the US, we might suggest further that they are also a manifestation of ongoing language wars in which 'symbolic exchange' is clearly implicated. The faltering of the dot.com boom and the general stagnation of the American stock market are a good deal more complicated than Cooper and other neo-Marxists might seem to appreciate. Valid as their arguments may be, there is also

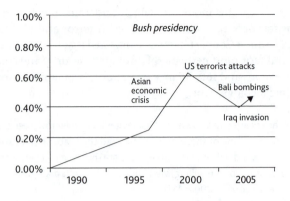

Figure 6.1 Relative US Economic Performance by Market Returns

an important case to be made that the symbolic exchange of capital has become a critical aspect of the mediasphere and the formation of signifiers which have no substance beyond their uncompromising intertextuality. The war on Iraq, therefore, is not merely reactive: it is a part of a creative, conscious and unconscious volition of texts. It may well be that US administrators considered the economic value of an assault on Iraq, especially within a threat of US recession. But it is equally as important to measure these speculations against the broader sweep of motivations, that twisted logic of dreams that Žižek identifies in his account of the invasion.

For Naomi Klein, the new privatized Iraq must and can be challenged on purely legal grounds. Klein points correctly to America's continued unilateralism and contempt for international law. Citing the British Attorney General, Lord Goldsmith, Klein points out that 'the imposition of major structural economic reforms would not be authorised by international law' (Klein, 2003: 3). The US actions in Iraq clearly contravene the 1907 Hague and 1949 Geneva conventions on war and military occupation, as well as the US army's own code of war. The Iraq war and the war on terror are taking us, therefore, into new territories of meaning. Perhaps we are witnessing, through the mediasphere, a more clear revelation of the double-codes and paradoxes of modernism; and perhaps we are witnessing new mechanisms for the exercise of law.

Jane Mayar (2005) corroborates this view, arguing that the US administration's propensity for clandestine security strategies and commercial privatization have combined to produce the most heinous breaches of international law. Writing in the *New Yorker*, Mayar points to the 'outsourcing of torture' by which America seeks to maintain its fidelity to democratic principles by getting others to 'do their dirty work'. This 'rendition' strategy involves the submission of suspected terrorists to a third party, most notably Egypt, where torture is deployed as a matter of course. Mayar outlines numerous examples of this strategy, noting that the need to extract information quickly from suspects who do not distinguish between civilian and combatant targets has become a universal premise for the exercise of torture and the dramatic shift in the conception of human and civil rights. While, of course, this outsourcing of violence and the breach of law may be criticized on legal grounds, it is also of dubious strategic value. Information derived from torture has proved notoriously unreliable, implicating innocent people and leading to vastly erroneous conclusions: detainees under torture, it seems, will offer any information they believe the torturers want to hear, including false confessions. The experience of many of the detainees at Guantanamo Bay prison, as we shall see below, exposes the double-coding of American human rights and notions of law.

ORDEAL AND EXECUTION

Perhaps, as we have considered, the war on terror, the invasion of Iraq and the period of occupation are forming new paradigms in the exercise of law. Or perhaps, the mediasphere is merely exposing the inner machinations and modes of political violence that lie within the law – a further manifestation of the contingency of violence which characterizes the relationship between state and citizen. As we discussed in Chapters 1 and 2, violence is a central platform of televisual culture and text producers of all kinds, including radical militants, are prepared to use this platform in order to serve their particular interests, fiscal and political. Thus, just as David Kelly's death was part of a mediated ritual of judgement and punishment, militants in Iraq have conscripted the media in order to commit to trial those people whom they regard as part of the occupation process. Indeed, the hostage and execution process that has evolved in occupied Iraq bears many of the hallmarks of a medieval trial by ordeal, even as it is shaped as a media spectacle. The brutality of the executions, most likely perpetrated by Saudi or Yemeni militants, is without doubt a further expression of Islamicist hostility to western interventions in the Middle East. As with the victims of 9/11, Bali,

Beslan or London, the victims are less important to the perpetrators than the persuasive impact of the crimes – the sense of anxiety and deep fear they create for westerners, their global supporters and their governments. While there is a twisted logic to these executions, there is no doubt that they are generated as a media event, a spectacle within a global broadcast public sphere which inevitably implicates the messenger as much as the message.

While there have been well over 100 abductions during the occupation period, only a proportion of the captives have been actually executed. Abductions however, usually follow a similar pattern. The victim is videotaped, kneeling before three hooded men who are reading their demands. It appears that the captive is not aware whether he is to be executed at that moment or simply exposed to public scrutiny through the iteration of demands; in a sickening revelation to audiences, however, the kidnappers indicate their intention to execute a victim when they are wearing gloves – demonstrating, no doubt, that they do not want to contaminate their hands with infidels' blood. On occasions, certain kidnap groups will videotape the victim pleading for his/her life or importuning governments to meet the kidnappers' demands.

UK contract worker Ken Bigley, for example, was kept alive for nearly three weeks as his captors sought to have all females released from Iraqi prisons. Two videos were released during his captivity, and then a third showing his decapitation. The pattern of releasing videos to the Arabic TV networks, especially al-Jazeera and al-Arabia, is producing maximum anxiety for the occupation workers and their governments. In some instances, the government accedes to the demands of the militant abductors; the Filipino government, for example, accelerated the withdrawal of its troops from Iraq in return for the release of its national, Angelo de la Cruz. This concession, of course, infuriated the US and UK governments, which are refusing to negotiate with 'terrorists'. This policy is based on a belief that negotiation will constitute a success for the abductors, encouraging them to continue or even expand the abduction strategies.

The refusal to accede to the captors of Ken Bigley created considerable consternation in the United Kingdom, leading to a further deterioration in support for the Blair government. The public measured the government's hard-headed resolve against the simple humanity of Bigley and his family. As an employee of a private contracting company, Bigley too was tried by his captors and by domestic audiences in the UK. His death was barely absorbed by a shocked and sympathetic domestic polis when another hostage, Margaret Hassan, was presented to television audiences across the globe. Unlike Ken Bigley, however, Hassan worked for an international aid organization and had been living in Iraq for nearly thirty years. She was known to many local officials and political leaders, and her kidnap was broadly condemned. Even the leader of one of the major Islamic resistance groups, Abu Musab al-Zarqawy, called for her release. To no avail, however. Despite her well-publicized pleadings and terror, Hassan was publicly murdered by an unidentified group, who claimed that they represented the Iraqi resistance movement, a highly unlikely possibility.

These public executions, along with those of Korean Kim Sun-il and American Nicholas Berg were replayed in graphic detail on the Arabic networks and in censored form across the western world. The horror of these events bewildered and disturbed many non-Arabic audiences for whom violence of this kind had been banished to fictional horror or the cinema poetics of Quentin Tarantino films. The absence of death in reporting on Iraq, including the ban on the visual depiction of American bodies or coffins, had left the west ill-prepared for such atrocity. But in a sense, also like the medieval trial by ordeal or public executions that persisted well into the nineteenth century, the execution of hostages in Iraq seems to confirm the underlying violence and perversity of the enemy in the war on terror. The US government was at least able to draw a line in the sand between its own violence of justice and the violence being perpetrated by brutish and inhumane political criminals. Our modern sensibilities were thus protected from the graphic details of the events by our governments' commitment to justice and the rule of law. The law of brutes is no law at all.

The Internet, nevertheless, carried the video executions with at least one California-based website juxtaposing the beheadings with hardcore porn links and advertisements for 'Horsegirls' (Fisk, 2004b). More terrifying, perhaps, is that the media strategy of the Saudi militants is being adopted by local Iraqi subversives who abducted eight transport workers, a group including Kenyans, Egyptians and Indians. These relatively impecunious internationals, clearly seduced by the offer of better pay in Iraq, were abducted from the dangerous highways that link various Iraqi cities. The captors demanded that the companies employing the drivers withdraw their contracts and leave Iraq – just as other companies and various NGOs and donor organizations had done. The strategy seeks to weaken the American-dominated reconstruction process; in creating greater insecurity around the roadways, the militants are drawing the American forces back onto the transportation lines, rendering them more vulnerable to attack. In either case, the trial by ordeal strategy appears to be producing political and strategic effects. As the western media confines itself to its hotel barracks and as information continually seeps away into a vortex of competing perspectives, western audiences are finding it increasingly difficult to reconcile the images emanating from Iraq with the lofty ideals of US-propagated democracy.

AL-JAZEERA AND THE RULE OF LAW

The Nicholas Berg, Kim Sun-il and Ken Bigley trials by ordeal that have been loaded onto US-based websites seem strangely resonant within the mediasphere that facilitated the 'trial and execution' of David Kelly. In a way, the tragic deaths of these people are not themselves directly related to military engagement, but are the outcome of the mediaization of war and political violence. As we have noted, former British prime minister Margaret Thatcher once famously pronounced that publicity is the oxygen of terrorism. Yet her own pronouncements were the predicate of media 'air time'. Politicians and the political system we are calling 'broadcast democracy' survive on the same oxygen as terrorism. The victims of these trials by mediated ordeal are merely the victims of a political system that sustains itself on the discourse of persuasion within the context of a complex mediasphere. In the space between the present and the absent of this system, the 'gigantic' intervenes – language wars whose gravest consequences are inscribed as judgement and punishment on the bodies of its victims. But these victims are merely props on the screen of a horrific political narrative that continually reconstitutes itself through the east–west divide and a culture that transfixes our own imaginary of violence in the savage imagery of death and despair.

This is precisely the difficulty for the US government, whose efforts to control the local media and the dangerous prospect of alternative perspectives are limited by the context of shared oxygen: that is, democracy and free speech. The answer to this dilemma for the authority of the state, of course, is pronounced in the 'limits to freedom' argument – the idea that each individual must reconcile his or her freedom with the freedom of other individuals. A democratic political system is paraded as the vehicle for this reconciliation. Individual interests, especially in times of crisis, must always submit to the interests of the collective. The paradox, of course, is that the collective is ultimately represented in the interests of a particular set of individuals, a minority with delegated power – the government. Translated as a minority elite, the government itself has the exclusive privilege and right to define the collective interest. Thus, while privileged by the system of democracy and freedom of expression, the government is able to define the level of freedom that does not imperil the collective – how much freedom of speech is too much freedom, how much oxygen is too much to breathe?

The security laws in the US and in other democratic states represent a particular mechanism for managing this problem, especially as many individuals are not even aware of how their rights and freedoms have been reduced through the current context of the war on terror. In addition to the Patriot laws, the US government has also sought to control the free speech and free flow of information emanating from external organizations. Thus, the US has been able to close down the al-Jazeera bureau in Baghdad through the auspices of the Iraqi interim government. While this decision was announced to the al-Jazeera staff as a decision of the Allawi administration, it is clearly sponsored by the interests, if not the directives, of the US government. Donald Rumsfeld had made his feelings about al-Jazeera perfectly plain in a speech at the Chicago Council of Foreign Relations. According to Rumsfeld, al-Jazeera and the Saudi-based al-Arabia were indirectly supporting terrorism by harming the image of America in the Arab world. This was particularly the case when al-Jazeera and al-Arabia reported on Iraqi resistance activities and personnel, who, according to the US authorities, were given excessively sympathetic renderings by the Middle East networks.

In fact, al-Jazeera had already been targeted by US authorities during the invasion period. Al-Jazeera journalists were killed by American mortar fire as they entered Baghdad (see Chapter 4) and on March 24, 2003 al-Jazeera finance reporters had their press accreditation revoked by the New York stock exchange. In what was an extraordinary gesture, the stock exchange cited the al-Jazeera broadcast of captured American soldiers, a breach of Geneva conventions, as the reason for the revocation. In defence of its approach, al-Jazeera's Washington Bureau Chief, Hafez Mirazi, argued that:

There is a feeling in our newsroom that you need to be as realistic as possible and carry the image of war and the effect that war has on people. If you are in a war then your population shouldn't just eat their dinner and watch sanitized images on TV and video games produced by the technological whizzes in the Pentagon and say, 'This is war.' No. You really need to show every family what your men and women are going through. (Mirazi, cited in Kolodzy & Wade, 2003)

Of course, those supporting the al-Jazeera ban made no mention of the American networks' footage of captured Iraqi soldiers which had been broadcast globally during the advance on Baghdad. The truly distinguishing feature of al-Jazeera is this willingness to present the most gruesome details of the war, including images of dead civilians and soldiers on both sides of the conflict. The al-Jazeera policy insists that war is horror and that all of us, in essence, must be placed on trial by ordeal. If we are to commit our young men and women to inflict this horror on themselves and others, we must at least be prepared to witness it; our reward or compensation is then a decision based on the fullness of knowledge rather than a fantasy of Hollywood ideology.

The irony in Mirazi's commendation of freedom is unmistakable. What needs to be said, however, is that al-Jazeera's principles are entirely consistent with the American Constitution's Fifth Amendment and with the ideals of Carlyle's fourth estate. These principles hearken back even to the classical model of a participative democracy, a public sphere in which informed citizens discuss and debate the issues of the day. These principles of absolute free speech are compromised, however, within a context of political delegation which creates complex intersections of hierarchy, social authority and governmentality. Combined with the hierarchical formations associated with economic capitalism, these managerial nodes contribute to an uneven distribution of semiotic resources within society; in a context of language wars, it seems that absolute freedom of speech poses a threat to the discursive privilege of specific groups, including governments.

The rise of broadcast media creates further problems for a principle of absolute freedom of speech, at least inasmuch as it integrates information with a televisual culture constructed around the audience's visceral gratification, consumerism and visual pleasure. The narratization of information ('info-tainment') is linked to the predisposition of the modern networked media to overcompensate for its financial and semiotic deficits through the production of excess. Thus, the sensate pleasure of the audience becomes a primary production and financial objective for many corporate media companies.

In Chapter 1 we discussed the ways in which violence has been transformed as discourse in modern societies (see also Foucault, 1977a), most particularly as a media spectacle. Violence has thus become a central motif within a hyperreal consciousness; film texts, TV drama, sport, and video games all contribute to the formation of a mediascape which shapes the cultural, social and political underpinnings of violence. These underpinnings are consonant with the modes of violence which are exclusively controlled by the state and its democratically sanctioned authority. In other words, the discourses of state-sponsored violence are largely co-extensive with the discourses of violence which are presented through the media; information (infotainment) featuring violence is folded into this same cultural ambit.

As we have discussed, western governments, especially the Coalition governments, have been very careful to manage information, including information about the violence of war. We have also noted that specific media companies have voluntarily censored the graphic depiction of bodily violence. The notion of 'taste' has always been central to the companies' decision about what may or may not be 'appropriate' for domestic news presentation and consumption. The preferences, anxieties and occasioned moral outrage that constitute this 'taste' are clearly associated with the cultural politics of specific social groups. There is, for example, an astonishing contrast between the absence of dead and injured bodies in the Iraq invasion, and the presence of such bodies in the coverage of the Tsunami disaster: a body destroyed through political calamity is more offensive, it seems, than a body destroyed by natural disaster.

The al-Jazeera model, therefore, is unsustainable in a culture that has formed its modes of violence through these highly managed and culturally inscribed narratives. Direct images of the beheading of American citizens might seem to serve the political interests of those who support the occupation of Iraq, confirming the demonic and brutish nature of the Islamicists. The horror of the event, however, seems not to fit with public taste or with the modes of narratization which ensure the triumph of the victim–hero. Thus, the event may be talked about but not presented visually, even though the image is no less terrible than the killings shown nightly on TV dramas or in digital video games. The difference is not determined by the confronting 'reality' of the Iraq beheadings, as many may assume. Rather, the difference is the mode of narratization: the executions of hostages in Iraq are difficult to contain within the cultural boundaries of visceral pleasure and sanctioned political violence since they immediately involve human responsibility, morality and blame – issues that are extremely difficult to manage. The Allawi interim administration, directed by the Americans, closed the al-Jazeera Baghdad bureau because it was not constrained by the same political concerns as the US. Muhammad Bashar al-Faidhi, a spokesman for the Association of Muslim Scholars, has criticized the closure of the al-Jazeera office, expressing his disappointment that Iraqis cannot yet be trusted with freedom of speech: 'There are a lot of tragedies that have gone unreported. We used to wonder why Aljazeera had not been reporting those facts ... but when we learned about American pressure on the channel, we understood why' (cited on aljazeera.net). The 'why' refers here not only to the pressure of American political interests, but to the global mediasphere and its uncompromising language wars in to which al-Jazeera has been drawn.

IMAGES OF VIOLENCE:
PHOTOGRAPHS AND THE TRANSFORMATIVE PUBLIC SPHERE

Hariman and Lucaites (2003) argue that the public sphere is certainly a contingency of mass mediation but it is forged largely in terms of a shared social construction. Unlike the postmodernists, who doubt the existence of an integrated public, nor indeed an integrated individual subject-identity, Hariman and Lucaites argue that a 'public' exists when the collective of individuals evolves an actual self-awareness and sense of historical agency. This is only possible, according to Hariman and Lucaites, when 'individual auditors see themselves in the collective representations that are the materials of public culture' (2003: 36). Photo images generated through the news media constitute a key element of this process since they are broadly disseminated and highly accessible:

> The daily stream of photojournalistic images, while merely supplemental to the task of reporting the news, defines the public through an act of common spectatorship. When the event shown is itself a part of national life, the public seems to *see itself*, and to see itself in terms of a particular conception of civic life. (Hariman & Lucaites, 2003: 36, emphasis added)

Returning to the structuralist–semiological conceptions of Roland Barthes and Umberto Eco, Hariman and Lucaites argue that photographic images engage inevitably in the social and political interactions which are an essential feature of public life; as Barthes argued some time ago, the aesthetic of the image may include or even exceed the controlling force of 'ideology' (2003: 38). These arguments, of course, were developed and employed by British cultural studies during the 1960s and 1970s; scholars from the Birmingham Centre for Contemporary Cultural Studies adapted Althusser's reworked Marxist concept of ideology, arguing that a text reader would become politically 'positioned' as s/he filtered and favoured specific meanings in accordance with dominant cultural values and norms (see Lewis, 2002a: 124–40). In certain circumstances, the BCCS scholars argued, this ideology could be challenged through an alignment of popular discourses within the culture of specific communities (the working class, youth, women, ethnic minorities and so on). Stuart Hall (1982) argued that Gramsci's conception of hegemony provided a leverage for these 'subordinate' social groups to negotiate against the rigidity and absolute control of social elites and their dominant ideology. The 'polysemy' or multiple meaning potential of a text may allow readers, that is, to escape the dominant reading, creating conditions for resistance and social change. Following Michel de Certeau (1984), a number of cultural studies scholars have suggested that alternative readings may, over time, contribute to widespread social change; the sexual revolution and changes in women's social roles over recent decades were brought about, at least in part, by the radicalization of teenage popular culture and texts which provided new spaces for sexual and gender expressivity. A text, therefore, may be an agent of social liberation or social control, depending on the socio-political and cultural circumstances of its reception. In many respects, this tension between control and liberation, the alternative potential that a text carries intrinsically in its meaning-making, constitutes an important mode of language war.

According to Hariman and Lucaites, an iconic photo, one which has assumed the status of 'universal' recognition and which experiences extended circulation over time, is particularly susceptible to this ambiguity, since on the one hand it engages directly with the political interests of the citizenry, and on the other it is maintained through the institutional and economic interests of media and other social elites. This tension between public and ideological interests 'is played out in the process by which collective memory is created through the ... appropriation of images over time' (Hariman & Lucaites, 2003: 38). In this sense, the iconic photo may well provide the essential material for social changes, a political representation around which the public rallies, and identifies itself and its interests. But these changes will inevitably prove evolutionary: 'their meanings and effects are likely to be established slowly, shift with changes in context and use, and be fully evident only in a history of both official and vernacular appropriations' (Hariman and Lucaites, 2003: 38). In other words, social changes may be deft and imperceptible as the opposition between elite (ideological) and public (resistant) interests are resolved through the momentum of the latter.

Hariman and Lucaites exemplify their theory through an analysis of the 'Accidental napalm attack' (*New York Times*, 1972), an 'iconic' photograph which depicts a naked girl who has been 'accidentally' burned by US troops during the America–Vietnam War. According to innumerable commentators, this photograph helped to galvanize public opposition to the American invasion of Vietnam. The publication of videos and photographs taken at Baghdad's Abu Ghraib prison was met with a similar prescience; many commentators believed that the images would radically alter public opinion and hence American foreign policy on the Middle East. These commentators, especially those who had been opposed to the invasion and occupation of Iraq, claimed that the images constituted a major blow for the Bush military project in the Middle East. In many respects, this prescience was forged around the sort of view propounded by Hariman and Lucaites, the idea that an integrated public sphere would rally around a mediated political conceit in order to create an effective social transformation. If this is the case, then photographic images would function as a corollary of writing democracy, enhancing the sort of integrated 'public sphere' paradigm encouraged by Jürgen Habermas and others. This idea will be tested in the discussion that follows.

ORDEALS AT ABU GHRAIB

Used as one of Saddam's torture camps, the prison at Abu Ghraib was refurbished and recommissioned by the US authorities after the fall of Baghdad (2003). The cells were cleaned and re-bricked, floors were tiled, and toilets, showers and a medical centre were installed in the new military prison. By September of 2003 there were several thousand Iraqis being 'detained' in the prison. These prisoners, however, were not primarily military personnel, but civilians who had been arrested during random military sweeps at checkpoints on the major highways. While some reports suggest that the inmates included around 107 'children' (*Sunday Herald*, 2004), it is certainly clear that teenagers of unspecified ages were detained at Abu Ghraib, along with women and men. All of these prisoners fell into one of the following three categories: common criminals, security detainees suspected of committing crimes against the Coalition, and a small number of 'high-value' insurgency leaders. The prison came under the broad command of army reserve Brigadier General Janis Karpinski. Karpinski, while having experience with intelligence and operations with the US Special Forces, had no prison experience. In Iraq she was placed in charge of the 800th Military Police Brigade, which included three large prisons and eight battalions in which there were 3,400 reservists, most of whom had no experience in penal operations or administration.

While Karpinski reported to the St Petersburg *Times* that her prison system was working exceptionally well, others within the system were feeling outraged by the extreme and routine abuses to which they were daily witness. One military police specialist, Joseph Darby, had been handed a CD from a fellow military policeman (MP), Charles Graner; the CD contained images of naked prisoners in various submissive and sexual poses. Darby reported the incident to his superiors and an investigation was undertaken by Major General Antonio Taguba. According to Taguba's report (February 26, 2004), the abuses at Abu Ghraib, first detailed by the International Red Cross, took place between October and December of 2003. As Seymour Hersh outlined in the *New Yorker*, Taguba's report, which was not available for public dissemination, identified 'sadistic, blatant, and wanton criminal abuses' at Abu Ghraib:

> Breaking chemical lights and pouring the phosphoric liquid on detainees; pouring cold water on naked detainees; beating detainees with a broom handle and a chair; threatening male detainees with rape; allowing a military guard to stitch the wound of a detainee who was injured after being slammed against the wall in his cell; sodomizing a detainee with a chemical light and perhaps a broom stick; and using military working dogs to frighten and intimidate detainees with threats of attack; and in one instance actually biting a detainee. (cited in Hersh, 2004: 1)

As well as the evidence provided by detainees, Taguba referred to photographs and videos which were taken by the prison guards themselves, but which were not included in the report because of their 'extreme sensitivity'. A number of these videos and photographs were later to be shown by the US TV programme *60 Minutes II* in stark revelations about the Abu Ghraib abuses.

While an 'independent' Pentagon review (August 2004) headed by former defence secretary James Schlesinger effectively rejected the idea of systematic abuse at Abu Ghraib, Taguba's report raised important questions about the ways in which the reservist prison officers and the professional prison interrogators operated. Taguba recommended disciplinary action against a number of reservists: Sergeant Ivan Frederick, Sergeant Javal Davis, Specialist Charles Graner, Specialist Megan Ambuhl, Specialist Sabrina Harman and Private Jeremy Svits. Private Lynndie England, who had become pregnant in Iraq, had already been reassigned to Fort Bragg in North Carolina. Frederick, the oldest and most senior of the group, was called before an Article 32 hearing, which had been convened in order to investigate whether there was sufficient evidence to court martial the accused personnel. Frederick's defence was principally built around the idea that the guards at the prison were following the orders and examples of senior officers. As Seymour Hersh explains, the evidence at the hearing seemed to indicate that abuse was 'largely routine'. Frederick himself had been explaining to friends and family that the military intelligence teams, including the CIA and interrogation specialists from private defence contractors, formed an elite corps within the prison. Their codes and modes of behaviour provided a model for the largely inexperienced MPs at Abu Ghraib.

While Frederick and the other guards accused of abuse would necessarily be seeking mitigation, there is certainly a sense, both in their behaviours and their defence, that there was a mood of 'anything goes' at the prison. The interrogations and intelligence practices are as much to be queried as the specific personnel. And while the Schlesinger review accepted that poor decisions had been made about the prison system's management and workforce requirements, intelligence and command systems need to be seriously investigated – most particularly in the context of accumulating revelations about US-sanctioned practices of torture and limitations on individual rights for 'suspected terrorists'. Taguba's report, in fact, broached these questions in its analysis of the practices of the CIA and private interrogation contractors. Specifically, the report recommended that several senior officers in the Military Intelligence and in the private CACI International interrogation unit be reprimanded and/or relieved of duty. These senior people, Taguba insisted, 'were either directly or indirectly responsible for the abuses at Abu Ghraib' (cited in Hersh,

2004: 6). Taguba was also highly critical of General Karpinski, who was 'rarely seen' in the prisons she was supposed to be running, and who tended to neglect strong evidence pointing to the possibilities of abuse and mismanagement.

Taguba's report, the subsequent hearings and trials of the guards represent an attempt by the US authorities to reinstate rule of law in their own occupation penal system. As local Iraqis were quick to note, the bearers of law and justice were themselves guilty of exploitation, brutality and tyranny. The grand projects of democracy and rule of law seemed duplicitous to a people whose safety and security were becoming increasingly imperilled by the US-led 'liberators'. Indeed, the public exposure of these tyrannies was an unintended effect of 'mediaization', and was only partially related to the exercise of the conquerors' ethical and legal responsibilities. The guards' videos and photographs, which represented their activities at Abu Ghraib prison, constituted the critical evidence for Taguba and ultimately the global publics. It is the guards' own 'productive' participation in media culture which leads them to judgement – that is, to the trials that are an intrinsic part of audience discernment within a 'broadcast democracy'. The texts produced by the guards become the conduit which engages citizens in the matrix of representations, ideas, images and persuasive perspectives that constitute the political mediasphere.

While these recordings are ultimately absorbed into the official discourses of democracy and law via the mainstream media, they are nevertheless generated through the democratic field of personal and community-based political expression. No matter how heinous this expression may appear, it is at least legitimate inasmuch as it is 'of the people', an iteration of personal and corporeal politics. In fact, the events at Abu Ghraib may have entirely escaped notice by the global media networks and US authorities had they not been represented for the visual and visceral pleasure of the guards themselves. A number of scholars and media commentators have questioned why the mainstream media took so long to absorb and develop the story. While the media made some attempt to explore the detention system, there seemed little interest or willingness to pursue the story – at least until the publication of the Abu Ghraib photographs. As Sherry Ricchiardi laments: 'During a town-hall style meeting with Pentagon workers on May 11 [2004], the defense secretary smugly noted that it was "the military, not the media" that discovered and reported the prisoner abuse at Abu Ghraib' (2004: 1). Despite reports from the International Red Cross and a number of minor or incidental media references, the Abu Ghraib abuses seemed to pass unnoticed until the airing of the photographs on *60 Minutes II* (April 28, 2004) and the publication of Seymour Hersh's article in the *New Yorker* two days later. Ricchiardi expresses her own confusion about the tardiness of media interest in the abuses, which only became a major international story three and a half months after the completion of Taguba's report. Ricchiardi cites several reasons for the torpid work of the US media:

> Media critics and newsroom professionals cite a wide array of factors: the Bush administration's penchant for secrecy and controlling the news agenda; extremely dangerous conditions that limited reporting by Western reporters in much of Iraq; the challenge of covering the multifaceted situation in the embattled country with a finite amount of reporting firepower. Some see a media still intimidated by the post 9/11 orgy of patriotism. Yet there's little doubt that missed cues and ignored signals were part of the mix. (2004: 3)

It is clearly the first of these reasons that most irritates Ricchiardi and other members of the more critical or 'liberal' media. The Bush administration's close management of information is seen as the nemesis of quality journalism and the primary challenge for on-the-ground reporters. However, what broke this silence on Abu Ghraib was less the work of professional journalists, and more the work of amateurs – the Abu Ghraib wardens themselves. Their own very direct participation in the mediasphere – the recording, publication and distribution of their narrative – is what actually exposed them to military authority and the broader conditions of the democratic legislative process. As the guards recorded their narrative – a fantasy of sexual, military and national power – they were engaging in a pleasure game which, to their own minds, accorded with the essentially vile imperatives of their duty. In terms of their own legal defence and the sexual politics of their bodies, the guards sought to explain their actions through an upward delegation of responsibility – to their senior officers, the US authorities and their culture generally. According to their defence lawyers, the guards were acting in accordance with what they perceived to be their 'duty' or more broadly their cultural expectations.

This impulse to representation illuminates the complex cultural, moral and legal web in which the guards' actions are bound. It was the transformation of the act to image which exposed the abuses at

Abu Ghraib prison to the surveillance and judgement of the public and the mediasphere. Secretary of Defense Rumsfeld might boast that it was the military itself which identified the activities of the Abu Ghraib night shift, but in fact these abuses were only an issue of concern when they became available to the contingencies of power that are constructed around a broadcast media, governments and their publics. Though not excusing the tardiness of the media's work, the editor of the *New York Times*, Bill Keller, claims that, 'Any honest editor will give you the same answer. It's the pictures. That's what did it. But it shouldn't require visual drama to make us pay attention to something like this' (cited in Ricchiardi, 2004: 3). These pictures provided not merely visual evidence of the abuse, however; they provided a discourse of emotional, moral and sexual stimulation which is the essential quality of a televisual media culture. The sexual presentation of this abuse, personified most dramatically in the photographs of Lynndie England, provided an 'acceptable' or 'recognizable' narrative framework for the violence. Unlike the beheading of American workers in Iraq, the sexual depictions stimulated a culturally consumable motif through which the interests of broadcasters, advertisers and audiences could congregate. Abu Ghraib, that is, made 'good copy' because the images combined the two vital ingredients of sex and violence within a political and moral context which seemed not to exceed the sensibilities of the media consumers.

Indeed, and like all good stories, the Abu Ghraib abuses stimulated a thoroughly 'human' response which aggregated moral and ideological issues within a profoundly emotional and 'affective' public engagement. The texts of the photographs contributed to a politics of rage which swept through the Arabic and western public spheres. They tarnished the moral authority of the United States' Coalition, stimulating new questions about the cultural condition of a nation which advances an ideological and ethical privilege over those whom it would depose and conquer. A US-commissioned report into Abu Ghraib compared it unfavourably with the typical conditions at Guantanamo Bay. Yet in both cases, the prisons have been established around a security and penal code which bears very little resemblance to the ideals of traditional democracy, citizens' rights or rule of law. The detainees also seem to be victims of a form of trial by ordeal, one in which they are implicated in the war of terror – essentially a media war – which strips them of signification as it seeks to deny them basic human rights and dignity. Their guilt, that is, is assumed by their entrapment in the web of terror.

The same, of course, might be said of the guards at Abu Ghraib whose own 'trials' have become amplified through their engagement in the vast politics of the war and the global mediasphere. Within the language wars that surround the photographs, the US authorities would like to suggest that the guards are aberrant and that democracy, rationalism and the rule of law will ultimately prevail over miscreants and sexual excess. For the viewers of al-Jazeera and al-Arabia television networks, however, the photographs must confirm some of their gravest fears about western values, sexual permissiveness and gender anarchy. Between the polar perspectives – one which reads 'aberration' and the other 'standards and norms' – the media creates its zone of doubt. The rationalism that is perpetually invoked by western governments and commentators seems continually to be subverted by the sensate experiences being generated through representation generally and the Abu Ghraib photographs in particular. Within a context of information and knowledge formation that is always incomplete, all players are on trial – the US, the guards, the detainees, US–western culture. The media absorbed the events and generated them through the non-rational, sensate discourses of the image. Through the advance of good and evil, the texts employ themselves in a forcefield of undecidability. The guards are guilty of excess. The media absorbs that excess into its own volition of deficit and overproduction. Abu Ghraib becomes another zone of reference, though many in its audience, while outraged, remain uncertain about its implications and meanings. The rationalism of Habermas' communicative action and regenerated public sphere is challenged by the emotional and sexual power of the broadcast image and a crisis of meaning which characterizes contemporary culture within the mediasphere.

THE BODY POLITIC AND ABU GHRAIB

Hariman and Lucaites' (2003) analysis of the 'Accidental napalm attack' suggests that it is the nakedness of the fleeing girl's body which is central to the photograph's social force and iconic durability. While images of the violence and brutality of the America–Vietnam War abound, the conflation of a non-prurient sexual innocence with the horrors of human conflict constructed a powerful anti-war motif. This motif provided a focus for the projection of a new and increasingly consensual public identity which functioned like a social superstructure, drawing together the attitudes and sensibilities of individual citizens into a more generalized political movement of opposition and change. As the child was an incidental or 'accidental' victim of America's moral and ideological expansionism, her nakedness personifies the pre-moral Christian purity of Eden. In a manner which Freud and Lacan may have envisaged as 'pre-language' or 'pre-discursive', the girl seems to be fleeing the brutal actualization of a discourse that is shaped in armed military conflict. She is escaping, that is, the force of democracy and its violent rule of law.

Many commentators have contrasted the media reporting in Vietnam and Iraq, suggesting very specifically that the American government and the mainstream media have deliberately obscured the horrors of military activities in the Gulf from public view (Rampton & Stauber, 2003, Waldman, 2004). The strategy of 'embedding' journalists, government legislation prohibiting the broadcast of images depicting American deaths, and the voluntary censorship by networks like Fox have all contributed to this obfuscation. Even so, global media publics have had considerably enhanced access to alternative representations of the Iraq invasion, most especially as they have been distributed through public broadcast systems and the Internet. To this extent, the horrors of the invasion – and of war generally – have been available to interested publics, including opinion leaders and groups opposed to the invasion. The Internet, in particular, has provided a global broadcast facility for the production and redistribution of images and stories presented by Arabic news networks such as al-Jazeera and al-Arabia. These broadcasters, along with a number of European, Canadian and Australian web-writers, have ensured that the horrors of the invasion and occupation of Iraq are being distributed to global audiences. These 'horrors', of course, include images of civilian bomb victims in Baghdad, American body-bags, the beheadings of captured workers, and the perspectives of resistance organizations like al-Qa'ida, the Muqawama and the Iraqi Islamic Army.

The Abu Ghraib photographs, therefore, are to be understood within this general context of mediated horror. Like the nakedness of the 'accidental napalm victim', the nakedness of the Iraqi detainees concentrates this horror through its archetypical other – sexual and sensate pleasure. The 'nude', in this instance, becomes the focus of opposing effects, intensifying the historical and cultural problematic of western corporeality, including, and most particularly, mind–body dualism. Expressed politically, this division, as intimated above, has stimulated the subjugation of bodily aesthetics by rational institutions and discourses like the public sphere and democracy. As we have also suggested, this hierarchical order is perpetually subverted by the image and the expressivities of a mediasphere which centralizes the aesthetic and sexual power of the individual body.

The nakedness of the Abu Ghraib detainees is profoundly implicated in this notion of a broadcast, participative democracy. This does not expunge the possibility or plausibility of a rational public sphere, but exists in concert with other political forms. Within these politics is a 'microphysics of power' which Michel Foucault (1977a, 1981, 1991) has famously called the politics of the self and the individual body; it is at the level of the body, Foucault reminds us, that politics are most powerfully and insistently experienced. The nakedness and sexual harnessing of the Iraqi prisoners' bodies, like the accidental napalm child, define the politics of the war in lurid and confronting detail. But less like the child, this nakedness is conscripted into a broadly constituted sexual politics that centres on culturally inscribed notions of identity, ethnicity, nation and class.

The 'shock' of the Abu Ghraib images, along with their political potential, is part of a highly sexualized cultural contention, one which centres specifically upon the power of female sexuality and the subordination of men. In discussing the war on Iraq, Wendy McElroy (2003) argues that the contiguity of military engagement is forcing western feminists to review their own solipsistic understandings of culture and the role of women. The feminism of the Middle East, according to McElroy, insists that women's liberation is absolutely integrated into religion, the family and men. Unlike the ideology of familiar second-wave feminism which identifies religion and the family with the hegemony of patriarchy, Middle Eastern feminism seeks continually to reconcile gender roles within an Islamic culture that is constituted around the identity of the devout, family matriarch. This leaves the liberal feminist in the west with a serious and confronting problem: 'Western feminists cannot resolve their ideology with that of Islam. War and its aftermath will bring the two movements into intimate contact and conflict. The result is likely to be a recasting of the definition of feminism' (McElroy, 2003).

To some extent, this ideological battle is personified through the photographs of the Abu Ghraib prison. The deep offence caused to Muslims and non-Muslims is clearly related to the rights, honour and sexual dignity of the prisoners, most of whom as we have noted are non-combatants, petty criminals and minor security suspects. The western female body articulates itself in the imagery of the Abu Ghraib photographs through the activation of a feminist, liberational fantasy. At the interface of these complex cultural and language wars, the female body is once again problematized; female GIs like Lynndie England subvert the Islamicist ideal, creating images of female power which clearly refer to dominatrix pornography. As an expression of liberated and powerful American femininity, the image of Lynndie England holding a naked Iraqi prisoner by a leash constitutes exactly the agonistic contiguity that Wendy McElroy anticipates and fears. The nakedness and submissive pose of the male Iraqi prisoner express an oppositional feminist aspiration of the 1960s in terms of a normative actualization: the ideal of liberated female sexuality and the ascendancy of sexual power is inscribed in a motif which asserts the supremacy of the western cultural ideal and the achievements of second-wave feminism. England and others at the prison express the power of the American conquest through direct feminist allusions.

Of course, many feminists in the US very quickly denounced the behaviour of the guards, but there can be no mitigating the simple idea that western feminism is complicit in the sexual expressivity of the Abu Ghraib photographs. Barbara Ehrenreich (2004) concedes as much, arguing that in the Abu Ghraib photographs 'you have everything that the Islamic fundamentalists believe characterizes western culture, all nicely arranged in one hideous image – imperial arrogance, sexual depravity ... and gender equality' (2004: 1). Ehrenreich goes on to suggest that patriarchal military conditioning is clearly to blame for the behaviour of the female guards at Abu Ghraib, noting that, 'The struggles for peace and social justice and against imperialist and racist arrogance, cannot, I am truly sorry to say, be folded into the struggle for gender equality' (2004: 4). Ehrenreich unwittingly betrays the paradox of her own sorrow, however, conceding that, even though she opposed the 1990–91 Gulf War, she was 'proud of our servicewomen and delighted that their presence irked their Saudi hosts' (2004: 2).

This 'delight' is precisely the delight being expressed by England, Ambuhl and Haman in their sexual games with the Abu Ghraib prisoners. The pleasure of their (western) subversive sexual power expresses precisely the intersection of two contending modes of meaning: the pleasure of sexual play, and the political pleasures which invert, as they assault, the authority and sexual–moral dignity of Islamic masculinity. Of course, we might simply account for these sexual pleasures in terms of the spoils of war; against its horrors, the wardens may have simply been creating textual narratives that are familiar in their home cultures. The spoils of conquest are constituted as visual and visceral pleasure, a pleasure which for the conquerors, at least, must have seemed a barely consequential, if vaguely nihilistic, resonance of the easy delight of sexual arousal. Within these representational narratives, the Iraqi enemy is reconfigured as playmate, even though the play exists within the framework of a complex and barely comprehensible set of hierarchical systems that embrace friendship, conquest, gender, sexuality, military structures, class, religions, nations and cultures. Within this confusion, the wardens at Abu Ghraib refer to the home culture, to televisualization and its reliable sequences of visual and sensory gratification. The guards invoke a familiar sexuality in which games have become an essential part of the liberational lexicon.

Thus the imperative to represent is a defining characteristic of contemporary televisual culture. The wardens at Abu Ghraib were, as much as anything else, ensnared in the momentum of visualization, creating images that they may have themselves engaged with in dominatrix pornography or popular culture texts; even music videos are replete with dominatrix motifs and allusions to bondage, leather and female sexual power. While we might consider that the context of horror and the twisted logic of the Iraq invasion should have disconnected any reference to popular (western) television fantasy, televisual culture situates sexual arousal within a prevalent and pervasive ontology of imagistic violence (Bok, 1999). Thus, it is not simply that the sexual play at Abu Ghraib was a relief from the actual horrors of warfare, it is also that the expressivities of sex and violence are part of the fundamental *episteme* of the home culture and its televisual hyperreality. The imperative to represent drives the actions of the wardens, both as actors within, and producers of, text. The guards video and photograph their exploits because that is how the world has been constructed for them – that is their *episteme* and their mode of expressive pleasure. But it is, of course, also their undoing. As they seek to share their texts with new audiences, the gaps in the meanings they are seeking to create return to destroy the narrative, deconstructing and then reconstructing the *episteme* within which they have been so naively and cruelly operating. As the exploits at the prison become 'news' for a broadening network of institutions, audiences and publics, the guards, like all creative text-makers, lose editorial control. The meaning of the text, thereby, escapes them, as it enters the globalizing field of the mediasphere.

Paul Virilio (1989, 2000, 2002) suggests that this culture of visualization is central to the whole project of military domination. While the guards at Abu Ghraib must have believed they were merely subscribing to a dominant sexual–cultural order, their actions subscribe more broadly to the technological imperative which, according to Virilio, drives the massive machinery of US-led global hegemony. The capacity of the US military to observe and record the global citizenry and its activities enables the US to maintain its interests and power across the world. The guards, both wittingly and unwittingly, participate in this process of surveillance, confirming the superiority of their nation and its modes of ideological domination. Barbara Ehrenreich, in fact, identifies some mitigation for the wardens, especially the women, who are mostly indigent, poorly educated and low-skilled workers with limited occupational options. Within the rigid and often brutally oppressive military hierarchy, women like Lynndie England are forced to adopt the patriarchal system in order to survive within its masculinist culture. This socially dubious mix of gender and class leaves the female soldiers with little choice but to obey the explicit and implicit commands of male material, symbolic and sexual interest. The hegemonic cultural practice of visualization thereby ensnares the female body into the web of a sexual order which is supported by masculine imperialism and technological rationality.

Taguba's report concedes that the processes of command and interrogation at Abu Ghraib leave much to be desired. While Brigadier General Karpinski was relieved of command in Iraq and numerous members of the 372nd division are facing criminal charges, the system of obedience and violence which prevailed at Abu Ghraib remains largely unaddressed. The Bush administration and Joint Chiefs of Staff appear to have managed the issue through a determined discourse of 'aberration'. This was not the true America or the true American mission. For those who oppose the mission, however, this is precisely the personification of a war that has no value, other than the materialist and hegemonic interests of the US elite. Abu Ghraib remains bewildering to many members of the community because it suggests or *connotes* a deep malaise within a culture that spawns such abuse. If the ends of freedom, democracy and justice can generate 'depravity' of this kind, then there can be no moral authority in its mission or the ideology which supports it.

THEATRE OF WAR

We cannot say with any confidence that the Abu Ghraib photographs, most specifically the image of the leashed prisoner, will assume the status of historical icon. We can say almost certainly, however, that these photographs have not substantially altered the thinking of the Coalition governments nor their citizenry in any measurable way. As further evidence of torture and abuse has come to light, including the 'breadbasket' abuses by British prison guards in Basrah, public despondency about the war seems only to deepen. Elections in the US and Australia in 2004 returned with increased majorities the incumbent conservative governments that had sponsored the invasion and occupation of Iraq. In the British elections in 2005 dissatisfaction with Tony Blair's management of the war was not enough to remove the Labour government from office, even though protest votes were directed to the Liberal Democrats. We might conclude, therefore, that the universal outrage with which the Abu Ghraib photographs were met seems not to have translated into a more generalized public expression within the institutionalized electoral system. The photographs, we might assume, were not sufficient in themselves to galvanize public protest against the war and force the removal of 'responsible' governments from power.

But of course nor were the reports of 100,000 civilian casualties in Iraq, the stories of social and political chaos, the beheadings of abducted workers, the savage ethnic tension, the relentless and hideously violent resistance, and the complete absence of weapons of mass destruction. Where they have engaged with the Iraq invasion at all, the Coalition publics seem only mildly concerned about its consequences and ramifications. Thus, while the *majority* of citizens within the US, Australia and the United Kingdom may respond negatively to polls and surveys about the Iraq invasion and occupation, these views seem only partially significant for the electors' actual political choices.

Habermas complains about the broadcast, image-based media because its affective and emotional impact disrupts the rational potential of the public. Commentators like Hariman and Lucaites counter his arguments, suggesting that a photograph, which is a highly accessible communicative form, enables broad sections of the community to 'identify' with the information, ideas and narrative of the image; social change becomes possible through the gradual and heaving reorientation of this identification toward a new position and presumably new knowledge. The problem with this theory of an aggregated public is the complex nature of the process of meaning-making, on the one hand, and the nature of the modern social 'polis', on the other.

If it is possible for a universal iconography to exist at all in contemporary mediated culture, then it can only be ephemeral and highly unstable. Global contiguities, social fragmentation, diversity and the proliferation of mediated information and imagery in televisual culture have contributed to a context of increasing semiotic instability. Thus, while communications may orient itself toward social and semiotic stability, televisualization, the pre-eminence of the image and the political context of the mediasphere seem predisposed to the problematization of stable universalities of meaning. In this sense, the universal meanings by which a public might identify itself and its collective consciousness can never be fixed or stable because they are always evolving and always seeking to overcome themselves and their own semiotic deficiency. Identification can only ever be a partial process since the complex associations–dissociations that function throughout a culture, especially a meaning-saturated televisual culture, continually override current options with new and evolving possibilities – these possibilities are themselves the outcome of a dynamic conflation of meaning-making processes that always bear with them the potential of non-meaning.

The Abu Ghraib photographs have contributed to the formation of new meanings, even as professional communicators seek to marshal a highly specific mode of understanding or *ideology*. The apparent success of the Bush administration in controlling the meanings and pursuant political damage of the Abu Ghraib photographs merely camouflages the irradiating effects of the event and its mediation. The meaning of Abu Ghraib lies somewhere in the broad conflation of possibilities and communicative fragments that pervade the culture and the publics' experiences of the Iraq war. But what is clear is that a notion of law, like its electoral and democratic source, has become problematized within the new mediasphere. Like David Kelly, Ken Bigley, Margaret Hassan and Nicholas Berg, the guards and inmates at Abu Ghraib were arraigned by a mediated war in which 'justice' becomes a central narrative in the counterclaims of violent, political adversaries. It is not 'law' that prevails over the Abu Ghraib guards, but a hollow resonance, a political expediency which exalts itself in the grand discourses of democracy and liberation.

CONCLUSIONS

1. A major objective of the invasion of Iraq was to establish democracy and 'rule of law'. These Enlightenment concepts have been transformed through the emergence of televisual culture and the global mediasphere.

2. Rule of law, in particular, must accommodate changes in the way politics and government operate within the mediasphere. The death of chemical and biological weapons expert David Kelly can be explained in part by these changes. Kelly became conscripted into the language wars surrounding the Iraq invasion and WMDs when he suggested to a media conduit that the British government's WMDs dossier (which was to be used as a justification for attacking Iraq) was effectively 'sexed up' in order to enhance its persuasive power.

3. The publication of Kelly's name and identity created the conditions for a virtual 'trial by media ordeal', which led eventually to his suicide.

4. Such mediated ordeals in the First World are directly linked to the occupation of Iraq. Different perspectives and meanings of the occupation continue to be generated, even in the period following the first free election in the post-Saddam period (January 2005). For conservative commentators Iraq is on the road to becoming a fully functioning, modern democratic state. For critics, the occupation is merely extending the agony and chaos wreaked by the invasion and the forced imposition of western institutions and values.

5. The abduction and 'execution' of foreign workers in Iraq is part of this generalized polemic. These individuals, their respective governments and home citizenry are engaged by militants in a mediated trial by ordeal, which challenges the rational order and ideology of democratic rule of law.

6. The mediated execution of Ken Bigley was particularly confronting for the British government, whose own credibility and moral authority had been compromised by the David Kelly affair and the continuing violence in Iraq.

7. The western media avoided showing the graphic details of the executions as part of its general management of the ideology of violence. Arab-based media networks like al-Jazeera, however, believe that global audiences should be exposed to the graphic details of war, especially when their governments and military are

directly engaged. This tell-all philosophy seeks also to enhance the capacity of effective, democratic decision-making.

8. Other commentators believe that democracy and the public sphere may be enhanced by the broad availability of information, including war photography. When the photographs of Abu Ghraib prison abuses were released for public scrutiny in the Coalition countries, a number of commentators believed that they would provide a catalyst for social change and the reversal of government policy on Iraq. This proved not to be the case.

9. The Abu Ghraib photographs and videos demonstrate, once again, that the mediasphere is replete with complex language wars which continually frustrate the restoration of a rational, communicative order and an integrated public sphere. The photographs may be seen as another mode of trial by ordeal whereby the inmates and guards in the prison are exposed to the judgements and multiple meanings of the global electronic polis. It was not the government or democratic rule of law that brought the guards to 'justice'. Rather it was a form of 'imperative to represent' and participate in the mediasphere that drew the guards into the language wars of the Iraq occupation.

Conclusion: Cultural Democracy, Difference and the End of Civilization

LANGUAGE WARS HERE AND OVER THERE

It has been argued throughout this book that 'democracy' evolved out of a desire to reconcile social difference without recourse to direct violence. Beyond this ideal, democracy has been framed as a discursive mechanism which subsumed violence within the interests and ideology of specific social groups, most particularly those that had vested interests in individual prosperity, capital and commerce. In the progress of democracy, however, violence didn't disappear; it was merely transferred into the institutional parentheses of 'responsible' government while simultaneously being recoded through social interaction and new modes of mediation. Thus, for all its undoubted benefits, the electoral system is shaded by the coercive power of military, paramilitary, penal, clandestine and surveillance organizations. 'Rule of law' is supported by a substratum of vicious contingency, a system by which 'difference' is only tolerated inasmuch as it submits to the unassailable right of the state to impose itself and its will over the citizenry. Paradoxically, however, the state is only tolerated inasmuch as its governments encode this propensity for violence in an imaginary which submits to the aspirations of individual freedom and economic prosperity. A deep contingency of violence is set, therefore, like a cold war, within the discourses of the state–citizen relationship.

This official coercive power corroborates, and contributes to, the broader distribution of violence in contemporary culture. We have noted, in particular, that violence is a critical component of media culture; out of the rationalized inscriptions of writing culture, violence has emerged as a central motif in televisual narrative and the more general cultural experiences of the mediasphere. The more or less explicit manifestations of conflict and harm have contributed significantly to the cultural transformations that Heidegger has called the 'world as picture'. In Heidegger's terms, this super-visualization constitutes the 'gigantic', that is the televisual spectacle. This gigantic leads inevitably to a hyperbolic response; the nation, economic capitalism and the media converge to create a hyperreality of excessive and obsessive signification in which the individual becomes lost in choice and an artifice of freedom.

While Heidegger's prescience is notoriously pessimistic, it alerts us to the importance of the televisual media as a conduit and agent for the production of specific interests and ideologies. The nation and economic capitalism are prefigured in televisual mediation, creating around the contingency of violence, discourses of heroic ascent which subtly and explicitly conflate the individual and the collective force of nation. Both fictional and news narratives inscribe the legitimization of violence in polemical or dramatic language wars, the outcomes of which are predetermined by the assertion of the ideological interests. In particular, the language wars that are producing the resurgent east–west divide are deeply embedded in the televisual discourses of nation and its engagement in the global processes of economic capitalism.

It has been consistently argued in this book that the media and culture are active agents in the evolving crisis of global terror and political violence. The media and culture are directly implicated in the wars of meaning which pervade contemporary politics. The grand ideals of the Enlightenment – Reason, Democracy, Truth – have been overrun and absorbed into the new panoply of meanings and meaning-contention which characterize the mediasphere. Through the force of a US-dominated global order, the networked media culture has become both context and weapon in the progress and articulation of violence. Information and ocular technologies have contributed to the transformations of democracy and the political ideal, creating new spaces for the waging of language war and the mad scramble for dominance. In this way, the ideal of truth has been double-coded, continuing as a spectre within the persuasive force of networked media and the image.

In fact, the 9/11 wars are articulated through these same patterns, most particularly as they are being waged through the aegis of a broadcast democracy. The borders between fiction, fact and persuasion are blurred by the pervasive presence of the image and the overproductive propensities of the media. While the news media and Internet are deluged with onsite reporting and analysis, fictional versions of the Iraq invasion are already proliferating. Emerging out of the powerful lineage of military cinema, a range of film projects have been developed, including *The Battle for Fallujah*, *Jarheed*, *The Tiger and the Snow* (comedy), *Gunner Palace* (documentary), and the somewhat bizarre Jerry Bruckheimer project on the 'liberation' of Private Jessica Lynch (*Saving Private Lynch*). What is evident through all these projects, however, is the absence of critical distance and artistic scepticism which might challenge the political and military hegemonies which authorized the Iraq invasion. The TV series *Over There*, written and directed by Steven Bochco, evinces a new mood of artistic patriotism which seeks to redeem American military heroics from the savage nihilism of Vietnam. Bochco's production, like his earlier series, *NYPD Blue*, focuses on the gritty and hard-edged experiences of the 'ordinary American'. In *Over There* Bochco specifically celebrates the US soldier in Iraq who is burdened by duty and the arduous demands of 'a tough job'. Like an embedded journalist, Bochco directs his camera through the vision of the US soldier, whose personal story must necessarily ascend, without challenging, the abstruse and abstract politics of US foreign policy. The business of the soldier is to endure hardship and prevail irrespective of, or in some ways despite, the great power and great civilization under which s/he labours.

We now know, of course, that these fictional perspectives are not only generated out of respect for national ideology; they are also a historical and highly strategic effect of government intervention. Casting off the failings of the Vietnam information experience, the US government and its military have embarked on very direct policies of media management. While the management of the news media has been discussed at length in the course of this book, it is also clear that the military is directly participating in the formation of fictional representations. Not only does the military encourage troops to produce their own video and photographic records of actual combat, rendering them available for 'newsreel' texts distributed through American cinemas, they are also contributing directly to those films and TV programmes which subscribe to the ideals and policies of the Department of Defense. Writing in the *Washington Post*, David Robb (2002) has pointed out that the Department's media liaison division assesses film and TV scripts in order to judge their ideological status. Those texts which submit to the persuasive interests of the Department, films like Tony Scott's *Top Gun*, are supported with equipment, aircraft, ships, personnel and artillery fire – those extremely expensive contextual elements which render the film 'believable'. Under these circumstances, scripts are assessed and often heavily edited to ensure that the military, military personnel, the government and the nation are presented in the best possible light. Those films which may be critical of war, the military or the US, films such as *Thin Red Line, Apocalypse Now!* or *The Windtalkers*, are denied the largesse of the Department of Defense.

At one level, this may seem fair enough. The military is not in the business of exposing itself to public or artistic critique. But in the context of 'democracy' and the Iraq invasion and occupation, culture is once again being marshalled in order to support a propagated east–west divide. Bochco's *Over There* is exceptional inasmuch as it enters the mediasphere while the war it represents is still being waged. The violent politics in which the state is engaged are drawn into the artifice of representationalism, contributing further to a broadcast democratic sphere in which the absent and the present clash in a confused predicate of semiotic disorder. The real, that is, encounters its fictional other in a greeting place of domestic doubt which, while reiterating the force of the east–west divide, moves us further away from the ideals and moral dignity of democracy. The intersection of propaganda, news reporting and fictional representation becomes the kaleidoscope of distrust through which the electronic polis views its values, its media and its political leaders.

DEMOCRACY AND GLOBAL CULTURE

The governments of the Coalition of the Willing very clearly have a vested interest in these propagated discursive divisions. The mobilization of violence that we have witnessed since the 9/11 attacks has been generated through a powerful confluence of interests designed to give clear expression to a collective imperative; this imperative is articulated through a mode of coercive action that fortifies the supreme project of democracy and capitalism against the forces of social, moral and political evil. To this end, the 'clash of civilizations' thesis becomes a useful weapon in the discourses of persuasion and propaganda. As the pinnacle of civilization, the Anglophones, dominated by the United States, seek to aggregate their citizenry through a propagated identity politics which forcefully aims to exclude alternative perspectives and modes of self-expression. As we have seen, the leaders of the Anglophonic Coalition have consciously distinguished themselves and their project of global governance from the enemy and all other national or transnational bodies that might question the US-ascribed civilizational order.

As we have also noted, however, these language wars are not so easily marshalled or contained. While the civilizational order and its many contingent parts seek to aggregate difference within a project of standardization, difference reasserts itself through the implacable efficacy of individual and community expressivity, as well as the intrinsic volatility of language itself. Difference, that is, re-emerges as a counter-flow to the hierarchical momentum of aggregated discursive and social formations. In a broadcast democracy, in particular, variant modes are finding expression through a range of global contiguities and cultural platforms. The idea of the civilizational divide is perpetually challenged not only by its own absurdity (Chan, 2005), but through the fissures that such ideologies inevitably create around and through their linguistic core. Even as media organizations like Fox seek to engender this dichotomous world, the subtleties of doubt re-emerge to destabilize the assumptions by which informational professionals and governments seek to fix their meanings. The fear that is inscribed in these assumptions, like the illusion of choice, returns to dispel this propagated certitude, compromising the very essence of the 'democracy' we are told will transform the Middle East and other renegade territories of difference.

The re-election of the government of Tony Blair in the UK, George Bush in the United States and John Howard in Australia might be seen as evidence of the failure of difference – evidence, that is, of the success of the civilizational argument and the propagated war on terror. The return of these governments, with increased majorities in the US and Australia, may be viewed as proof that the electronic polis are merely dupes of government and media ideological interests. But as we have noted, this form of electoral expression necessarily aggregates a plethora of interests into a single and not particularly representative choice of political imaginings. The limits of writing democracy were most clearly articulated in the 2004 US presidential elections where the Iraq invasion and occupation were subsumed within a peculiar personality contest which left voters with an extraordinarily opaque division of options. George W. Bush maintained his fidelity to the imaginary of the homespun guy, while his supporters viciously denigrated the aptitude and trustworthiness of his opponent, especially as a wartime leader. Bush's poor record on economic and social management – indeed his disastrous record on international policy – was generally obscured within the televisual context of propagated familiarity. Bush's strategically constructed neighbourly demeanour was carefully woven into his exceptional capacity to lead the nation in times of crisis. John Kerry was never able to match this tactical conflation of the exceptional–familiar, the essential nuance of broadcast mediation.

Even so, Bush and the Republicans barely moved the electorate toward his foreign policy 'mandate'. In the wash-up, only a little over 25 per cent of eligible voters bothered to choose George Bush, but this was enough to ensure success in this highly rarefied democratic process. Almost half the electorate didn't vote, perhaps because many of the electors felt disenfranchised or alienated by a system that is, for them at least, largely illusory. Bush's increased majority needs to be measured against the nearly three-quarters of Americans who didn't vote for him at all.

In Australia and the United Kingdom the rhetoric of an electoral sanction for the invasion seems equally problematic. Australians seem mesmerized by a war of distance, a war which amounts to little more than a confirmation of the nation's status as a minor power appending itself to the symbolic and military might of the United States. The supine and fawning demeanour of the Prime Minister, while offensive to many Australians, seems to have been bracketed by local concerns over mortgages and real estate valuations. A similar mood, of course, has been descending in the UK where Tony Blair's integrity and honesty have been cast into doubt by the failure to find WMDs and his handling of the David Kelly and Ken Bigley affairs. The deployment of British troops in Iraq and Blair's unflinching fidelity to US foreign policy had always been unpopular in the UK; the ongoing problems in occupied Iraq seem only to have fortified existing doubts, leading to the continued decline in Blair's personal approval ratings. Thus, the return of the Labour government in the 2005 elections was achieved in spite of the Prime Minister's evangelical mission in the Middle East – not because of it.

In Iraq the first post-Saddam democratic election produced a not dissimilar effect. While over 100,000 Iraqi civilians (mostly women and children) were killed in the violent gestation of democracy, only around 58 per cent of registered voters went to the polls. Against the background of threats and intimidation, this figure is probably quite compelling. However, the greater proportion of the minority Sunni Muslim population didn't vote, leaving a profound gap in the constituency of the new 'responsible' government, and in the democratic ideals of representation, reconciliation and participation. More alarming, perhaps, for the Coalition sponsors of the regime change, has been the ascendancy of the Shi'ite religious party the United Iraqi Alliance, which received around 50 per cent of the cast votes. The US-sponsored secularist party, led by interim Prime Minister Iyad Allawi (14 per cent), finished third behind the Kurds (26 per cent). The significant electoral support for the United Iraqi Alliance reflects the importance placed on religion and the leadership of the party's patron the Grand Ayatollah Ali al-Sistani. It also marks Iraq's move from a clearly secular state under Saddam Hussein to what we have called a 'transitional' state (Chapter 2) whereby religion becomes more fully infused with the practices of politics and government. While this mutation may reflect the greater disposition of the country's majority, it is surely a cause for further anxiety for those in the Coalition who consider themselves the apex of the civilizational order. A fear of Islamicism, which inspired the US to support Saddam Hussein in the first place, may re-emerge through the influence and theocratic disposition of Sistani and the United Iraqi Alliance. The failure of the Allawi alliance must surely disappoint the American and British aspirations for an uncomplicated and secular political system in Iraq which would be sympathetic to western goals of economic integration and an ongoing military presence.

Equally problematic, of course, is the potential of this electoral outcome to exclude the significant differences marked by ethnicity and gender. We know that at least 44 people were killed and over 100 injured during the election period, and the violence being perpetrated around ethnic, ideological and religious resistance has continued largely unabated. The appointment of a Kurdish president, Jalal Talabani, and Shi'ite Prime Minister, Ibrahim Jaafari, after several months of extremely complex and tense negotiations, has not led to a reduction in violence and insurgency. While Jaafari's ministry includes seven Kurds, some Sunnis and a Christian within the majority Shi'ite government, this new multi-ethnic democracy seems not to have convinced the insurgents. With so much damage having been perpetrated in Iraq, the new democracy has not assuaged the intent or brutality of those groups which see the whole project of US interventionism and the congregation of radical difference in Iraq as irresolvable, except through combat and violence. This contention of a fundamentally masculinist politics, however, somewhat distracts from other important contentions, especially those that are constituted around the experiences of women. As several commentators have noted, the ascendancy of the conservative religious parties clearly threatens the liberational aspirations of many women who seek to emancipate their lives from the restrictions imposed by patriarchal Islamicism. While the freedoms of women are enshrined in the interim constitution, the results of the election have reignited the concerns of secularists and other groups that women will be denied full participation in government, public administration, education and work. The success of the United Iraqi Alliance has stimulated new debates about the role of women and the constraints on the free expression of gender.

THE *HIJAB* AND GLOBAL POLITICS

The principal problem for the new democracy in Iraq is similar to that experienced in all other democratic states. The interests of the 'majority' must be mediated against the interests of individuals, minorities and the elected elite which exercises its power through the auspices of representation and responsibility. This 'mediation', in fact, is transposed through the mediation of communicational channels (the media). Difference is absorbed into the complex matrix of representational processes: the interests of ethnic groups, political parties, communities, classes and women are all shaded into the ideals of resolvability. Where difference threatens the whole, it is crushed. Where it can be deployed for social good or the interests of capital, then it will be released as commodity for consumer choice (cuisine, clothing style, tourism products). As innumerable theorists of globalization have noted, the integration of this form of commodified difference into the western capitalist hegemony has created new forms of consumable difference which largely assuage the dangers of radical or absolute difference (see Hall, 1991a, 1991b).

In a profound way, these new forms of cultural contiguity – in particular the presence of the Islamic or Oriental other in the midst of the western majority – test the capacities of the Euro-American democratic ideal. Migration and the contiguities generated by media representations of 'over there' bring the 'other' directly into contact with the western imaginary, including the imaginary of the east–west divide. Little doubt, the well-publicized plight of Afghan women under the Taliban regime brought particular sensibilities of difference and similarity into the political–cultural horizon of many liberal westerners. Bringing to bear their own standards and values, these liberals were forced to confront the political dilemma of invasion against the liberation of a particular social group, women, who had been incarcerated by a brutal political regime. The ideals of tolerance (of difference) were challenged by a radical difference which was essentially repugnant to the contemporary value system of the west.

Through cultural contiguities and the clash of values, democracy is forced to confront its own intrinsic contradictions.

This issue has been foregrounded through the practice of political kidnap and trial in occupied Iraq. It was particularly evident in the kidnap in August 2004 of two French journalists, Georges Malbrunot and Christian Chesnot, whose nation and government had been strong opponents of the American-led invasion. In this case, the kidnappers were demanding that the French government withdraw new legislation which banned the wearing of religious symbols, including the Muslim headscarf or *hijab*, in publicly funded schools.

The *hijab* represents a particularly resonant issue for relationships between democratic secularism and religiosity which extends the simple oppositionalism of the east–west divide. Women wear the *hijab* as an indication of Muslim identity, historical connection, femininity and religious faith. Like other religious iconography that can be worn as personal adornment, the *hijab* may be more or less extant, ranging from a full headdress, cloak and visor to a simple headscarf. The French government, which for decades tolerated the wearing of religious iconography (the Catholic Cross, the Star of David, the scull cap) in its public schools, has decided to reassert a more aggressive secularism. Since 1989 when the first *hijab* case appeared in France, schools have independently banned the headscarf, raising significant issues around equal opportunity and civil rights. The decision by the government to standardize legislation and ban all religious symbols from public schools seems merely to have amplified the issues from the community to state and global levels. Of course, the separation of church and state has been highly valued in French political life since France, unlike England and Germany, had no reformation and the Catholic Church remained powerful and highly visible in community and state affairs. Secularism, therefore, became explicitly embedded in the establishment of the modern, democratic governance. The church was bordered and constrained from excessive interference in the matters of secular life. The decision to ban the headscarf and all other religious iconography from state institutions hearkens back to the significant language wars of rationalism, democratic liberalism and the power of the state to protect the material welfare of its citizens.

With the rise of Islamic militantism and a significant number of migrants from Islamic north Africa, France, like many other nations in the developed west, has found it necessary to confront once again the basis of its own statehood and national interests. Globalization, in fact, bringing new modes of cultural cosmopolitanism, seems to have drawn to the surface some latent but significant anxieties about the essence of the state and the cultural contingencies of 'being French'. Comparable secular nations such as the UK, Germany and Australia have not been tempted to adopt a similar model; nor indeed has the United States, which has a far more theologically ambient modern history. Supporters of the legislation from the non-Muslim French community declare a deep affiliation with western French values; democracy is protected against a faithfulness that is arbitrary and fixed within a cosmology that has no material or rational basis. The right-wing French magazine *L'Express* goes further with these claims, arguing that the pluralism promoted by 'liberals' necessarily collapses within a religious context that says all but the Islamic perspective is fallacious. *L'Express* argues that the French opposition Socialist Party's neutrality on the issue is anti-French, as it is constructed on a cynical electoral platform aimed at attracting the votes of Moroccan immigrants.

This issue poses some significant problems for the Left and liberal-minded political thinkers in France. While appearing in some respects to contravene human rights, the legislation covers all religious symbology, not just the Muslim *hijab*. Even so, there is also little doubt that the primary target of the legislation is the community of 5 million Muslims living in France, and their particular form of religious expression. A number of feminists have, over the past two decades, been vociferous in their denunciation of the *hijab*, largely because it represents a form of patriarchal oppression. Prominent Iranian expatriot scholar Shardrot Djafman supports this view, arguing in a 50-page booklet entitled *Down Hijab* that the mandatory wearing of the headdress, especially the Iranian chador or veil, is designed to oppress women and deny their sexuality. Djafman makes clear that the oppressive regime of the Iranian ayotollahs is symbolized in the compulsory mode of dress and the denial of fundamental freedoms to women. According to this perspective, the state and religion should be separated and the spaces provided by the republic should be free from religious impositions and laws. According to this view, the putative 'freedom' that is sought by Muslim women in France and elsewhere across the globe is a fantasy which disguises the power of patriarchal ideology: women never choose to wear the *hijab*; they are simply trained by a traditional, male-dominated community to wear it.

While many in the Muslim community in France and elsewhere might sympathize with Djafman's perspective, others would argue that choice is the critical factor, and that the government is denying the civil rights of the Muslim community by imposing its secular values. This standardization of the western experience constitutes a form of assimilation, a hegemony which submits the theological values of the Muslim faith to the traditions of Eurocentricism. The arguments become circular. But what is very clear is that the introduction of the new law is creating its own forms of resistance and the intensification of identity. As Manuel Castells has outlined, resistance becomes of itself a powerful force in the building of an essential identity. The young Muslim women who have defied or circumvented the law in some way are expressing a form of ideological martyrdom which the *hijab* law seeks specifically to undermine.

As they are forced to confront this fundamental contradiction in the heritage of western civil–democratic society, Muslims in the west have often resorted to the identity–resistance politics offered by Islam; this politics, as we have frequently noted, reverences struggle against adversity and the suppression of faith. Muslims in France, thereby, have been subjected to the rationalist paradigm which they believed would universally protect them and their rights as citizens. What many are discovering, of course, is that modernism bears fundamental flaws and contradictions which may, at any moment, condemn the citizen to an accommodation of the rights and freedoms of others. In this particular instance, the conflict of rights and the meaning of the *hijab* are expressed through longstanding language wars – secularism–faith, rationalism–devotion, freedom of expression–public responsibility. It is a tragic but telling irony that the French journalists who were captured by the Iraqi Islamic Army have also been 'tried' through the exchange of Enlightenment values within the global mediasphere; as journalists, they represented the new mediated public sphere to which they may have been martyred. While they may or may not have supported the new laws banning the *hijab* in French public schools, their fate may have been entirely determined by the outcome of these difficult ideological and ethical encounters. It is, perhaps, a testament to the ideals of modernism and civil society that Muslim leaders in France appealed publicly for the release of the two French journalists, making clear that their consternations over the *hijab* issue should not be confused with the events in Iraq. It is also a peculiar irony that the planned protests against the new law, protests that would have been conducted through media publicity, were largely abandoned as a show of support for the captured journalists.

The release in December 2004 of the two journalists was purportedly achieved through this powerful alliance of secular and religious advocacy. The denunciation by Muslim leaders of the abduction and the abandonment of planned protests might well have convinced the kidnappers of the sincerity of the French opposition to the Iraq invasion. Writing in *Le Figaro*, Georges Malbrunot said that he and Chesnot had seen nationals from Macedonia and Iraq who had later been executed. The release of the French journalists was a direct result of the French government's opposition to the war, an opposition which treads a fine line between an engagement with difference and the assertion of the country's own all-encompassing ideology. Like the lives of the French journalists, this ideology may have easily been sacrificed to the broader ideological interests of the east–west divide.

WORLD GOVERNMENT: BEWARE THE FAITHFUL

In many respects, the debates over the *hijab* in France parallel similar contentions over secularism being played out in the United States. A number of American school councils, encouraged perhaps by the evangelical spirit of the Bush administration, have reinstated creationism into the curriculum, overriding the epistemological project of rationalist, scientific evolution theory. The comparison with France, of course, ends as we recognize that this resistant anti-modernism in the US is, in fact, a form of hyper-modernism, one which appends its irrational religiosity to a hegemonic military and technological rationalism. American evangelism, articulated and encouraged specifically through the Bush administration, becomes a tool for the world crusade which would draw all nations and peoples into the bosom of global capitalism, American idealism and institutional democracy. The invocation of (a Christian) god and the discourse of 'the chosen' infuses with incandescent fury the neoconservative goal of American world governance and unassailable economic and military primacy (Chomsky, 2003a). In many respects, this is precisely the idea behind Tariq Ali's characterization of the war of terror as a 'clash of fundamentalisms'. In essence, the global jihad is a reaction to American-dominated global capitalism and a materialism which dignifies itself through a form of national(ist) apotheosis.

These arguments bring us full circle. But perhaps we need to consider the possibility of a world governance that may be constructed around a co-operative model and international rule of law. America and its allies have sought to impose on the world their own version of liberal democracy, regarding it as the antithesis of anarchy, barbarianism and totalitarianism. Using itself as the paradigm of advanced western civilization, prosperity and power, the US feels entirely justified in bringing all other social entities into its ideological and ethical ambit. There are, of course, alternative models of world governance. Danilo Zolo (1997), in his reflection on the first Gulf War, explores these alternatives through a basic polemic – one side constructed around the model of an enhanced United Nations, the other around a form of de-bordered cosmopolitan pacifism. In the first instance, Zolo applies the work of Norberto Bobbio, who argues that the collaborative actions of the United Nations provide a template for the formation of a functional global governance. While conceding that the positive outcomes of the war against Iraq need necessarily to be reconciled with various negative implications, Bobbio nevertheless insists that the original Gulf War represents the first time in history that the collective action of states was generated through a genuine application of rule of law. Using this consensual law as a guiding principle, Bobbio suggests that the move from global anarchy and military conflict is only possible when states themselves subscribe to a consensual model which delegates authority to a 'third party'. As in Hobbes' account of the leviathan, the sovereign state would act in self-interest; a fundamental survival instinct would drive the sovereign state to submit to a third power, a global government, which would have the authority to control the actions of all members through the exercise of law. This consensus would proceed through four basic stages: first, a preliminary, negative treaty which would establish the ground rules of non-aggression between those states intending to develop a more permanent council; second, a positive treaty by which the sovereign states would establish rules for the resolution of differences, thereby avoiding violence; third, submission to a common power capable of administering the laws and delivering justice; and finally, the establishment of civil and community rights which would form the basis for protection against the excess of 'third party'-governmental power.

This approach, of course, parallels the governance and judiciary models of modern democracy. The global government represents the interests of member states but returns power through the auspices of responsible government. The protection of individual, community and civil rights forms the basis of the responsibility, ensuring that the overriding power of the world body does not become despotic and infringe on the freedoms and diversity of its constituent membership. The first Gulf War may be viewed as an incomplete, though promising framework for Bobbio's approach. Chapter VII of the United Nations Charter sanctions a military response to illegal international action; this military response would be directly controlled by the UN and its Security Council. It is clearly arguable that the Iraqi invasion of Kuwait in 1990 constituted a breach of international law, and thus the US-led military response was 'authorized' by the UN. The actions of the United Nations forces, under the general command of the United States, were sanctioned by the Security Council and thus were not determined by a single sovereign power. The UN forces' attack on Iraq was therefore 'legal' as it was framed by the Charter as international law.

The fallibility of this model might also be located in the first Gulf War when the United States administration under George Bush senior took *unilateral* action, amassing vast forces in Saudi Arabia and commencing from November 8, 1990 massive air strikes against the sovereign territory of Iraq. The war immediately exposed itself as something more than just the protection of Kuwaiti sovereignty as the US began to exercise its own sovereign interests without reference to the United Nations or the Security Council (Zolo, 1997: 35). As numerous commentators have noted, the first Gulf War failed clearly to demonstrate how military action should be justified against the alternative strategy of sanctions and diplomatic persuasion. The deaths of between 40,000 and 200,000 Iraqi civilians, mostly from US air strikes, raise serious questions about the human cost of this second-level unilateralism – especially as we consider that the civilians had very little say in their government's policy-making and the invasion of Kuwait. The lingering image of the war is of the United States placing heavy pressure on the Security Council, in much the same way as it did during the lead-up to the Afghanistan invasion and second Gulf War. In the latter case, of course, the Security Council refused to submit to the pressure, and the United States, along with its Anglophonic allies, exercised its unilateral power. Richard Falk (1991), who has explored numerous models of international government, suggests, in fact, that the greatest impediment to global law is precisely this form of national or 'statist' imperative. Statist imperatives include the competition for national economic advantage and economic growth objectives; technological and stem-based competition; diversion of international institutions to the service of national interest (as in the American 'use' of the UN); political barriers to movement of people across national borders; and the refusal to pursue effective international demographic policy.

Any optimism that may have derived from the first Gulf War, particularly around the effectiveness of a UN global governance model, has been severely compromised by the George W. Bush administration. The 'statist' imperative might seem to explain the US's reluctance to sign the Kyoto Protocol and the international treaty banning land mines, as well as its pursuit of war crimes exemption from the International Criminal Court. These abrogations of international responsibility, which place the US alongside nations such as Libya, Iran and North Korea, indicate to the world that the US is absolutely uninterested in submitting to an international authority which is not centred on US power. The bypass, and indeed derision, of the UN Security Council and 'old Europe' during the Iraq invasion crisis in 2002–03 further confirmed the Bush administration's hegemonic approach to international politics.

Even so, the ideal of a cosmopolitan governance is not necessarily destroyed by the current wave of unilateralism. There are those, even within the current administration, who demonstrate considerable respect for the ideal, if not the organizational framework, of the United Nations. Former secretary of state Colin Powell, for example, tried to reconcile his government's interests with the UN Charter and processes. While he was not successful, the aspirations of the UN remain redolent for many governments of the developed world and/ or their parliamentary oppositions. Powell himself sought to work through the United Nations over the ethnic and refugee crisis in the Sudan. The global effort in the Sudan, and in the areas of Asia affected by the tsunami disaster, might yet prove to be an ideal context for the exercise of cosmopolitan governance. Moreover, if America's only success in Iraq, the removal of Saddam from power, continues to be subsumed within a protracted social, humanitarian and political calamity, then there may well be a resurgent interest in a more collaborative, UN-style approach to international tensions. Certainly, in the second Bush administration, particularly through the assertions of Secretary of State Condoleezza Rice, there have been clear signs that America is seeking to re-establish its collaborative engagement with Europe, most particularly with France and Germany.

On the other side of this resurgent interest in Europe, however, is the reaffirmation of the 'two civilizations' polemic. Even as Bush courts Europe and seeks to reform the United Nations model to better suit US interests, the global hierarchy is reconsolidated. Indeed, the problem with the UN model, even if it were evolved in terms of Bobbio's prescience, is the uneven and incomplete nature of representation. The US, which largely sponsors the organization and which distinguishes itself as a unique economic and military power, seeks a representational model that is commensurate with its global status. If the aim of a cosmopolitan global governance is the standardization of the constituent parts and the abrogation of political crime and political violence, then the representational model seems to falter precisely around the question of power. The European Union, which might seem to provide a regional paradigm for the global framework, is largely constructed around an economic interdependence which now seeks to articulate itself within a political and legal framework. Even so, the Union is clearly dominated by the interests of its four primary sponsors, members of the OECD club who have comparable power, status and levels of economic development. Yet even within this framework, debates around the viability of the Union remain, and there are certainly those member states which continue to experience considerable apoplexy around the problematics of identity, history and culture. Moreover and as the current context of political violence indicates, the precariousness of affiliations is exposed when senior members so radically diverge in their opinions, actions and military allegiances. In so stridently and publicly aligning itself with the US, the United Kingdom is placing itself within the political vectors of a superpower which is showing very little sympathy for organizations like the EU-sponsored International War Crimes Tribunal. Indeed, the strong anti-European rhetoric that has come from the White House over the Iraq invasion has clearly isolated the UK from other major EU partners, France and Germany.

The events of 9/11 demonstrated above all other things the continuing force of patriotism and a nationalism which draws from the depths of culture and history. The bloom of American flags and the sense of national family that issued from the 9/11 attacks were quite bewildering – and frightening – for many of the global polis outside the United States. Upon reflection, however, they should not have been so. The force of American global domination and the sense of a unique historical status are repeated unceasingly in American cultural texts. For all its diversity and pluralism, there seems a deeply rooted conviction that America has no parallel, that it is both the salvation and the centre of civilizational progress. The conjuration of this patriotic and jingoistic certitude, as we have indicated, now binds itself to an evangelical spirit in the Bush administration, creating the conditions for a revivified crusade. Where once it was the communists, now it appears to be the Islamicists who provide the focus for this sense of America's historical destiny. The limits of political representation in a global sphere are matched, therefore, by the representational force of the mediasphere. Of course, and as the present electoral processes in the US are indicating, not everyone supports George Bush. But the choice that is available to the American electorate seems to be one of shadows. The implosion of institutional political difference, which was discussed earlier, expresses itself in the limited policy options that the major political parties offer. The real choice for Americans appears to be between voting and not voting. In the absence of significant alternatives, the rejection of institutional politics seems the most powerful option – especially for those members of the community who are marginalized by the force field of hierarchical capitalism.

To this extent, the mediasphere provides new spaces for global political participation. While many commentators complain that the media has evolved through corporatization in the service of government information management and plutocratic interests, these criticisms seriously underestimate the cultural capacity and potential of the mediasphere. This capacity is evident in the expressive content of the margins – alternative information and ideas which challenge directly the unanimity of highly managed, mass mediated texts. These ideas, of course, are extremely important for framing and stimulating the pluralism necessary for an effective (writing-based) democratic public sphere. But they are also critical for the formation of the broadcast mediasphere within which multiple flows of information and perspective continue to proliferate, and by which individuals generate their own communities and modes of political consciousness that conflate the public and private zones of social life. While we have considered the problematics of doubt which are necessarily implicated in the proliferation, it is also necessary to acknowledge the potential of the mediasphere to provide critical and creative spaces for new modes of political expressivity. This potential is not guaranteed to produce the positive outcomes envisaged by theorists like Giles Deleuze and Felix Guattari, and the growing army of new media scholars who seem to assume that a form of 'digitopia' will issue from the rise of interactivity (see Lewis, 1998, Lewis & Best, 2002). It does, however, suggest that the broadcast media, including the interactive media, may provide the tools for managing our doubt in ways that allow expressive creativity to subsume excessive negativity within a general sphere of language war.

The more modest aspiration of this book, therefore, is to reconcile differences rather than resolve or expunge them. The disputes and contentiousness which are inscribed in language and culture are not to be averted or occluded within a saccharine triumphalism – the positive over the negative, democracy over anarchy, good over evil. They are to be released through the fundamental practice of cultural expressivity which resists a recourse to violence, terror and the suppression of community. It is not a matter of releasing the people of the Middle East, Chechnya, South Asia, Africa or South East Asia to their own fate. It is not a matter of standardizing the west and its constituent nations against the uncivilized forces of darkness within and outside its borders. It is rather a matter of looking squarely at the global divisions which continue to condemn the vast majority of humanity to desperation and misery. It is a matter of rehabilitating that misery through a new and invigorated language of compassion and care, a language that is not constrained by the excesses of avarice and fear.

If those of us in the west are to circumvent political violence, then the ocular technologies which constitute its weaponry must be drawn back into the service of the global polis, unleashing their potential for absolute freedom of speech and the multiplication of perspectives. The mediasphere, that is, cannot be constrained by the regulatory interests of the state and information managers, but must be largely unhindered in the pursuit of ideas, knowledge, information and pleasures. Indeed, it is only through doubt, expressive freedom and a limitless access to the oracular technologies that an effective intervention in the horrors of political violence is possible. It is not enough, therefore, to await the semiotic collapse of ideology; we are all responsible for the active engagement of doubt and expression in those language wars which beset the interests of our humanity.

In many respects, this doubt is far less threatening than the certitude that delivered the human hell of 9/11 and the belligerent patriotism that rushed to fill its void. It is this certitude on all sides which lies behind the violence of state and resistant terrorism, and which has led to the deaths of so many people across the globe.

If this context of political violence demonstrates anything, it is surely that those with the greatest faith are proving to be the most dangerous of all beings. Only those with a murderous conviction could possibly override the precious sensibilities of life and the simple beauty of human community. Only those who have already assumed control of good and evil could seek to triumph over the mysteries and incandescent power of a poetry that lies beyond the capture of dogma and absolute knowledge.

References

Abuza, Z. (2003) *Militant Islam in South East Asia: Crucible of Terror*, Lynne Rienner Publishers, London.

Adorno, T. (1994) 'On popular music' in J. Storey, ed., *Cultural Theory and Popular Culture: A Reader*, Harvester Wheatsheaf, Hemel Hempstead.

Akerman, P. (2003) 'Remembering Bali', *Sunday Telegraph*, October 5.

Ali, T. (2002) *The Clash of Fundamentalisms: Crusades, Jihads and Modernity*, Verso, London.

American Civil Liberties Union (2004) 'As House Committees consider latest "Patriot 2" provision, ACLU urges Congress to reject further expansion of government powers', *ACLU News*, May 5, <www.aclu.org/>.

Anderson, B. (1990) *Language and Power: Exploring Political Cultures in Indonesia*, Cornell University Press, Ithaca, NY.

—— (1991) *Imagined Communities: Reflections on the Origin and Spread of Nationalism*, Revised Edition, Verso, London.

Ang, I. (1996) *Living Room Wars: Rethinking Media Audiences for a Postmodern World*, Routledge, London.

Anggraeni, D. (2003) *Who did this to our Bali?* Indra Publishing, Melbourne.

Appadurai, A. (1990) 'Disjuncture and difference in the global cultural economy' in M. Featherstone, ed., *Global Culture: Nationalism, Globalization and Modernity*, Sage, London.

—— (1996) *Modernity at Large: The Cultural Dimensions of Globalization*, University of Minneapolis Press, Minnesota.

Ashley, J. (2004) 'Blair's trial by ordeal hasn't slaked his appetite for power: post-Hutton the prime minister's authority is in tatters', *Guardian*, February 4, <www.guardian.co.uk>.

Bakhtin, M. and Medvedev, P. N. (1978) *The Formal Method in Literary Scholarship*, trans. A. J. Wehrie, The Johns Hopkins University Press, Baltimore.

Barthes, R. (1975) *The Pleasure of the Text*, trans. R. Miller, Hill and Wang, New York.

—— (1977) *Image, Music, Text*, Fontana, Glasgow.

Bataille, G. (1987) *Eroticism*, trans. Mary Dalwood, Boyars, London.

Baudrillard, J. (1987a) *The Evil Demon of Images*, trans. P. Patton, P. Foss and P. Tanguy, Power Publications, Sydney.

—— (1987b) 'Forget Baudrillard' in *Forget Foucault*, trans. P. Beitchmann, P. L. Hildreth and M. Polizzotti, Semiotext(e), New York.

—— (1990) *Seduction*, trans. B. Singer, Culturetext, New York.

—— (1993) *The Transparency of Evil: Essays on Extreme Phenomena*, trans. J. Benedict, Verso, London.

—— (1994) *Simulacra and Simulation*, University of Michigan Press, Ann Arbor.

—— (1995) *The Gulf War Did Not Take Place*, Power Publications, New South Wales.

—— (1996) *The Perfect Crime*, trans. C. Turner, Verso, London.

—— (2002a) *The Spirit of Terrorism and Requiem for the Twin Towers*, trans. C. Turner, Verso, London.

—— (2002b) *Screened Out*, trans. C. Turner, Verso, London.

BBC News (2002) 'Blair condemns "evil" Bali bomb attack', *BBC News*, October 14, <www.bbcnews.com>.

Beard, M. (2001) *London Review of Books*, September 11 Special Edition, October 4.

Best, K. (2004) 'Visual imaging technologies, embodied sympathy and control in the 9/11 wars', Published Proceedings, Sources of Insecurity Conference, Melbourne, November.

Bhabha, H. (1987) 'Interrogating identity' in H. Bhabha, ed., *Identity: The Real Me*, ICA, London.

—— (1994) *The Location of Culture*, Routledge, London.

Blondhelm, M. and Liebes, T. (2003) 'From disaster marathon to media event: live television's performance on September 11, 2001 and September 11, 2002' in A. M. Noll, ed., *Crisis Communications: Lessons from September 11*, Rowman and Littlefield, Lanham, Maryland.

Bok, S. (1999) *Mayhem: Violence as Public Entertainment*, Perseus, New York.

Boller, D. (1993) 'The information superhighway: roadmap for renewed public purpose', *Tikkum*, 8, 4.

Bourdieu, P. (1984) *Distinction: A Social Critique of the Judgement of Taste*, Routledge, London.

—— (1998) *On Television and Journalism*, Pluto Press, London.

Brisard, J.-C. and Dasquié, G. (2002) *Forbidden Truth: US–Taliban Secret Oil Diplomacy and the Failed Hunt for Bin Laden*, trans. L. Rounds, Thunder's Mouth Press, New York.

Burchell, G., Gordon, C. and Miller, P. (eds) (1991) *The Foucault Effect: Studies in Governmentality*, University of Chicago Press, Chicago.

Bush, G. W. (2001) 'September 11: address to the nation', The White House, <www.whitehouse.gov/news/release/2001/09/20010911-16/html>.

—— (2002) 'The threat of Iraq' Address to Congress, the White House, October 7, <www.whitehouse.gov/news/releases/2002/10/20021007-8.html>.

Carey, J. (1991) *Communication as Culture*, Unwin Hyman, Boston.

—— (2003) 'The functions and uses of media during the September 11 crisis and its aftermath' in A. M. Noll, ed., *Crisis Communications: Lessons from September 11*, Rowman and Littlefield, Lanham, Maryland.

Carlyle, T. (1905) *On Heroes: Hero Worship and Heroics in History*, H. Allenson, London.

Carruthers, S. (2000) *The Media at War: Communication and Conflict in the Twentieth Century*, Macmillan, London.

Castells, M. (1997) *The Power of Identity*, Blackwell, Oxford.

Chan, S. (2005) *Out of Evil: New International Politics and Old Doctrines of War*, University of Michigan Press, Michigan.

Chitty, N. (2003) 'Introduction: subjects of terrorism and media' in N. Chitty, R. Rush and M. Semeti, *Studies in Terrorism: Media Scholarship and the Enigma of Terror*, Southbound, Penang.

Chomsky, N. (1989) *Necessary Illusions: Thought Control in Democratic Societies*, Pluto Press, London.

—— (2001) *September 11*, Unwin, Crows Nest.

—— (2003a) *Middle East Illusions*, Rowman and Littlefield, Lanham, Maryland.

—— (2003b) *Hegemony or Survival*, Metropolitan Books, New York.

Cohen, E. (2002) *Supreme Command: Soldiers, Statesmen and Leadership in Wartime*, Free Press, New York.

Connor, L. and Vickers, A. (2003) 'Crisis, citizenship and cosmopolitanism: living in a local and global risk society in Bali', *Indonesia*, April, 75.

Cooper, S. (2004) 'Perpetual war within the state of exception', *Arena Journal*, 21.

Crockatt, R. (2003) *America Embattled: September 11, Anti-Americanism and the Global Order*, Routledge, London.

Cullison, A. (2004) 'Inside al-Qaeda's hard drive: budget squabbles, baby pictures, office rivalries – and the path to 9/11', *Atlantic Monthly*, September 1.

Darling, J. (2002) *The Healing of Bali*, DVD.

de Certeau, M. (1984) *The Practice of Everyday Life*, trans. Steven Rendall, University of California Press, Berkeley

—— (1988) *The Writing of History*, trans. T. Conley, University of Columbia Press, New York.

Deleuze, G. and Guattari, F. (1987) *A Thousand Plateaus: Capitalism and Schizophrenia*, trans. B. Massumi, University of Minnesota Press, Minneapolis.

Derrida, J. (1974) *Of Grammatology*, trans. Gayatri Chakravorty Spivak, The Johns Hopkins University Press, Baltimore.

—— (1982) 'Signature event context' in *Margins of Philosophy*, University of Chicago Press, Chicago, 307–20.

Docker, J. (2002) 'Plenty of hope, an infinite amount of hope – but not for us: cultural studies in the shadow of catastrophe', *Arena Journal*, 19.

Dodson, L. (2002) 'We're all at risk, warns sombre PM', *Age*, October 14, 4.

Dubecki, L. (2003) 'Politicians pay tribute to Bali victims', *Age*, October 10.

During, S. (1999) 'Popular culture on a global scale: a challenge for cultural studies?' in H. Mackay and T. O'Sullivan, eds, *The Media Reader*, Sage, London.

Ehrenreich, B. (2004) 'Feminism and Abu Ghraib', *Sunday LA Times*, May 17.

Eisenstein, E. (1983) *The Printing Revolution in Early Modern Europe*, Cambridge University Press, Cambridge.

el-Nawawy, M. and Iskandar, A. (2002) *Al-Jazeera: How the Free Arab Network Scooped the World and Changed the Middle East*, Westview, Cambridge, Mass.

Ess, C. (1994) 'The political computer: Hypertext, democracy and Habermas' in G. Landow, ed., *Hyper/Text/Theory*, The Johns Hopkins University Press, Baltimore.

Falk, R. A. (1991) 'Reflections on the Gulf War experience: force and war in the United Nations system', *Juridisk Tiaskrifi*, 3, 1.

Featherstone, M. (2002) 'Islam encountering globalization: an introduction' in A. Mohammadi, ed., *Islam Encountering Globalization*, Routledge-Curzon, London.

Finnegan, R. (2003) 'Bali bombings: an investigator's analysis', *Jakarta Post*, January.

Fiske, J. (1989) *Understanding Popular Culture*, Unwin Hyman, Boston.

Fisk, R. (1999) 'Interview', *Progressive*, <www.progressive.org/0901/intv1201.html>.

—— (2003) 'Does the US military want to kill journalists?' *Independent*, April 8, reprinted in *Znet*, <www.zmag.org/content/showartcle.cfm?sectionID=15&ItemID=3419>.

—— (2004a) 'So this is what they call the new, "free" Iraq', *Information Clearing House*, July 16, <www.informationclearinghouse,info.article6429.htm>.

—— (2004b) 'Four missiles, 14 deaths and the crisis of information in Baghdad', July 19, <www.selvesandothers.org/article2444.htm>.

Foucault, M. (1972) *The Archaeology of Knowledge and the Discourse on Language*, trans. A. M. Sheridan, Pantheon, New York.

—— (1974) *The Order of Things: An Archaeology of the Human Sciences*, Tavistock Publications, London.

—— (1977a) *Discipline and Punish: The Birth of the Prison*, trans. A. M. Sheridan, Penguin, London.

—— (1977b) *Language, Counter-memory, Practice: Selected Essays and Interviews*, trans. Donald F. Bouchard and Sherry Simon, Blackwell, Oxford.

—— (1981) *The History of Sexuality, Volume One*, trans. R. Hurley, Penguin, London.

—— (1991) 'Governmentality' in G. Burchell, C. Gordon and P. Miller, eds, *The Foucault Effect: Studies in Governmentality*, University of Chicago Press, Chicago.

Gallup Poll (2001) 'Popular support for George Bush', <www.gallup.com>.

—— (2003) <www.gallup.com>.

Giddens, A. (1994) *Beyond Left and Right: The Future of Radical Politics*, Polity, Cambridge.

Gouldner, A. (1979) *The Future of Intellectuals and the Rise of the New Class*, Seabury Press, New York.

Greenwald, R. (2004) *Outfoxed: Rupert Murdoch's War on Journalism*, DVD.

Habermas, J. (1989) *The Structural Transformation of the Public Sphere: An Inquiry into a Category of Bourgeois Society*, MIT Press, Cambridge, Mass.

Hall, S. (1982) 'The rediscovery of ideology: The return of the repressed in media studies' in M. Gurentch, T. Bennett, J. Curran and J. Wooloat, eds, *Culture, Society and the Media*, Methuen, London.

—— (1991a) 'The local and the global: globalization and ethnicity' in A. King, ed., *Culture, Globalization and the World System*, State University of New York at Binghampton, Binghampton.

—— (1991b) 'Old and new identities, old and new ethnicities' in A. King, ed., *Culture, Globalization and the World System*, State University of New York at Binghampton, Binghampton.

Halliday, F. (2002) 'West encountering Islam: Islamophobia reconsidered' in A. Mohammadi, ed., *Islam Encountering Globalization*, Routledge-Curzon, London.

Hamilton, A. (1990) 'Aborigines, Asians and the national imaginary', *Australian Cultural History*, 9, 14–35.

Hanson, V. (2004) 'The mind of our enemies', *National Review Online*, January 30 <www.nationreview.com>.

Hariman, R. and Lucaites, J. (2003) 'Public identity and collective memory in US iconic photography: The image of "Accidental napalm"', *Critical Studies in Media Communication*, March, 20, 1.

Harris, J. (2001) *Depoliticizing Development: The World Bank and Social Capital*, Anthem Press, London.

Heidegger, M. (1952) *Being and Time*, trans. J. Macquarie and E. Robinson, Harper, New York.

—— (1977) 'The age of the world picture' in *The Question Concerning Technology and Other Essays*, trans. William Lovitt, Garland Publishing, New York.

Heinberg, R. (2003) *The Party's Over: Oil, War and the Fate of Industrial Societies*, New Society Publishers, New York.

Held, D. (1995) *Democracy and the Global Order: From the Modern State to Cosmopolitan Governance*, Polity, Cambridge.

Held, D., McGraw, A., Goliblatt, D. and Perraton, J. (1999) *Global Transformations: Politics, Economics and Culture*, Polity, Cambridge.

Herman, E. and Chomsky, N. (1988) *Manufacturing Consent: The Political Economy of the Mass Media*, Pantheon Books, New York.

Herman, E. and McChesney, R. (1999) 'Global media in the late 1990's' in H. Mackay and T. O'Sullivan, eds, *The Media Reader*, Sage, London,

Hersh, S. (2004) 'Torture at Abu Ghraib', *New Yorker Fact*, May 10, <www.newyorker.com/fact>.

Hess, S. and Kalb, N. (eds) (2003) *The Media and the War on Terrorism*, Brookings Institution Press, New York.

Holland, K. (2002) 'Poem on the Bali Bombing', Zionist Federation Newsletter, November/December, 31, <www.I-deas.com>.

Horkheimer, M. and Adorno, T. (1972) 'The culture industry: Enlightenment as mass deception' in *Dialectic of Enlightenment*, Seabury Press, New York.

Huntington, S. (1993) 'The clash of civilizations', *Foreign Affairs*, Summer, 72, 3.

—— (1996) *The Clash of Civilizations and the Remaking of the World Order*, Simon and Schuster, New York.

—— (2004) *Who Are We? The Challenge to America's National Identity*, Simon and Schuster, New York.

International Crisis Group (2003) *The Perils of Private Security in Indonesia: Guards and Militias on Bali and Lombok*, November.

—— (2004) 'Indonesia: Violence erupts again in Ambon', *Asia Briefing*, May 17.

Jameson, F. (1981) *The Political Unconscious: Narrative as a Socially Symbolic Act*, Methuen, London.

—— (1991) *Postmodernism, or, the Cultural Logics of Late Capitalism*, Verso, London.

Jenkins, H. (1992) *Textual Poachers: Television Fans and Participatory Culture*, Routledge, London.

Joint Standing Committee (2004) Report on Intelligence, US government.

Joint Standing Committee on Foreign Affairs, Trade and Defence (2004) Report on ASIO, intelligence and Iraq's weapons of mass destruction.

Kagan, R. (2002) 'Power and weakness', *Policy Review Online*, <www.policyreview.org.JUN02.kagan.html>,

Kagan, R. and Kristol, W. (2004a) 'Iraq One Year Later', *Weekly Standard*, March 22.

—— (2004b) 'The right war for the right reasons', *Weekly Standard*, February 27.

Kakutani, M. (2003) 'How books have shaped U.S. policy', *New York Times*, April 5.

Kaplan, L. F. and Kristol, W. (2003) *The War over Iraq: Saddam's Tyranny and America's Mission*, Encounter Books, San Francisco.

Karim, K. (2000a) *The Media and Global Violence*, Black Rose, Montreal.

—— (2000b) *The Islamic Peril: Media and Global Violence*, Black Rose, Montreal.

—— (2002) 'Muslim encounters with new media: towards an inter-civilizational discourse on globality?' in A. Mohammadi, ed., *Islam Encountering Globalization*, Routledge-Curzon, London.

Keane, J. (2004) *Violence and Democracy*, Cambridge University Press, Cambridge.

Kellner, D. (1989) *Jean Baudrillard: From Marxism to Postmodernism and Beyond*, Polity, Cambridge.

Klein, N. (2002) *No Logo: No Space, No Choice, No Jobs*, Picador, New York.

—— (2003) 'Iraq is not America's to sell', *Guardian*, November 7, <www.guardian.co.uk/comment/>.

Knightley, P. (1989) *The First Casualty*, Pan, London.

Kolodzy, J. and Wade, S. (2003) 'Stocks are down and Al Jazzera are out', *American Journalism Review*, May, 25, 16.

Kristeva, J. (1984) *Revolution and Poetic Language*, trans. M. Waller, Columbia University Press, New York.

Kristol, W. (2004) 'Project for the new American century', <www.newamericancentury.org/>.

Lacan, J. (1977) *Ecrits: A Selection*, Tavistock, London.

Laclau, E. (1991) *Emancipations*, Polity, Cambridge, London.

Laclau, E. and Mouffe, C. (1985) *Hegemony and Socialist Strategy: Toward a Radical Democratic Politics*, Verso, London.

Landow, G. (1992) *Hypertext: The Convergence of Contemporary Critical Theory and Technology*, The Johns Hopkins University Press, Baltimore.

Lanham, R. (1993) *The Electronic Word: Democracy, Technology and the Arts*, University of Chicago Press, Chicago.

Laqueur, W. (1987) *The Age of Terrorism*, George Weidenfeld and Nicolson, London.

—— (2003) *No End to War: Terrorism in the Twenty First Century*, Continuum, New York.

Levy, P. (1998) *Becoming Virtual: Reality in the Digital Age*, trans. Robert Bononno, Plenum Trade, New York.

Lewis, Belinda and Lewis, J. (2004) 'After the glow: challenges and opportunities for community sustainability in the context of the Bali bombings', Published proceedings, Sources of Insecurity Conference, Melbourne, November.

Lewis, Bernard (1990) 'The roots of Muslim rage', *Atlantic Monthly*, September, 266.

—— (2001) *What Went Wrong? Western Impact and Middle Eastern Responses*, Oxford University Press, Oxford.

—— (2003) *The Crisis of Islam: Holy War and Unholy Terror*, The Modern Library, New York.

Lewis, J. (1995) 'Putu goes to Paris: global imagining and the Australian imaginary of the east', *Kunapipi*, 7, 2.

—— (1997) 'The inhuman state: nature, media, government', *Media International Australia*, February, 83.

—— (1998) 'Digitopians: transculturalism, computers and the politics of hope', *International Journal of Cultural Studies*, 1, 3.

—— (2000) 'Manufacturing dissent: new democracy and the era of computer communication', *International Journal of Cultural Studies*, January.

—— (2002a) *Cultural Studies*, Sage, London.

—— (2002b) 'Propagating terror: 9/11 and the mediation of war', *Media International Australia*, August, 104, 90–1.

—— (2002c) 'In search of the postmodern surfer: territory, terror and masculinity' in K. Gilbert, ed., *Some Like it Hot*, Meyer and Meyer, Oxford.

—— (2003) 'The electronic polis: media, democracy and the invasion of Iraq', *Reconstruction*, summer, 3, 3.

Lewis, J. and Best, K. (2002) 'After Y2K: time, Andre the Giant and other democratic avatars', Published Proceedings, International Conference on Cultural Attitudes to Technology and Communication, Montreal, Ca., Suny Press.

—— (2005) 'Pure filth: apocalyptic hedonism and the postmodern', *Scope*, May.

Lewis J. and Lewis, Belinda (2004a) 'After infinite justice: Australia, the media and the terror of national identity', Conference on Diversity in Organizations, Communities and Nations, July.

—— (2004b) 'Crisis of contiguity: communities and contention in the context of the Bali bombings', Published Proceedings, Sources of Insecurity Conference, Melbourne, November.

Lucy, N. (1995) *Debating Derrida*, Melbourne University Press, Melbourne.

Luow, E. (2001) *The Media and Cultural Production*, Sage, London.

Lyon, D. (2003) *Surveillance after September 11*, Polity, Cambridge.

Lyotard, J.-F. (1984) *The Postmodern Condition: A Report on Knowledge*, trans. G. Bennington and B. Massumi, University of Minnesota Press, Minneapolis.

—— (1991) *The Inhuman: Reflections on Time*, trans. Geoffrey Bennington and Rachel Bowlby, Polity, Cambridge.

MacArthur, J. (1992) *Censorship and Propaganda in the Gulf War*, Hill and Wang, New York.

—— (2004) *Second Front: Censorship and Propaganda in the 1991 Gulf War*, Revised edition, University of California Press, Berkeley.

Mackay, H. and O'Sullivan, T. (eds) (1999) *The Media Reader*, Sage, London.

Mackay, N. (2004) 'Bush planned Iraq "regime change" before becoming president', *Sunday Herald Online*, October 31, <www.sundayherald.com/>.

Macmillan, Margaret (2001) *Paris 1919: Six Months that Changed the World*, Random House, New York.

MacRae, G. (2003) 'Art and peace in the safest place in the world: a culture of apoliticism – Bali' in T. Reuter, ed., *Inequality, Crisis and Social Change in Indonesia*, Routledge-Curzon, London.

Mailer, N. (2003) *Why Are We at War?* Random House, New York.

Maududi, M. (1967) *The Islamic Law and Constitution*, trans. K. Ahmad, Islamic Publications, Lahore.

Mayar, J. (2005) 'Outsourcing terror: the secret history of America's "extraordinary rendition" program', *New Yorker*, February 14.

McElroy, W. (2003) 'Iraq War may kill feminism as we know it', Online essay, July 23, <www.wendymcelroy.com>.

McGuigan, J. (1996) *Culture and the Public Sphere*, Routledge, London.

—— (ed.) (1997) *Cultural Methodologies*, Sage, London.

McLuhan, M. (1969) *Counterblast*, Rapp and Whiting, London.

Milner, A. (2002) *Re-imagining Culture*, Sage, London.

Mohammadi, A. (ed.) (2002) *Islam Encountering Globalization*, Routledge-Curzon, London.

Moore, M. (2001) *Stupid White Men*, Regan Books, New York.

Moores, S. (1993) *Interpreting Audiences: The Ethnography of Media Consumption*, Sage, London.

Mumdani, M. (2002) 'Good Muslim, bad Muslim: a political perspective on culture and terrorism' in E. Hershberg and K. Moore, eds, *Critical Views of September 11: Analyses from around the World*, The New Press, New York.

Nacos, B. (2002) *Mass Mediated Terrorism: The Central Role of the Media in Terrorism and Counter Terrorism*, Rowman and Littlefield, London.

Nairn, T. (2002) 'Globalization and the unchosen', *Arena Journal*, no. 19.

Negroponte, N. (1995) *Being Digital*, Hodder and Stoughton, Sydney.

Noll, A. M. (ed.) *Crisis Communications: Lessons from September 11*, Rowman and Littlefield, Lanham, Maryland.

Noor, F. (2004) 'The expulsion of Sidney Jones', *Muslim Wake-up*, October 31, <www.muslimwakeup.com/>.

Norris, C. (1987) *Derrida*, Fontana, London.

—— (1992) *Uncritical Theory: Postmodernism, Intellectuals and the Gulf War*, Lawrence and Wishart, London.

Norris, P., Kern, N. and Just, M. (eds) (2003) *Framing Terrorism: The News Media, the Government and the Public*, Routledge, London.

Olivero, A. (1998) *The State of Terror*, State University of New York Press, Albany.

Ong, W. (1982) *Orality and Literacy*, Methuen, New York.

Orr, M. (2003) *Intertextuality*, Polity, London.

Pasqualini, R. (2003) 'The first casualty of war: wartime reporting and ethnic community broadcasting', *Ethnic Broadcaster*, Autumn, 32–5.

Perigoe, R. (2005) 'Racist discourses after 9/11 in two Montreal daily newspapers', unpublished PhD thesis, RMIT University.

Philo, G. and Berry, M. (2004) *Bad News from Israel*, Pluto Press, London.

Pilger, J. (2003) 'Newspapers and radioinfo', <www.radioinfo.com.au/>.

Pinsdorf, M. (1994) 'Image makers of desert storm: Bush, Powell and Scwarzkopf' in T. McCain and L. Shyles, eds, *The 100 Hour War: Communication in the Gulf*, Greenwood Press, Westport.

Poster, M. (1995) *The Second Media Age*, Polity, Cambridge.

Postman, N. (1987) *Amusing Ourselves to Death: Public Discourse in the Age of Show Business*, Methuen, London.

Prayudi (2004) 'Media reporting of ethnic violence in post-Suharto Indonesia', unpublished Masters thesis, RMIT University.

Quinlan, M. (2004) 'Iraq: the indictment', *Tablet*, March 13, 8–10.

Radway, J. (1987) *Reading the Romance: Women, Patriarchy and Popular Literature*, Verso, London.

Rampton, S. and Stauber, J. (2003) *Weapons of Mass Deception: The Uses of Propaganda in Bush's War on Iraq*, Hodder and Stoughton, Sydney.

Rantahen, T. (2005) *The Media and Globalization*, Sage, London.

Rarey, J. (2003) 'The murder of David Kelly', *From the Wilderness Publications*, October, <www.fromthewilderness.com>.

Reuter, T. (ed.) (2003) *Inequality, Crisis and Social Change in Indonesia*, Routledge-Curzon, London.

Rheingold, H. (1993) *The Virtual Community: Homesteading on the Electronic Frontier*, Addison Wesley, Reading, Mass.

Ricchiardi, S. (2004) 'Missed Signals', *American Journalism Review*, August/September.

Riddell, M. (2004) 'Don't shoot the messenger', *Observer*, June 27.

Robb, D. (2002) 'To the shores of Hollywood: Marine Corps fights to polish image in "Windtalkers"', *Washington Post*, June 15.

Roberts, L., Lafta, R., Garfield, R., Khudhain, J. and Burnham, G. (2004) 'Mortality before and after the 2003 invasion of Iraq: cluster sample survey', *Lancet*, October 30, 364, 9445, <www.thelancet.com/journal/vol354/iss9445>.

Said, E. W. (1978) *Orientalism*, Pantheon Books, New York.

—— (1993) *Culture and Imperialism*, Chatto and Windus, London.

Salusinszky, I. (2003) 'The harm left in a treacherous thought', *Australian*, April, 9.

Schmid, A. P. (1983) *Political Terrorism: A Research Guide to Concepts, Theories, Data Bases and Literature*, Transaction Press, New Brunswick, NJ.

Schumpeter, J. (1989) *Capitalism, Socialism and Democracy*, Allen and Unwin, London.

Sherlock, S. (2002) 'The Bali bombing: what it means for Indonesia', Australian Government Foreign Affairs, Defence and Trade Group, *Current Issues Brief*, 4.

Silberstein S. (2002) *War of Words: Language, Politics and 9/11*, Routledge, London.

Smith, J. (2004) 'The Gnostic Baudrillard: A philosophy of terrorism seeking pure appearance', *International Journal of Baudrillard Studies*, July, 1, 2.

Sontag, S. (2001) 'On the cowardice of the 9/11 attackers', *New Yorker*, September 21.

—— (2003) *Regarding the Pain of Others*, Farrar, Strauss and Ciroux, New York.

Stauber, J. (1995) *Toxic Waste is Good for You*, Common Courage Press, Monroe, ME.

Sunday Herald (2004) 'Iraqi's Child Prisons', <www.sundayherald.com/43796>.

Taylor, P. M. (1992) *War and the Media: Propaganda and Persuasion in the Gulf War*, Manchester University Press, Manchester.

Tester, K. (1994) *Media, Culture and Morality*, Routledge, London.

The Economist (2002) 'The no-longer-lucky-country', *The Economist*, October 12.

Traynor, I. (2003) 'US plays aid card to fix war crimes exemption', *Guardian*, June 12.

Tuman, J. (2003) *Communicating Terror: The Rhetorical Dimensions of Terrorism*, Sage, London.

Unger, C. (2004) *The House of Bush, The House of Saud: The Secret Relationship between Two of the World's Most Powerful Dynasties*, Scribner, New York.

United Nations Development Program (2003) *Bali Beyond the Tragedy: Impact and Challenges for Tourism-led Recovery in Indonesia*.

United States Department of Defense (1986) DOD directive, 2000.12, 'Protection of DOD resources against terrorist acts', June 16.

United States Department of Defense (2003) 'Public Affairs Guidance (PAG) on embedding media during possible future operations/deployment in the U.S. Central Commands (CENTCOM) area of responsibility (AOR)', <www.defenselink.mil/news/Feb2003/d20030228pag.pdf>.

United States Government (2004) The 9/11 Commission Report.

Updike, J. (2001) Untitled contribution to the *New Yorker*, 24 September, p. 28.

Vickers, A. (1990) *Bali: Paradise Created*, Penguin, London.

—— (2003) 'Being Modern in Bali after Suharto' in T. Reuter, ed., *Inequality, Crisis and Social Change in Indonesia*, Routledge-Curzon, London.

Virilio, P. (1989) *War and Cinema*, trans. P. Camiller, Verso, London.

—— (1994) *The Vision Machine*, British Film Institute, London.

—— (2000) *Polar Inertia*, trans. P. Camiller, Sage, London.

—— (2002) *Ground Zero*, trans. C. Turner, Verso, London.

Waldman, P. (2004) *Fraud: The Strategy Behind the Bush Lies and Why the Media didn't Tell You*, Sourcebooks, Naperville, Ill.

Wilkinson, P. (1997) 'The media and terrorism: a reassessment', *Terrorism and Political Violence*, summer, 9, 2.

Williams, R. (1981) *Culture*, Fontana, London.

Wood, A. and Thompson, P. (2003) 'An interesting day: President Bush's movements and actions on 9/11', The Center for Co-operative Research, <www.cooperativeresearch.org/timeline/main/essayaninterestiongday.html>.

Woodward, B. (2004) *Plan of Attack*, Simon and Schuster, New York.

Young, P. and Jesser, P. (1997) *The Media and the Military*, Macmillan, London.

Žižek, S. (2004) 'Iraq's false promises', *Foreign Policy*, January/February, <www.lacan.com/zizek-iraq2.htm>.

Zolo, D. (1992) *Democracy and Complexity*, Polity, Cambridge.

—— (1997) *Cosmopolis: Prospects for World Government*, trans. D. McKie, Polity, Cambridge.

Index